HARVARD
BUSINESS SCHOOL
Executive Education

"Ammerman and Groysberg have captured the real-life issues that continue to limit women. *Glass Half-Broken* should be a mandatory read for every CEO and CHRO—men and women."

—**SOFIA CHANG,** President, WarnerMedia

"Through a rare combination of history, storytelling, and research, Ammerman and Groysberg build a framework to both understand and address the persistent lack of women at the highest levels in the workplace. Both inspirational and challenging, *Glass Half-Broken* is a valuable resource for the post–#MeToo world."

—**MARYBETH HAYS**, board member and adviser, former EVP, Walmart US

"With a primary focus on gender equity for professional women in all their diversity, *Glass Half-Broken* is a major contribution in support of the American democratic promise of inclusion and equal opportunity for all. In a model of lucid analysis with compelling case studies, Ammerman and Groysberg identify the bias and structural barriers that still confront women in business school and the workplace, and, optimistic about the future, they lay out strategies for transforming organizational culture, ending the gender gap, and advancing women to positions of leadership."

—**STEVEN C. ROCKEFELLER,** Professor of Religion, Emeritus, Middlebury College; former Chair, Board of Trustees, Rockefeller Brothers Fund

GLASS HALF-BROKEN

Shattering the Barriers That Still Hold Women Back at Work

COLLEEN AMMERMAN
AND BORIS GROYSBERG

Harvard Business Review Press
Boston, Massachusetts

HBR Press Quantity Sales Discounts

Harvard Business Review Press titles are available at significant quantity discounts when purchased in bulk for client gifts, sales promotions, and premiums. Special editions, including books with corporate logos, customized covers, and letters from the company or CEO printed in the front matter, as well as excerpts of existing books, can also be created in large quantities for special needs.

For details and discount information for both print and
ebook formats, contact booksales@harvardbusiness.org,
tel. 800-988-0886, or www.hbr.org/bulksales.

Library of Congress Cataloging-in-Publication Data

Names: Ammerman, Colleen, author. | Groysberg, Boris, author.
Title: Glass half-broken : shattering the barriers that still hold women back at work /
    Colleen Ammerman and Boris Groysberg.
Description: [Boston, Massachusetts] : Harvard Business Review Press, [2021] | Includes index. |
Identifiers: LCCN 2020047840 (print) | LCCN 2020047841 (ebook) |
    ISBN 9781633695931 (hardcover) | ISBN 9781633695948 (ebook)
Subjects: LCSH: Glass ceiling (Employment discrimination) | Women—Employment. |
    Corporate culture. | Organizational change.
Classification: LCC HD6050 .A66 2021 (print) | LCC HD6050 (ebook) | DDC 331.4/133—dc23
LC record available at https://lccn.loc.gov/2020047840
LC ebook record available at https://lccn.loc.gov/2020047841

ISBN: 978-1-63369-593-1
eISBN: 978-1-63369-594-8

The paper used in this publication meets the requirements of the American
National Standard for Permanence of Paper for Publications and Documents in Libraries and
Archives Z39.48-1992.

To the people who most inspire us to work toward equality
Colleen's mother
and
Boris's parents, sister, wife, and children

CONTENTS

INTRODUCTION

The Stalled Workplace Revolution 1

PART ONE

OFFICE OBSTACLE COURSE

1. **Aiming High and Falling to Earth** 11
Women in Early and Midcareer

   Reaching for the Top . . . 33
   The Honorable Barbara Hackman Franklin

2. **Scarce, Scrutinized, and Still Climbing** 39
Women in Leadership

   Leading with Purpose . . . 57
   Ana Paula Pessoa

3. **Cracks in the Ceiling** 65
Women on Corporate Boards

   Paving the Way and Paying It Forward . . . 85
   Michele Hooper

PART TWO

CLEARING THE PATH TO GENDER EQUALITY AT WORK

4. **Allies on the Sidelines**   95
   The Role of Men

   Championing Gender Equality in the Media . . . 119
   Ros Atkins

5. **Becoming a Glass-Shattering Organization**   129
   A Systemic Approach to Closing Gender Gaps

   The Glass-Shattering Framework . . . 166

   Settling for Equality . . . 169
   Qualcomm

6. **Day-to-Day Parity**   173
   How to Manage for Gender Equity and Inclusion

   Bringing Inclusive Management to Wall Street . . . 199
   Jack Rivkin

CONCLUSION
A Breakthrough Moment   205

   From Innovator to Advocate . . . 215
   Ilene H. Lang

EPILOGUE
Gender Balance Sheet   221
A Harvard Business School Case Study

   A Pioneer's Path . . . 251
   Professor Regina E. Herzlinger

Notes . . . 257

Index . . . 279

Acknowledgments . . . 287

About the Authors . . . 293

THE STALLED WORKPLACE REVOLUTION

In 2019, women made up the majority of college-educated US workers for the first time ever, and the gap between the percentage of women versus men in the labor force was the lowest on record.[1] Other developed countries have also seen women enter the labor force in greater numbers—even Japan, where women's workforce participation has long lagged behind other large economies, has experienced an uptick in recent years.[2] While the Covid-19 pandemic upended the global economy in early 2020 and chipped away at these gains, such milestones ought to suggest that women are becoming more and more represented in positions of leadership across business and society. The hard-fought battles of the twentieth century to provide gender-equal access to education, job training, and employment opportunities enable women today to pursue careers without being denied entry into degree programs, without being summarily barred from certain occupations or ranks, and without the threat of being dismissed when they get married.

But women in fact remain underrepresented, often dramatically so, in positions of power. The proportion of female CEOs struggles to break 10 percent across a variety of indices. The gender pay gap is showing little movement, largely because high-paying jobs are the most gender-imbalanced. Today's most remunerative fields, particularly high finance and tech, are also those where women are most scarce. But even in fields that employ roughly equal proportions of men and women or where women actually make up the majority, leadership ranks remain male-dominated. Female CEOs are about as rare in the health care sector as they are in any other, despite a huge supply of women; three-quarters of the health care workforce is female.[3]

In 2020, just thirteen of the companies on *Fortune's* Global 500 list—the world's largest companies by revenue—were led by women, and none of those female CEOs were women of color.[4] (As this book went to press, Citigroup joined the list, announcing that longtime executive Jane Fraser would become CEO in early 2021.) In the United States, women have received the majority of undergraduate degrees, prerequisites for high-earning jobs, since the 1980s.[5] Across all racial and ethnic categories tracked by the federal government, women earn more than half of college degrees.[6] The gates have been opened, and women have stepped through—yet they have found themselves staring down a set of obstacles that can't be adjudicated away.

Glass Half-Broken: Shattering the Barriers That Still Hold Women Back at Work is an exploration of the moment we've arrived at, with women's progress into positions of leadership and authority stalled for years, and why the status quo persists. The book is also about the individual and institutional strategies deployed to overcome these barriers, how well they have worked, and what it will take to create real change.

Our own institution, Harvard Business School (HBS), started educating women in 1937 yet didn't begin admitting women students directly to our MBA program until 1963. Like many other schools, HBS initially approached the presence of women students as a challenge of integration—that is, how to add and assimilate women to the classroom and the campus. Underlying was the assumption that the school's existing norms and practices need not be altered, the so-called add-women-and-stir approach. More recently, HBS has taken a candid look at its history and at the ways in which we continue to fall short of aims to provide equal opportunities and supports for all students, regardless of gender, race, or any other identity category. In the epilogue, we will explore the school's decades-long, and ongoing, journey toward equality. Both of us have been deeply involved in the efforts to make HBS a place where every member of the community, from students to faculty and staff, is able to thrive and contribute to our shared educational mission. We, along with numerous colleagues, have worked to improve our curricula, advance research on inequality and inclusion, and use the school's platform to communicate with leaders who can change the culture of business.

This book is our attempt to take what we've learned from this work and provide educators, managers, and anyone who wants to better understand why gender parity remains elusive with a clear view of the structures and mindsets that perpetuate inequities as well as a guide for dismantling them. We are indebted to the many scholars who have conducted critical and groundbreaking research on gender in organizations and in leadership. Throughout this book, we cite the work of numerous researchers from the fields of organizational behavior, psychology, economics, sociology, and law, including a number of our HBS colleagues as well as some of our own past research. Our aim has been to synthesize the most critical findings and explain what they mean for women's careers in real workplaces and what they suggest about how to effect change.

In addition, we conducted a series of new research projects, surveying and interviewing women and men around the world at all career stages and levels of organizational hierarchy, from undergraduates just starting out to seasoned executives serving on corporate boards. Across all these projects, more than three hundred people were interviewed. In addition, we collected survey responses from more than 275 women executives. We heard from people on every continent except Antarctica. They were working in sales, marketing, operations, human resources, and other functions across all manner of industries.

Most worked in for-profit companies, both privately held and publicly traded, but a sizable minority were employed at nonprofits and academic institutions. They came from all sorts of socioeconomic and cultural backgrounds, and their stories were inspiring and often moving. They confirm much of what we know from academic research about how and why gender disparities persist, but they also offer the texture and vividness of first-person experience, helping us to absorb and more fully understand the effects of the biases and barriers long studied by researchers.

Our interviews also shed light on how women have overcome obstacles and how both women and men are trying to take down barriers. Most of the people we spoke to have thought deeply not only about their own careers but also about how to enable those around them to succeed. Throughout the book we have included profiles of real women and men; the trailblazers in these stories reflect the transformations in women's opportunities as well as the ways their potential is still stymied. Moreover, they are a reminder that big changes—to society, to business, to major institutions—are always the collective work of committed individual actors. We hope that these stories likewise remind readers that they too have the power to be change agents.

The book is organized into two sections, with the first half of the book focused on how, despite decades of corporate initiatives, public policy programs, and grassroots activism, gender-based inequities continue to limit women's careers and maintain the male-dominated status quo in leadership. The second half of the book zeroes in on how to eliminate gender gaps in organizations, with chapters devoted to what men can do to be effective allies, what companies need to do at an organizational level to drive systemic change, and what individual managers should do to promote equity on a day-to-day basis.

Chapter 1 focuses on the barriers to advancement that begin early in women's careers and the obstacles to leadership that keep even high-achieving women from the uppermost echelons. We talk to women on the rise: some about to graduate from college, others earning MBAs, and some a handful of years into their postgrad careers. They are already quite accomplished, products of competitive, elite environments where their ambitions were encouraged and their hard work rewarded. Those on the cusp of careers generally believe that the path to success is clear. But women who have been working for just a few years—sometimes as little as twelve months out of college—are already starting to observe an unequal playing field.

As they move further into their careers, they are beset by the roadblocks that characterize today's workplace: Skepticism about and stigma for working mothers, a lack of role models who share their gender (compounded for women of color who are highly unlikely to see leaders who look like them), and the first signs of the double bind that forces women to choose between being liked and being respected, with career costs no matter which tack they take. In Chapter 2, we talk to women who have made it through this gauntlet and risen to senior executive roles in companies around the world. We learn about the factors that made their success possible, in particular the outsize impact made by the small number of female role models in view. We also identify how gender-based barriers evolve, like a drug-resistant affliction, to create new disadvantages for women leaders. The female executives we studied were often still navigating the double bind while being the only woman at their level or in their immediate peer group, which added a new level of scrutiny. Even though they had more power than at any other point in their careers, they spent significant time managing how male colleagues at all levels perceived and received them—a distraction from and a burden on their actual work. While they have made it further than most other women of their cohorts, they continue to be thwarted in their attempts to reach parity with the men around them.

Chapter 3 takes us higher still in the corporate hierarchy, where there are even fewer women: We go into the corporate boardroom. Gender diversity, or the lack thereof, on company boards has garnered increasing attention in recent years, but interest outpaces progress. We look at how various actors—from governments to investors to women directors themselves—are exerting pressure on boards and why corporate governance, with its enormous influence on business and society, remains essentially the purview of white men.

We acknowledge that the population we focus on at each of these stages is an elite one: graduates of top schools, employees of name-brand companies, highly paid executives. Women in low-wage jobs, the service industry, trades, domestic work, and the informal economy are fighting very different, more fundamental battles—for a living wage, basic job protections, and safe working conditions, among other vital needs. The obstacles faced by the professional women we have studied should never be the sole focus of the conversation about gender and work, but the fact that even this privileged group remains fundamentally thwarted by gender inequality is a stark reminder of just how much that inequality continues to shape organizations and careers. Gender barriers cannot be elided by the advantages of education and income; they will limit all women's opportunities until they are uprooted and dismantled.

In Part 2, we turn to action. Chapter 4 focuses on the most underutilized weapon in the battle against gender inequality: men. They themselves stand to gain, we argue, from combating gender stereotypes, and they are disproportionately in positions to shape policy and culture—yet their voices are often absent from conversations about gender inequality. In this chapter we explore why men remain largely on the sidelines, the untapped potential of male advocates, and how men at all levels, not just high-profile leaders, can create meaningful change.

Chapter 5 shifts from individual actors to organizations, asking what practices companies can put in place to address, prevent, and mitigate the barriers hindering women's careers. We synthesize our own and others' research about all aspects of talent management, from hiring to evaluation to retention, offering a practical framework that organizations can start applying tomorrow. Drawing on behavioral science, studies of organizational structure and culture, and our own interviews with women and men across dozens of companies, we adapt the insights of research to the day-to-day processes involved in people management.

In the final chapter, we offer guidance that anyone who manages people can implement. While systems and structures are critical, they don't determine the totality of anyone's experience at work. A rigorous performance evaluation process designed to be fair can't overcome a team culture where women are systematically denied opportunities to work on mission-critical projects and whose contributions are thus less impressive. This chapter addresses the day-to-day practices and micromoments that add up over time. Leading equitably and inclusively requires a willingness to learn, to be uncomfortable at times, and to critically reflect on how we see others and ourselves—qualities that reside in the manager, not the task list he or she executes.

All told, we hope this book will educate, inspire, and motivate. Although workplace gender gaps have become a hot topic in recent years, the reasons for their persistence are often misunderstood or underexamined. All too frequently, women misinterpret organizational obstacles as personal inadequacies. Without the language to identify the subtle biases hindering their progress, they internalize the failures of their companies and industries as their own and become even less likely to achieve their leadership potential. And when men don't understand how their female colleagues contend with a very different set of circumstances right in the same organization, they too might easily assume that gender imbalances in power and pay reflect merit, not structural barriers.

We hope that readers come away with a better understanding of the systemic disadvantages that aspiring and actual female leaders face and then turn a clear eye on their own teams, departments, and companies. But this book is also meant to remind readers of how far we've come. Subtle yet obdurate barriers continue to stand in the way of gender parity, but the glass is riddled with cracks.

PART ONE

OFFICE OBSTACLE COURSE

CHAPTER 1

AIMING HIGH AND FALLING TO EARTH

Women in Early and Midcareer

To a woman graduating from college today, the lack of women in the senior ranks of business (as well as other fields) looks like an historical artifact. By the time she is the age of one of the few dozen female *Fortune* 500 CEOs, she reasons, company hierarchies should more or less reflect the proportion of women in her cohort. She has learned, likely throughout her entire educational career, about female leaders whose breakthroughs made it possible for later generations to rise. She may have read about someone such as former secretary of commerce Barbara Franklin, whose story appears after this chapter, who demonstrates that women can hold their own in the halls of power and help clear the way for women who come after them.

We conducted in-depth interviews with more than two dozen graduating seniors and found that women—and men too—reared on the rhetoric of "women's empowerment" and accustomed to sharing the classroom and the playing field anticipated a future in which women leaders are commonplace. Given the well-known benefits of a college degree, young alumnae launching professional careers might reasonably assume that gender inequality will have little to no impact on their professional trajectories. While they are well aware of the lingering impacts of discriminatory practices and biased attitudes, by and large they believe that the underrepresentation of women in leadership, in the words of one graduate, "is changing" and that, perhaps more importantly, "it won't matter because I'll kick all their asses anyway."

She is not alone in her optimistic, hard-charging outlook. A 2015 survey of millennial women found that about half of women in the workforce for three or fewer years (at an average age of twenty-five) believed they would be able to rise to the most senior level of their current organization.[1] In the same survey, women cited "opportunities for career progression" as the most attractive employer trait. In an ongoing study of MBA graduates that we are involved with, millennial women ranked "opportunities for career growth" as their second-most important overall concern, after "quality of relationships," exactly the same as millennial men ranked their concerns.[2] Is it any wonder that young women entering the white-collar workforce view professional success as both desirable and attainable? Today's college graduates grew up in an era when women comprised almost 50 percent of the US workforce and "girl power" was a bright thread woven into the pop cultural products that orbited them at every stage, from children's books to T-shirt slogans to hit songs.[3]

This doesn't mean young women are ignorant about lingering gender inequality. Having been witness to the debates about and painful disappointments associated with "having it all," women entering the white-collar workforce are keenly aware of the prevailing sense that family demands interfere with women's careers and see the friction between parenting and work as a general social problem. "I think work-life balance means maternity leave and childcare and universal preschool," noted one young woman. A 2015 study of unmarried, childless men and women between the ages of eighteen and thirty-two found that women were cognizant of the effect these kinds of supports would have on their futures. They were more likely to express a preference for an egalitarian relationship, in which they and a future spouse equally shared the responsibilities of breadwinning and caregiving, if told they'd have access to paid family leave, subsidized childcare, and flexible work options.[4] And it is not the case that young women—or men, for that matter—are uninformed about structural gender discrimination in the workplace. Indeed, it would be hard for them to be unaware: A search of the ABI/ProQuest database for newspaper and magazine articles on workplace gender gaps, bias, and discrimination published between 2000 and 2016 yields over five thousand results, even before the onslaught of media coverage sparked by the #MeToo movement.

For our research into women's early professional experiences, we interviewed more than two dozen undergraduate students a few months before their graduation and then one year later. We also followed up with a subset of these graduates five years after that, when they had become more firmly established in their careers. When asked as graduating seniors about their expectations for how or whether gender might play a role in their paths, both men and women were quick to acknowledge the existence of inequities. Graduating men acknowledged their privileged position as they looked ahead to starting their postcollege jobs: "I know there's a lot of sexism in the workplace, and I do anticipate in many contexts being treated like a more responsible person just because I'm a man, a white man," one said. One of his female peers, who planned to attend law school, pointed out that "a field like law is still mostly male-dominated. I don't know the statistics on this—I might be wrong. But I know that especially the older people in all these different firms are more likely to be men and there aren't that many women at that level, from a couple of decades ago." One of her peers, who had been hired to join a health care consulting firm postgraduation, had much the same assessment: "I know that at my firm there are definitely females, but there's not too many females at the partner level. But that could have just been because of how things were back in the day."

The notion that "kicking their asses" will overcome any potential discrimination authorizes the sense of agency that young women are encouraged to feel in the face of lingering inequality. As another graduating student asserted, "The way I comport myself shows that I'm serious about what I'm doing, and as soon as you get to know me, the gender part doesn't really matter anymore." Having internalized years of confidence-boosting messages about their potential, early-career women may even speculate that prior generations were lacking not only opportunity but also drive: "When you look at these [consulting] firms, if you look at the top tiers—like partners—there are very, very few women. From my perspective, I feel like there is self-selection, to a certain extent," mused one. From her vantage point, gender doesn't loom large in a cohort equally balanced between men and women: "At least, going in with my class at [a firm], there's going to be a lot of women. I don't really foresee any sort of issue."

But this progress narrative is belied not just by research on gender barriers to career advancement but also by what these same women experienced as their careers took shape. Take our interviewee Carla,[5] a senior who was awarded a prestigious fellowship with an international marketing firm. She recounted "fl[ying] out to London for an interview, [and] they flew in executives from everywhere in the world to London, and everyone on the other side of the table was a man, and that was sort of weird." But, she pondered as she looked ahead to the fellowship, "it was also interesting, because of everyone who was applying, there were only eight guys and twenty-two girls. So, it's also thinking about the shift there, and how in twenty years, the other side of the table is going to look a little bit different." Carla's belief that the executive side of the table will seat more women implies, of course, her own opportunity to ascend to such a role over the next two decades. But one year later, her faith had been tested: "When I met one of the CEOs of the company with all the fellows in New York, where we finished the fellowship, he happened to remember all the guys' names and none of the girls' names. . . . The most senior person in the room was a woman, and the more senior fellow is a woman, and he didn't remember her name, but he remembered the first-year guy in my class."

The way that the women in Carla's group of fellows seemed to be almost invisible to a senior leader of the firm is not an isolated anecdote. A large body of research confirms that women are perceived by superiors, peers, and subordinates in ways that diminish their status. Women get praised in performance evaluations, often for stereotypically feminine traits such as willingness to help out, yet receive lower numerical performance ratings and fewer career-developing "stretch" assignments than their male peers.[6] Women's contributions to their teams' successes go undervalued and unrecognized; unless their achievements are explicitly called out to observers, women are seen as less competent and having inferior leadership capabilities compared to male peers.[7] And women experience backlash when they are not helpful, even though the kinds of tasks they get criticized for avoiding, such as planning events and taking meeting notes, are neither highly valued by their employers nor associated with career advancement and rewards.[8]

The incongruity between Carla's ambitions and the view of women's suitability for leadership implied by the forgetful CEO sets up what will become an ever-widening gap between aspirations and attainment for young women embarking on white-collar careers. The emergence of this gap will recapitulate a pattern that has endured since women began entering professional jobs in large numbers. Our own research on baby boomer and Generation X Harvard Business School (HBS) alumni, who embarked on their post-MBA careers in the 1980s and 1990s, offers a case in point: Men and women had virtually the same values, rating "work that is meaningful and satisfying," "professional accomplishments," and "opportunities for career growth and development" as all highly important. That is, both men and women with the same elite pedigree aspired to fulfilling careers characterized by achievement and advancement—hardly a stunning insight. But these women saw their actual professional outcomes fall short: They were less likely than men of their same age to be in senior management or even in supervisory roles at all. And it isn't at all clear that these women simply self-selected into less powerful positions: The women expressed lower satisfaction with multiple dimensions of their careers, compared to men in their cohorts.[9]

Lowered Horizons: Emerging into Careers

Six years after the aspiring lawyer quoted above graduated, now admitted to the bar and working at a large firm, her confidence had faltered:

> It took a while for it to sink in, especially in my first year here, how often I was the most junior person in the room and the only woman. . . . There are plenty of women at this law firm, but it's still frequently the case that you can be on a conference call with twelve people, standing in a room with ten people, and you look around and someone's supposed to get water—and guess what, that's you. . . . The fact that it kept happening, that it wasn't just a one-time occurrence, it starts to get to you . . . especially the fortieth time a man speaks with a complete lack of respect for you or your time or efforts. It does add up, and it gets to a certain volume where you know it's not coincidental. If I'm planning a lunch with five people and two people have to back out at the last minute—I started to notice that it is often the women of color who have last-minute [assignments] that come up, and these are often not substantive assignments . . . and it's painful after a while to see this and to see how it happens.

She is not alone in finding what a difference a few years can make. After five years in the finance industry, another young woman found that the lack of female leadership at her firm was not an unfortunate relic of past norms: "I definitely felt isolated and different from my peers. And there's definitely a lack of role models . . . there are fewer women overall, and then as you go up to higher and higher positions there are fewer and fewer women. I definitely felt like a minority and felt there were fewer role models for me." According to the study of millennial women referenced above, by the time they are in their early thirties, the proportion who see themselves as likely to attain senior leadership has dropped ten points, to 39 percent.[10] These diminished expectations are likely rooted in experience; an annual "Women in the Workplace" survey conducted by McKinsey and Lean In has found that women in entry-level jobs are 18 percent less likely to be promoted than their male peers.[11] A raft of studies has come to similar conclusions. As leadership scholars Alice Eagly and Linda Carli observe in reviewing the literature, "Men generally have a promotion advantage even when characteristics such as job experience are controlled."[12] Very few women fully overcome this disadvantage. As is well known, just 5 percent of companies in the S&P 500 have a female CEO.[13] More broadly, the World Economic Forum notes that women's global presence in managerial and other senior positions in both the public and private sectors "is not trending toward equal representation."[14]

One female MBA graduate (class of '13) described, "Right out of undergrad, at least at my [consulting] firm, the [male-to-female] ratio was about 50/50. You generally just feel like a human being, as opposed to a female human being, and no one ever treated me differently. I got top ratings. I always felt like I was a strong performer." But this equilibrium tends to be short-lived. Promoted to a management role after business school, this same consultant noticed that "increasingly, I'm the only female voice in the room." A 2014 MBA, working at a different firm, described the same trajectory:

If you're doing good work, and if you're doing problem-solving effectively at the junior level . . . I do think that men and women are treated very, very equally. Of course, there is unconscious bias, but in general I do think at the junior level, I didn't feel disadvantaged or different. I would say as a manager, it's very different now. . . . I still have the attitude that if I keep my head down and work hard, I'll get ahead, and I still believe that's very true. I still believe [my firm] is a very meritocratic place. But I see my male colleagues doing really smart things to get recognition and to build relationships—and be seen to have a lot of the credit— that I would never see a woman do. . . . Most of the partners are men, and they engage in a certain way and look for certain things.

This consultant's emerging sense that her male peers have better access to key internal networks and colleagues is borne out by research across a range of highly remunerative fields from venture capital[15] to investment banking[16] to law.[17] In industries such as these, where the apprenticeship model reigns, such relationships are critical for advancement. As the consultant went on to explain, mentorship and sponsorship from senior colleagues are unevenly distributed at her firm:

A big consideration is, if I try to build a platform to partner, who's going to help me build it? And that's sort of where I'm struggling. . . . I was talking recently with a group of women at my level who all feel like, "I want to be partner, I like the work, but I don't know who's going to help me get there." And we stepped back and asked, "Why is it that none of us feel like we really have someone, that we've built a community of people to help us build that platform, while a lot of our male colleagues have?"

It should be no surprise, then, that women's representation begins to drop off higher up the ranks. While 48 percent of entry-level workers are women, that proportion shrinks to 30 percent at the vice president level and down to 25 percent at higher strata, according to a 2017 study.[18] This underrepresentation fuels a vicious circle: As women move into managerial roles and notice that their cohort is not as gender-balanced as it once was, they may begin to wonder how long they will remain in the pipeline. Even if overt bias or explicit discrimination has not figured in their experiences, they see that men's and women's trajectories are starting to unfold differently. And women's sense that they are not on a solid path to leadership is also reinforced when they find themselves steered away from or without access to development opportunities. For example, in multinational companies, global postings are a key stage on the path to senior ranks, yet 18 percent of millennial women do not believe they have equal opportunities to undertake international assignments, and they are less likely than their male peers to believe that their employer provides equal access to such assignments.[19]

Overall, women under age thirty are less certain than their male peers that they can reach the top level of their organizations.[20] And they are right. Even among HBS alumni, a gender disparity in career outcomes persists: Among those in mid- to late career, women are less likely than men to have direct reports or profit-and-loss responsibilities or to be in the highest echelons of leadership, either as members of top management or as corporate board directors.[21] As women move beyond the first few years of their working lives (when it may indeed appear that their gender won't matter), the pool of women shrinks with each ascending level of organizational hierarchy.

While the diminishing number of women in positions of increasing responsibility and power is clear, there is far less consensus about why and how the leaks spring and, in turn, what should be done to plug them. One widely held belief maintains that the real driver of gender gaps is that women's aspirations trend downward over time, widening the distance between their goals and leadership roles. Implied is the notion that women's underrepresentation in leadership is therefore inevitable or at least has less to do with organizational barriers than with individual decisions. Even among high-achieving women themselves, this conventional wisdom dominates: In our alumni study, 85 percent of HBS's female graduates identified "prioritizing family over work" as the number one barrier to women's career advancement, and women were no less likely than men to cite this explanation.[22]

The prevalence of this belief is perhaps unsurprising, given that work-family conflict dominated media reporting of gender and work between 2001 and 2009[23] and continues to figure prominently in discussions about women's careers, including in the firestorm of coverage ignited by Anne-Marie Slaughter's 2012 *Atlantic* article "Why Women Still Can't Have It All" (and her 2015 follow-up book, *Unfinished Business: Women, Men, Work, Family*). But the explanatory power of this narrative is limited. Our study of HBS alumni found that the gender gap in top management was not explained by women's greater likelihood to have made career moves—such as taking time out, declining a promotion, or choosing a job with more flexibility—to accommodate their family responsibilities. Even when controlling for any combination of family accommodations as well as factors such as age, number of children, industry, and company size, the gender gap between men and women at senior levels persisted.[24] And it isn't at all clear that family demands are what drive women's job exits: Just 2 percent of women planning to leave their current company were doing so to focus on family responsibilities, according to a survey of more than seventy thousand workers.[25]

When Organizations Depress Women's Flight Paths

Despite shaky evidence, this narrative of women's careers being stymied by their own lack of interest shapes how organizations interpret a dearth of women in their leadership ranks and, in turn, efforts to rectify the imbalance. As a result, companies can fail to address—or even see—what is really driving their gender disparities. One such cautionary tale comes from a large consulting firm that brought in a team of outside researchers to study the lack of women at the senior level and recommend changes that would enable more women to rise. What the team found wasn't what the firm expected. While the firm had assumed that more women were quitting and doing so primarily because they couldn't keep pace with job demands, in fact men and women were leaving at about the same rate. Moreover, the firm's culture of round-the-clock hours—driven largely by a norm of overdelivering to clients as a way of one-upping coworkers—was experienced by both men and women as exhausting and dispiriting. Extensive interviews made clear that this culture was causing all employees, not just women, to feel that their jobs prevented them from being fully present in the rest of their lives, including as parents. Yet, despite commissioning the data, the firm's leaders rejected and discarded it. Instead of tackling the overwork that was leaving employees, regardless of gender, unhappy and unwell, they doubled down on the belief that women were simply less suited to the challenges of high-level roles.

The solution, in the eyes of the firm's leaders, was to continue encouraging women (but not men, who were also struggling with excessive work) to take advantage of family-accommodation policies such as flex time and reduced schedules. But using those benefits pushed women off the leadership track and reinforced notions that they couldn't handle the demands of higher-level roles, ultimately perpetuating the very problem that the firm had hoped to solve.[26] When workplaces funnel women into lower-status, less rewarding jobs out of a well-meaning desire to "support" their careers, they further entrench the expectation that women's primary role is outside the office. At the same time, gender inequality at home reinforces a cultural norm that associates men with paid work and women with caregiving. Women in dual-career heterosexual partnerships do the majority of housework and caregiving; even among affluent couples who outsource much of the labor, women take on the lion's share of managing and coordinating such work.[27]

Among HBS alumnae—a highly educated, high-achieving segment of women workers—the proportion of millennial women expecting to interrupt their careers to care for children is more than twice as high (37 percent) as that of baby boomer women (17 percent) who expected the same when they first started out. Generation X alumnae were also less likely (28 percent) than millennial women to anticipate career interruptions for children. Younger women's lowered expectations for egalitarian caregiving are a reminder that progress toward gender equality is stalled at home, not just at work, in ways that reinforce women's disadvantage in both domains. Indeed, millennial women's tempered outlook reflects the reality that earlier generations of women experienced; significantly larger proportions of Generation X and baby boomer alumnae reported being in traditional marriages where they did most of the childcare and their careers took a back seat than they had expected when they graduated.[28] More recently, the coronavirus pandemic laid bare the extent to which mothers are still expected to choose between career and family. Amid the sudden closure of schools and day care centers as well as the risks associated with having a nanny, babysitter, or relative provide care, women with young children reduced their work hours four to five times more than did fathers.[29] While the long-term effects of the pandemic on women's employment remain to be seen, it seems likely that for many families, increased childcare demands will inspire the adoption of bifurcated gender roles that impede women's careers.

Despite clear indications that external pressures spur women to ratchet back their ambitions, the belief that women don't want to pursue leadership persists. Even as the recent college graduates in our study professed a strong interest in gender equality in their workplaces, they often attributed a lack of women in their companies or on their teams to women's lower career ambition. In the words of one alumnus working in Europe for a major US-based consulting firm, "It is difficult to find women that are both qualified and willing to work the extremely long hours of consulting. It becomes a hard choice between career and family, given that the work gets in the way of meaningful time with family, and many women find it hard to make that choice." The corollary is implicit: Men don't find it as hard to make the same choice. And yet, as the consulting firm mentioned above found (but didn't quite believe), men *do* suffer when expected to sacrifice time with their families. But in response they tend to deploy different coping strategies, such as quietly trimming their hours or limiting their availability without asking for formal accommodations, thereby flying under the radar and avoiding being branded as undercommitted.[30] Meanwhile, women are bombarded with messages about the impossibility of managing career and family. A female executive can hardly get through an interview without being asked, sometimes with an undercurrent of incredulity, how she balances the two. And women who don't follow a traditional path can sometimes experience more than just skepticism about their ability to juggle work and home: One series of studies found that men with wives who do not work viewed their female colleagues negatively and were more likely to deny promotion opportunities to women.[31]

These messages create some dissonance for young women in particular, coupled as they are with exhortations about women's power and potential. (Girls can do anything except be both mothers and leaders.) One college senior claimed that she did not anticipate being treated differently from men in future work settings but also noted, in the same breath, that "in any field, the women and children thing is going to be an issue." It isn't clear if she thinks that the "women and children thing" is going to present difficulties for *her*, but she understands work-family conflict to be gendered and to be an "issue" for women's experiences at work.

Family responsibilities are generally seen as problematic by young employees, according to a study of millennial workers: 44 percent of women and 49 percent of men believe that in their organizations, taking advantage of flexibility and work-life balance programs has negative consequences.[32] These young professionals are not wrong, according to scholars who study the issue. The use of such programs and policies is associated with slowed wage growth and diminished promotion opportunities.[33] Researchers have even coined a term for it: flexibility stigma. These are obstacles placed in women's paths by their employers, not their children. As sociologist Pamela Stone found in a landmark study of highly educated women who leave the workforce, such workers are less likely to have "opted out" due to a diminished or vanished professional ambition than to have been pushed out by diminished opportunities, vanished mentors and sponsors, and organizational cultures that ascribe lowered status to mothers, even if they had previously been top performers.[34] These shifts may take women by surprise, particularly if they have been on an upward trajectory. Is it any wonder that talented lawyers, bankers, tech workers, and consultants believe that they will be able to maintain their careers after becoming parents by dint of hard work and strategic planning, the qualities that have enabled them to succeed thus far? What they may fail to anticipate are the ways in which the context will morph into one that devalues their work and is riddled with unanticipated roadblocks to career growth.

Imagine you are, say, a midlevel manager at a large professional services firm. You started at the firm after college and returned after getting your MBA four years go. You are aiming to make partner. You have received stellar performance evaluations, you are cultivating relationships with a few key executives, and you make it known to your boss that you are eager for stretch assignments that will help you develop and demonstrate your potential. You and your spouse decide to start a family, and upon your child's birth you take advantage of your firm's industry-standard parental leave. When you return to work, you schedule a meeting with your boss. You want to propose that you'll focus on local clients for the next year and have the flexibility to leave the office around four o'clock to pick up your son from day care, when the norm in your department is to work in the office or at the client site until at least seven o'clock. You explain that you'll be back online after the nighttime routine and won't be working less, just working more hours from home. You remember that when you first came to the firm these kinds of arrangements were touted, along with the maternity leave you just took, as key components of the company's benefits scheme. You even recall one of the partners who spoke at a women employees' forum pointing them out as central to the firm's commitment to retaining and promoting women. Just to be sure you have the right information, you skim through the human resources intranet to confirm that your proposed plans are explicitly presented as options.

In the meeting, you also remind your boss about several upcoming milestones that the two of you have discussed as crucial to your career track. And you point out that you are exceptionally well qualified to lead a major project with a prominent client who happens to be located in your home city. Even though you've been with the firm for almost eight years and know that your supervisor has been impressed by your work, the conversation doesn't go as you'd expected. Your manager agrees to your requests but cuts the meeting short. In the coming months, you find that your boss doesn't seem as happy with your work, which is puzzling given that your output on the local projects meets or exceeds your past performance. You are disappointed when your manager tasks a younger male colleague with a high-profile assignment that is right in your wheelhouse, but when you ask to be put on the project your boss says simply that your coworker is a "better fit," even though he is less familiar with the industry. As time passes, you realize that you continue to be passed over for exactly the kinds of projects that would propel you to partnership. You also find that the senior colleagues who once sought you out for expertise or special requests have stopped doing so.

Unbeknownst to you, your request to modify your working arrangement triggered the flexibility stigma present in your workplace. Researchers describe the effects of this stigma as "both reputational and concrete":

> When caregiving constraints become salient at work, the quality of work assignments suffers. This alone can doom a career, given that career development is highly dependent on on-the-job highly specialized training. Yet negative career consequences are overdetermined: other penalties include the difficulty of finding mentors and sponsors, which again is vital for career progress in elite jobs.[35]

Experiencing both reputational and concrete effects, you feel increasingly disconnected from your job, once a source of deep meaning and satisfaction. In frustration, you decide to apply for a similar role at a competing firm, knowing that they have more women partners than your current employer. You are encouraged when the hiring manager calls you for an interview. Despite feeling that you aced the interview, you never hear back. Though you tell yourself they must have just wanted someone with different experience, you can't help but wonder if the fact that you are a parent of a young child played a role. Although the hiring manager didn't ask you about your family, you know that several former colleagues and friends work closely with her. When you hear that an old college friend was hired—a young father of two with a stay-at-home spouse—you can't help but wonder if he was viewed as a safer bet than you. Your nagging feeling that the hiring field wasn't quite level has a name, again grounded in social science: the motherhood penalty. Women with children are less likely to be hired than men—with or without children—or women without children. And we know why: Mothers are viewed as less committed and less competent than any of those other groups.[36] The penalty is gender-specific. The "daddy bonus," by contrast, means that men with children, especially professionals who are white, college-educated, and in households with a traditionally gendered division of labor, are paid more than childless men even when controlling for number of hours worked.[37]

At this point, faced with stymied career growth, you may very well decide to opt out of the workforce if financially feasible, but in context this decision looks less like a desire to leave than a reflection of how unrewarding it is to stay. Is it any wonder that it is ambitious women, those with elite pedigrees and impressive track records, who pause or abandon their careers? The deep sense of satisfaction they derive from work fades when opportunities to learn, grow, and lead are foreclosed. The high-flying MBA who drops out of the paid workforce is simply an extreme example of women's continued frustration at workplaces that prevent them from realizing their full potential.

How to Succeed in Business
(and Why It's Still Harder for Women)

Upon gaining admission to top law, medical, and business schools in the mid-twentieth century, growing numbers of women sought professional degrees to mitigate their structural disadvantage in the pursuit of jobs and promotions. One woman's 1980s-era memoir about earning her MBA described her decision to apply to business school: "So often, it seemed, women lacked the necessary authority to take control of a situation and be listened to. When I thought about my business and the work I would do helping people market and finance their ideas, I imagined myself sitting in front of a banker and trying to convince him or her to lend money to my client. When that image came to mind, so did an MBA. It was there like a silent partner, helping to shore up my credibility."[38] An MBA or other professional degree still remains a signal to employers, not only of the quality of a prospective employee's training but also his or her ambition and career orientation. An ever-increasing number of women have followed these early graduates' paths. Today 45 percent of applicants to graduate business schools are women.[39]

An MBA, particularly one from a top school, should—in theory—help to mitigate the effects of unequally distributed opportunities and counter gender stereotypes that render women less credible in certain settings. Business educators are undoubtedly aware that part of the value proposition they offer to women is an increased likelihood of ascending to ranks where there are few who share their gender. The Forté Foundation, a nonprofit promoting business education for and to women, states on its website (in a section titled "The Value of an MBA for Women") that "women with MBAs are more confident and content in their careers and earn more than their MBA-less counterparts." It goes on, "An MBA is an integral stop on the Path to the Boardroom." The website also notes three high-profile female leaders—former CEO Indra Nooyi of PepsiCo, Facebook COO Sheryl Sandberg, and Ellen Kullman, former CEO of DuPont—who hold MBAs.[40] Business education, this pitch suggests, will give ambitious women the footing to succeed in what remains a man's world.

Yet stepping into an MBA classroom can make women keenly aware that they remain underrepresented. A minority of faculty are women, and the protagonists of case studies—widely used as teaching materials around the world—are most commonly men (specifically, white and heterosexual men). In the words of a 2015 MBA graduate, the lack of women in cases "seemed like a shame, given that 40 percent of my classmates are women. . . . I don't think my gender had any sort of negative [impact] on my experience, but I feel like the academic experience was certainly more male-biased." Research has demonstrated that the representation of women in educational spaces does affect how women students perform and how they see their future options.[41] When we analyzed HBS's own curriculum, we found that three-quarters of cases taught in the first year (when all students take the same set of courses) featured male leaders. Given these numbers, it is unsurprising that women MBA students sometimes feel out of place. When asked about the extent to which gender as well as other social identities such as race were addressed in the curriculum, a 2013 graduate said, "Not at all, that I noticed. It didn't come up at all, and I think it was very poorly integrated." And it is not only women students who notice the absence of discussion around issues of gender diversity. A 2015 male graduate observed, "I don't really remember it taking up more than five minutes of conversation. You'd like it to be woven throughout, not just 'Today we're doing gender, tomorrow you can forget about it.'"

Course materials aren't the only signals that female business students receive. Another 2015 graduate noted how gender dynamics in the classroom can undermine women's sense of belonging: "I think it's harder for women to speak up in the classroom setting, and I think it's subconscious, because of how women are judged more harshly compared to their peers. . . . I think that's very true in the classroom setting. I think it impacts female students." Outside the classroom, women MBA students navigate other dynamics that make their gender salient. As one recalled, "It's funny, my guy friends who set up golf pools or sports brackets didn't even invite females, or think it would make sense to [invite women]. That always just made me laugh, because I like golf! I would golf with my guy friends—yet to them it would be male-oriented." Another noted, "Socially there were still things where it didn't really feel equal. There was definitely a finance crew that you could never really become friends with because you were a female, even if you had previous finance experience or future ambitions. There were those sorts of stereotypes that were frustrating, but I kind of chose to not even go to battle with them."

The educational climate at business school affects more than women's experiences in the classroom; it also influences how they articulate their ambitions. A 2017 study of students at a top-tier institution found that when unmarried women believed their responses to questions about their career aspirations and goals would be seen by their fellow students, they reported a desired salary $18,000 lower than when their responses would not be seen by classmates. They also said they were willing to travel seven fewer days per month and work four fewer hours and reported being less professionally ambitious and having lower leadership tendencies.[42] As these findings make clear, women are contending with contradictory expectations. Even in a setting where, by definition, everyone wants to advance their career and increase their earning power, women are well aware that these very characteristics may make them appear "too" ambitious and make it harder for them to find life partners.

This vexing choice intensifies as these same women move through their careers, manifesting not only in the conflicts women themselves wrestle with but also in how they are perceived in the workplace. Because characteristics stereotypically associated with leadership are in tension with those associated with femininity, women in positions of power tend to be viewed as competent but cold or nice but ineffective.[43] Discomfort with women in leadership roles is rooted in a contradiction between the "good woman" and the "good leader."[44] The existence of this double bind is not a secret. Indeed, women students may learn about it in organizational behavior or leadership courses. There is no shortage of books, workshops, curricula, or support groups that aim to help women navigate it, and any executive-level woman can recall the delicate balancing act.

At the start of their careers, young women may believe they can cultivate an image as both a "good woman" and "good leader," allowing them to earn professional rewards while avoiding pejorative labels such as "sharp-elbowed" and "domineering." In short, they strive to be seen as competent *and* likable—a respected leader who has warm, genuine relationships. Indeed, when we asked college students in their final semester to name women they viewed as epitomizing success, both women and men described the women they identified—ranging from celebrities to professors to industry leaders to students' own family members—as admirable not only for their professional achievements and influence ("Someone like Samantha Powers, very well respected in the field academically but also brings to bear her experience in policy") but also for coupling career with the roles of wife and mother ("and also managed to get married to that law school professor"). Even when students did not highlight these family roles in describing what they found admirable about the women they identified, when prompted to share what they might ask these women, the students frequently said they would ask them about how they managed their work-life balance. One graduating senior, who had accepted a consulting job to begin after graduation and planned to get an MBA, summed up the dual imperative for women:

> One of my parents' friends is actually a woman who has two children, and she is a partner at a consulting firm. For someone like that to be able to have the best of both worlds—that's something that I've been talking about a lot: women who are able to have a family, and not just have it, but be able to actually spend time with them and be a good mother but at the same time still develop her career. That's something that I really respect.

This student's praise for the female partner "still develop[ing] her career" while not just having children but "be[ing] a good mother" mirrors the dominant narrative about motherhood as the primary impediment to women's career advancement. The female partner stands in as the exception that proves the rule: someone who inhabits the role of good leader (evidenced by her promotion to partner) as well as good woman (demonstrated in her maternal devotion). But the female partner is, in fact, simply an exception—fewer than 20 percent of managing directors and partners in major professional service firms are women.

What happens to women who do reach leadership? Their stories make clear that assumptions about caregiving are far from the only factor that contributes to women's underrepresentation in the C-suite and other executive ranks. Gender becomes more salient as women ascend to more senior positions, and this marginal status becomes more pronounced as female peers leak from the pipeline. Because manifestations of bias evolve from one career stage to the next, women are tasked with identifying and navigating new forms of subtle discrimination just as they are taking on increasingly challenging roles and new responsibilities. What may have long been a successful strategy of keeping one's head down and paying little attention to gender differences often falters when women rise in the ranks, even as their high-level jobs afford the kind of autonomy and flexibility that allows them to manage their family responsibilities more easily.

Striking the perfect balance between expectations for women and those for leaders is by definition impossible, yet women in leadership roles spend significant time and mental resources attempting to achieve it—time over and above the demands of their actual jobs. As one vice president of sales we spoke to noted, "It's not about work. The problem is never about work. Because on work, I deliver." As women navigate the increasing complexities that come with the expanded scope and responsibility of more senior roles, they must simultaneously manage the challenges of being outliers—another kind of second shift. The higher a woman ascends, the more noticeable her difference from the masculine norm, a realization that often dawns on women as they climb higher and find themselves the only woman in the room. We spoke to dozens of women in executive roles, many of whom were aiming for promotion to the C-suite at the time of our interviews. The next chapter explores their experiences and the tactics they deployed to navigate the evolving obstacle course.

REACHING FOR THE TOP

The Honorable Barbara Hackman Franklin

n the 1950s, college-educated women had few options for pursuing a professional life—and those who did were expected to leave their jobs behind when they married. Barbara Franklin intended to carve a different path. She recalls, "I'm not sure I could have defined what success was—but I knew I wanted a career." Encouraged by a father who said "You can do anything you want, but do it well," Franklin set off for college at Penn State with high, if slightly hazy, aspirations. ("I think my mother never really approved of the whole idea," she notes.)

A trailblazing path did unfold, as did a long-running habit of making her way into places that were the traditional province of men. In 1962, Franklin's last year of college, came a call from the dean of women. Harvard Business School, which offered, in partnership with Radcliffe College, a certificate program for women called the Harvard-Radcliffe Program in Business Administration, had begun allowing women graduates of that program to attend the second year of its traditional MBA curriculum. For the first time since the school's founding in 1908, women were being awarded Harvard MBAs. Franklin was considering graduate work in political science and law school, but she knew that a professional degree from Harvard would open the door to opportunities few women had yet accessed.

At the time Franklin didn't see her ambition as particularly remarkable, but she did know she was an outlier. At HBS, her minority status was front and center: "The challenging part was just all those men. There were six hundred–something, and there were very few of us women. I think we started with fourteen in the class of '64." While some male classmates were hostile toward their presence, most were fairly neutral, and some were openly supportive. But even if men's attitudes toward women students were, on balance, friendly, Franklin and her female peers were not always treated equally:

> We women all had that same experience of being called on by a professor and laying out the case, and nobody would say anything. The discussion would go on from there, and then later someone would say the same thing, often in some of the same words, and it would be welcomed as an astute comment. And you wanted to say, "But I said that!"

There were more explicit obstacles too. An eminent professor denied Franklin and several of her female classmates seats in his wildly popular course, a policy the school's administration declined to dissuade him from. "He wouldn't have any women. He was very clear about that," she remembers.

After graduating Franklin pushed on, joining the Singer Company in New York City as the company's first female employee with an MBA and the only woman in the department she was hired into. As Franklin's career unfolded, she set her sights on corporate leadership: "When I started to get into organizations, I was always looking at the top of it, and so my aspiration would have been that—to get to the top of it." And despite the challenges of working in the overwhelmingly male workplace of the time, Franklin seemed to be on her way there: "There were three women assistant vice presidents [at what is now Citibank], and I was one of them. I was the young one, and I would have been on the fast track, if there was such a thing, to become a full vice president." That Franklin was on a path to upper management is all the more noteworthy because she had no female role models, and certainly no women at the bank were in a position to mentor her. "There were no women full vice presidents," she recalls. In fact, "there were just not a whole lot of women anywhere who were not secretaries."

It wasn't lost on Franklin that her emerging leadership deviated from conventional expectations:

> I married someone who wasn't all that keen about my career. He said my career objectives, my career, would be fine—but that's not what he meant, ultimately. I think this kind of miscommunication happens today, too. We talk about the same things, and use the same words, but the meanings are not the same, particularly when it has to do with women's aspirations.

That early marriage soon ended, and Franklin later remarried. Today, she counts her thirty-year dual-career union with a "wonderfully supportive" spouse as an important part of her journey.

As it happened, enabling women's aspirations would become Franklin's own professional mission in a remarkable career turn. In the early 1970s, she was recruited to head a White House initiative on women in government and served as staff assistant to the president, leading an effort to recruit women into high-level professional and policy roles in federal government. By the time Franklin finished, the number of women in such jobs had more than tripled. Her success was unsurprising to business school classmate Ed Hajim, who commented to the *Harvard Crimson* years later that "anything she has undertaken, public or private, whatever she's involved in, it improves."[45]

As the staff leader of the program, Franklin turned lofty pronouncements about the need for more women in government into day-in, day-out operations:

> It was a managerial effort, meaning that the president required action plans for advancing women from all of his cabinet secretaries and agency heads, and those plans were monitored. They

were monitored by me, and there would be reports that would then go up the line, that the president would get. If a cabinet secretary did what he was supposed to do and met his—they were all men then—targets, he got a note from the president saying "Well done on this." That makes a difference. If he did not, then he got a different kind of note. And I know that because I was drafting them.

Franklin's work, along with the visible support of President Nixon, helped to shift the national conversation about women in the workforce at a time when, as she notes, "there was not a consensus in our society about women and careers." Although Nixon's efforts to promote women in the federal workforce began after a reporter's question about the issue at a 1969 press conference, Franklin speculates that it was not just political expediency that inspired him.[46] Nixon was undoubtedly responding to pressure from the women's movement, especially because "Republican women were making noise—it wasn't just the other side of the aisle." But Franklin points out that First Lady Pat Nixon was "really a self-made woman" who had paid her way through college in the 1930s and worked for the American Red Cross and the federal Office of Price Administration early in her marriage to the president. "I do think that she had a role—whispering in his ear, or whatever it might have been. And they had two daughters."

Franklin's own career path, already unconventional, continued to be groundbreaking. In the 1980s, she served on the boards of seven publicly traded companies at a time when almost no women sat in company boardrooms. In the early 1990s, she was appointed secretary of commerce by President George H. W. Bush, becoming the highest-ranking woman in his administration. Her public service includes four terms on the Advisory Committee for Trade Policy and Negotiations during the 1980s and 1990s as well as being appointed an alternate representative to the 44th United Nations General Assembly. Near the end of her tenure as secretary of commerce, she was asked by President Bush to pursue a controversial mission to renew US-China economic relations, which had stalled after the Chinese government's 1989 crackdown on pro-democracy protests in Tiananmen Square. The prospect of friendlier relations with China was unpopular in the wake of Tiananmen Square: Some Republican members of Congress viewed the trip as tacit approval of communism, while Democrats decried human rights violations. Amid negative press, in the final weeks of the Bush administration Franklin traveled to Beijing to hold talks with Chinese officials about trade relations and to encourage new business agreements. By the time she departed a few days later, almost $1 billion worth of contracts for American companies had been signed, setting the stage for an ongoing trade relationship. Today, we are accustomed to seeing female cabinet officials undertake high-profile international missions, but none had done so prior to Franklin's 1992 visit to China.

Franklin has had stints on the boards of nearly twenty companies, and she chaired the National Association of Corporate Directors from 2009 to 2013. As she continued to ascend in her career, she found that while some obstacles "got cleared away" as social norms, laws, and policies shifted, others "popped up that are more invisible. It's harder when there's a prejudice or stereotype in somebody's head." As a corporate board member, she found that although many male colleagues were welcoming, "one had to dance around on eggshells a little bit . . . to be accepted as a member of the group— and be respected as a member of the group." Franklin acknowledges that while much has changed since the early days of her career, there is still resistance to women in leadership roles: "There just is."

Despite the persistence of such obstacles, Franklin does see cause for optimism. Although women are still a minority in boardrooms and other leadership ranks, "today there are more clusters of women. You step in not having to walk around on eggshells as much as I did in the early days, because automatically there's some respect. There are gradations of that [respect], but it's a whole lot better than it was thirty years ago." Franklin also believes that today's women leaders have a role to play in growing the numbers: "I have made it a point when I am leaving any group, like a board, that if I have anything to do with selecting a successor, I try to make sure that it's a woman."

Franklin has not restricted her efforts to advance women's career opportunities to conversations with her corporate colleagues. "I've gone to see several different deans at Harvard Business School over the years," she says. "I remember once, I prepared a good three minutes, point by point, on what I believed the school needed to think about and maybe change. I think it's been tough going. It took a number of folks to break down some of the barriers that were a part of the culture of the school, and I'm proud of where Harvard Business School has come. I really am. And it needs to keep going."

CHAPTER 2

SCARCE, SCRUTINIZED, AND STILL CLIMBING

Women in Leadership

Recall the voices of undergraduates from the previous chapter, who noticed a lack of women in the senior ranks of the fields and firms they were on the cusp of entering. "The legal field is still mostly male-dominated," one aspiring law student noted. "There's not many women at the partner level," said another of the consulting firm she would soon be joining. "All the executives on the other side of the table," observed another student after a job interview, "were men." Recall too how students explained these disparities as the vestige of practices that no longer prevailed. These young women assumed with confidence that for their own careers, "the gender part doesn't really matter anymore."

They were partly right—gender matters far less than it once did. No longer limited to pink-collar support jobs, women have arrived at a place of greater opportunity and certainly far less de jure discrimination. But inequalities persist. While some women have broken through to the top ranks of leadership, the proportion remains far lower than that of their participation in the labor force. Of the US workers employed in professional occupations, 52 percent were women as of 2017, yet the proportion of women executives and senior-level officials in the S&P 500 was just half that, at 26.5 percent.[1] Women are even more scarce at the highest heights of business; as of May 2020, 7.4 percent of companies in the *Fortune* 500 were led by a female CEO. And that proportion was an all-time high.[2] Historically, there are just eighty-seven women who have ever served as CEO of a *Fortune* 500 company.[3] In 2018, a *New York Times* article quickly went viral for pointing out that there were fewer women CEOs in the *Fortune* 500 than there were male CEOs named James.[4] Only two Black women have appeared on the list: Ursula Burns, CEO of Xerox from 2009 to 2017, and Mary Winston, who served as interim CEO of Bed Bath & Beyond for six months in 2019.[5] With the departure of Pepsi-Co's Indra Nooyi late in 2018, the business community kicked off 2019 with under 1 percent of *Fortune* 500 CEO seats held by women of color.[6]

The data are clear: Women start to vanish as the corporate hierarchy ascends. Many of those who get almost to the peak are unable to break through to CEO or similar roles, watching as white men continue to dominate the most high-status, lucrative projects or lines of business. To take just one real-world example, in Pricewater-houseCoopers's *Building on a Culture of Belonging: 2020 PwC Diversity & Inclusion Transparency Report*, the firm revealed that three-quarters of its largest audit accounts were led by white male partners. During that fiscal year, the firm had worked with 90 percent of the companies in the *Fortune* 500, but just 19 percent of those key engagements were led by women or nonwhite men.[7]

To study the women who had managed to reach senior ranks, we conducted in-depth interviews with seventy-five executives across twenty-six countries, all of whom were partners, vice presidents, division heads, or C-suite leaders at multinational and other large companies at the time of our interviews. We asked all of them about the influence of gender on their career paths and what conditions and strategies contributed to their success. Their experiences highlight the most obdurate obstacles women face—factors that even highly accomplished leaders continue to come up against—and also reveal the strengths and limitations of common strategies for overcoming them. The women we interviewed are survivors. They got the crucial breaks, the senior colleagues willing to go to bat for them, and the opportunities to lead high-profile projects. For every woman we spoke to there are unknown scores of others, equally skilled and ambitious, who never made it to the executive level. Understanding how these women leaders navigated uneven terrain can help us understand what needs to change for more of their peers to succeed.

The Outlier Effect

The women we spoke to were keenly aware that their gender made them conspicuous, for better *and* worse. One, a chief operating officer in the energy industry, reflected: "I've always been in male-dominated environments at work and in businesses. I think one of the early lessons I got was that women are visible in such environments, and that goes both ways. It means that if you fail, and everyone does in some areas, it's highly visible, and everyone knows it. On the other hand, if you succeed, it's also highly visible." A number of interviewees put this positive spin on minority status, including one CEO: "In one way, it's a huge advantage to stand out. People don't expect [a woman] when you walk into a meeting." But even she acknowledged that it came at a cost: "You're always a bit of a misfit in a social circle, and work is not just about getting a deal done; it's also about the environment and the people that you work with." One executive at a large insurance company found that being a woman of color compounded this challenge:

I'm a female non-European in a predominantly white-dominated environment. It made people just not sure how to relate to me.

People become very cautious in how they deal with me. And it takes a much longer time to build their trust or build relationships because I'm alien to them. I'm too foreign; I'm nonmale, and I'm non-European. It took a very long time to build any rapport or working relationship.

Women in powerful roles stand out not only because they are rare but also because leadership archetypes align with men and masculinity. Decades of research have demonstrated this, and our interviewees felt it firsthand, as one finance executive observed: "There's a kind of a masculine norm. This doesn't have to be a vicious or a negative norm, but it's a norm that says you are different, you're abnormal." Simply put, traditional beliefs about women—that they are communally oriented, emotionally sensitive, and attuned to others' needs— contrast with the attributes thought to characterize leadership, such as authoritativeness, independence, and rationality.[8] Even though gender roles have evolved over time, the archetypal leader remains male. Asking a group of professionals to draw an "effective leader" yields sketches of men and captions about "his" qualities, as one management professor found while leading workshops in multiple companies.[9] Meanwhile, women in positions of authority shake up our expectations—of women and of leaders—so much that we may even assume, consciously or not, that our women colleagues don't *want* to wield power. One CFO of a biotechnology company continued to observe her colleagues defaulting to junior male candidates for promotion, long after she herself was an executive: "I've asked men, when they're promoting someone, 'Did you consider these women?' and they would just automatically have the assumption 'Well, she's probably not interested.'"

Being evaluated against the masculine norm was typical for the women we spoke to and meant a higher bar to clear. A senior vice president at an entertainment company described the resulting tax on her ambitions: "I have really had to work my way into the boys' club, so to speak. Just for women in Asia, working in my capacity amongst men is really rare." A marketing executive said she "felt like I was entering an all-boys' club and [being] summarily dismissed at the start. I think I had to work really hard to build up credibility." For women in client-centered fields such as consulting, struggling to build rapport with male clients was a common experience. Some went so far as to forego working with certain industries or companies to avoid cultures where "the barriers are too high," as a female partner at a consulting firm put it.[10]

One phenomenon came up again and again in our interviews: When women approached the uppermost ranks at their companies, skepticism about their suitability for leadership suddenly came to the fore. Their performance wasn't typically in question, but their fit for leadership was. One banking executive pointed out that men may be willing to work with women but less happy to have them as true peers: "In your thirties, they're hoping you're going to get married, have children, and never come back. In your forties, they start taking you as real head-to-head competition." Sometimes the messages undermining women's ambitions were explicit; one woman was told that she would never become CEO because she was "the wrong fit" for the top job. (She was later appointed CEO.)[11] Other times it's subtler, as this sales executive described:

In the first fifteen years of my career, I never thought of myself as a woman leader. I was just a business executive or a business manager, just like any other male colleague of mine. And I never ever thought of myself as a woman leader. But I have started feeling that in the last two years. I don't know if the reason is because when you reach senior positions, you somehow begin to feel that you are not moving as fast as others. I particularly feel, do I make certain men insecure when they are around me? Do I make a boss feel insecure about me? These kinds of thoughts never used to occur to me, but they've started occurring to me in the last two years.

The women in our study who hit the proverbial glass ceiling are not unique. In 2018, the Australian Parliament offered an exemplary case of a high-achieving female leader's stalled momentum when Julie Bishop stood for election to lead the Liberal Party, the first woman ever to do so. Although Bishop had been the party's deputy head for more than a decade and had higher public approval ratings than her two male opponents, she lost with less than 13 percent support from fellow lawmakers.[12] Despite Bishop's widely lauded track record as foreign minister and popularity with voters, the top job, where she would have wielded real power over the party, was off limits. In a private sector example, former Pinterest chief operating officer Françoise Brougher sued the company in 2020, alleging that she was excluded from decision-making, was compensated less than male colleagues, and was fired after voicing her discontent with gender discrimination. Brougher, a sought-after tech executive with stints at Square and Google, was stunned to encounter these obstacles after being personally recruited to the company by its CEO just two years earlier. "Here is a glass ceiling I never hit into until my 50s that I suddenly did, very violently," Brougher told the *New York Times*. "You don't see it all. And then you hit it."[13]

Under the Microscope

Like Brougher, the women we interviewed typically didn't anticipate late-career barriers. For many who started out in the 1980s and 1990s, especially in industries with a significant proportion of women, gender seemed incidental until suddenly it was paramount. A vice president at a large media conglomerate explained:

> There were lots of "web girls" and "women in new media" organizations, and I never wanted to be a part of it. I was so busy. I thought, "I don't have the time for this. I don't even understand what they're on about. Just get to work. Work hard and you'll be fine." And it's interesting that, up to a certain level in your career, that's true. But not when you're really trying to break through

the final layer—which is kind of where I'm at now—especially in this day and age where [organizations] are increasingly complicated. I ran into it first at [my previous company], which is big telecom and male-dominated. They had very little patience or tolerance for diversity on the management team. I think their blueprints for senior managers are male-dominated. They're really having to wrap their heads around how women fit in.

The resistance women faced was just that: a drag on their velocity, slowing down their advancement. One finance executive estimated that it slowed her trajectory by a decade:

I am absolutely certain that if I had been a man, both in the way I would have behaved and in the way I would have been perceived, I would have definitely had a more rapid career. I can't say that I'm unhappy with the result of it but I think I would have liked to reach the level I am today in my forties rather than in my late fifties, and I definitely think that gender played a role.

As part of our research, we also spoke to a smaller sample of men in senior roles. They rarely spoke about a need to manage perceptions within their companies as part of their career development, while women described spending considerable energy and effort to do so. Women recounted stories such as that of a longtime energy executive who took great pains to help her male colleagues feel comfortable in her presence and empathize with their feelings of uncertainty about how to relate to her. She and others expressed a need to strike a delicate balance between not alienating men and pushing back against gender bias when it felt career-threatening. The relationship management and image management that ambitious woman perform is often described with the metaphor of the tightrope, but it might be more accurately characterized as an invisible weight. For the women in our study, managing how others perceive and react to their gender added a cognitive and practical burden onto already demanding job responsibilities. To take just one example, we looked at the data from men and women within a single industry, consulting, for an apples-to-apples comparison and found that while developing a "personal brand" was seen as key for everyone, what that actually meant was more complex and more onerous for women. Everyone had to specialize, pursue visibility, and hone a long-term vision to craft an effective personal brand, but on top of all that women had to focus on finding an appropriate leadership style and practice communicating assertively. Women in the industry also cited the need to actively seek out developmental feedback in order to understand where they needed to grow and improve, whereas men simply spoke of the need to work on their shortcomings.[14] This difference echoes research finding that women are less likely than men to receive practical feedback, instead getting vague praise that doesn't provide actionable recommendations or even distorted feedback that obviates or minimizes constructive criticism.[15]

The more senior a woman is, the more likely she is to be the only woman in the room, facing an increasing need to manage perceptions and shore up credibility as she moves up the ranks. A banking executive in our study explained: "I have seen that when women reach higher levels, more than complimenting her on her ability, people tend to say, 'Oh, she's been close to this person, that person,' whether there is a relationship or not." Persistent stereotypes about women's innate capabilities fuel some of these doubts, as was noted by an energy industry vice president who recalled multiple colleagues who felt "they'd never come across a woman who's good at math." (Indeed, a 2017 study found that a belief that women are worse than men at math does make employers less likely to hire women, even when the performance of individual women is just as strong as that of male candidates.[16]) In one 2018 study, women who were often the only female employee in their work environment were especially likely to say their judgment was questioned, that they had to provide extra evidence of their competence, or that they were mistaken for someone in a much lower-level role.[17] One of our interviewees, an executive at a multinational food company, echoed these findings: "I find it much more difficult to be taken seriously. I had to become much more prepared than I feel a male colleague has to. I have to be much surer of what I'm saying to be taken seriously or to be credible." And another woman in a very different industry, banking, made the same assessment: "I've been in quite male-dominated environments where women have certainly had to work harder and smarter than their peers to break through to the top ranks." And women of color tend to experience an even higher "burden of proof" and yet another layer of scrutiny as they navigate their careers.[18]

Having to undergo stricter scrutiny than male colleagues and co-workers came up again and again in our interviews. One top executive at a global consulting firm explained that "as a woman, and as a Black woman, I had to work five times more to be noticed." An officer at a large insurance company said, "Gender mattered a lot. It didn't mean that I missed out on opportunities; it just meant that I felt I had to work a whole lot harder than anyone else." This higher bar meant not only that women had to work harder for recognition but also that their missteps were viewed in a harsher light. "There is no tolerance for a female to have an off day," said one vice president at a packaging company. "You'll be labeled as emotional or someone that can't handle [her job]." A banking executive described an unforgiving double standard: "I do think that women get criticized much more for behaviors than men. If a woman loses it, she's seen as emotional. Whereas if men lose it, that is seen as just par for the course; he's just being strong, or whatever. And I think women therefore have to be incredibly careful about their behavior at all times."

This need for vigilance is not mere anecdote; studies have found that women who exhibit emotions such as anger in the workplace are indeed seen as less competent than men who do the same.[19] Black women experience an extra burden, as the executive above felt. Researchers have found that Black female leaders are judged more harshly for organizational failures than white men, Black men, or white women.[20] For women of color especially, a reputation for competence is both harder to attain and more easily lost. Even women at the top of their game feel the threat and protect themselves accordingly. Recent research on executive compensation found that female CEOs negotiate for higher severance pay in their contracts than men do, suggesting that women stepping into high-profile leadership roles realize they could be "more dispensable than their male counterparts."[21]

Nevertheless, She Persists

To their credit, many companies notice and attempt to remedy gender disparity in promotion and advancement. But too often such efforts spend scant time on the kinds of biases our interviewees spoke of in favor of creating family accommodations. At the same time, their organizational cultures stigmatize flexible hours and other "family friendly" policies such that they actually undermine the careers of women who take advantage of them.[22] Our interviewees were senior executives who had largely solved or resolved the challenges of balancing their work and family roles but still struggled to fully actualize their career aims. A number of them found that as they ascended in the hierarchy, they gained more autonomy and flexibility, making it in fact easier for them to manage competing demands as they took on more responsibility at work. Unfortunately, a focus on work-family conflict as the most important and most explanatory driver of women's underrepresentation in leadership obscures and distracts from other obstacles, including biased attitudes and behaviors, meaning less effort is spent on mitigating discrimination even when it is a more pressing factor.[23] One CEO in the transportation industry saw exactly this phenomenon play out many times:

> You saw a huge number of people who were leaving who were really talented, and the reasons they gave as they walked out the door were not the reasons that they actually left. The reasons

they gave you as they walked out the door were "too many hours, too tough a job, can't have a family and do this, work-life balance." And then you get right down to it—it's really that they're feeling underrecognized. It takes women longer to get the same achievement level as men, and they get tired of not being heard and not being listened to.

If company policies to accommodate parenting were not the primary reason that the women we spoke to had been able to stay on a leadership track, what factors—both individual and organizational—had been instrumental in their success? The women we interviewed were often the only remaining members of their cohorts; one, a senior vice president at a real estate investment group, crunched the numbers as she described her journey:

> When I was at [an investment bank], in my class there would have been twenty analysts starting out; it dropped down to about fifteen people by the time you got to the associate class, and then by the time you reached the VP level, there were maybe ten of us left from the initial class. You generally get 50 percent attrition—by which time I was the only female. When we started off, the class was closer to 40 percent female. By the time you get to the VP level, it's literally 10 percent. And the numbers get worse at the managing director level.

How had the women we spoke to maintained an upward trajectory as peers walked out the door or found themselves stalled at lower levels? Part of the answer clearly lay in their ability and willingness to respond to the contradictory demands that stem from the norms about gender and leadership discussed above. Making one's ambitions known could come at a cost, as a finance executive told us: "When women say 'I want a raise' or 'I want this,' they're sometimes treated as though they're being pushy, whereas it's expected or anticipated that men will say 'I deserve this.'" At the same time, when the default assumption is that women are "probably not interested" in stepping into higher-level roles, as the biotech CFO quoted above found that her colleagues believed, not being explicit about one's aspirations could easily mean never moving up. After this chapter is a profile of Ana Paula Pessoa, a high-flying media executive, tech investor, and corporate director who may not have achieved any of these powerful roles if she hadn't spoken up about her desire to take on new opportunities, even if they meant relocating to a new city—something one manager initially presumed she wouldn't be open to doing.

Women get to leadership by threading the thinnest of needles—being direct enough about their ambitions to counter assumptions that they don't want or can't handle top jobs, but without being branded as overly aggressive or unpleasant. In environments where the masculine norm shapes expectations, women labored to articulate, clarify, and stress their aspirations to leadership. A retired agribusiness leader summed up the balancing act:

> You don't want people making assumptions for you, as in "Oh, she never said she would be interested in being CEO. Maybe that's not her gig. She wants to be middle-level management, or she likes sales or blah blah blah." Don't let them make assumptions for you, but do it in a way that's not in your face, as in "I want your job, I want to be the CEO. I'm going to be the CEO." Instead, say it in a way such as, "I would like to have the opportunity to continue to progress in this company, and my ultimate goal would be, I'd love to be the CEO or I'd love to be one of the members of the executive team."

Managing this tradeoff between competence and likeability exacts a mental tax, as women strive to be seen as capable ("I'd love to be the CEO") without alienating (by being too "in your face" about that goal) the peers and superiors whose endorsement they need to advance. As we sifted through the data from our interviews, an underlying factor that enabled women to take on this work day after day

became apparent: They had quite consciously and deliberately cultivated a sense of resilience. "Part of the challenge is that in an environment where there are very few [women leaders], you look up and
you see one, maybe two, and you almost self-doubt," one consulting
executive said, explaining the need for nurturing her leadership ambitions. Women in our study often reframed the experience of being
in the minority, as a CFO described: "I have worked very much in environments that were geared more towards men than towards
women, and I think it has influenced me to become a stronger person, because you have to have the will to succeed and really want to
succeed in that environment." Similarly, a finance executive turned
hostility into motivation:

> There was one man who just had it out against me at the firm.
> There was a promotion that I wanted, that I thought I deserved,
> and I was told at the end of the year that the reason I didn't get it
> was because of this particular person—they thought that he
> would quit if I was promoted. I didn't even know how to respond.
> It was so infuriating. There was no logic. I just thought, you're
> going to make a suboptimal decision because of one person in
> the organization? I questioned if I wanted to keep working there.
> But I thought, I am going to prove him wrong, and ultimately,
> I did. And that guy ended up reporting to me. He quit about
> three months into reporting to me, but I treated him as fairly as
> anyone else.

Deciding to ignore or mentally minimize bias or other obstacles
was a common tactic. As a human resource executive put it, "I dismiss it. I don't really give it any space." Another woman, at a food-
services company, described a singular focus that helped her quell
anxieties as she strived to advance: "I never stopped to consider—
maybe I should back off or not, or maybe I'll wait for somebody to ask
me. I just thought, I want to do this, and I went and did it." A thick skin
proved to be as useful as any business acumen. Women executives told

us many stories of having the proverbial last laugh, including one recounted by the president of a chemical company. She recalled being an invited guest at a meeting of local businesspeople early on in her career:

> I looked in, and I realized there's not one woman in here.
> I [thought I] must be in the wrong place. But I saw my name and figured no, I'm in the right place. I sat down, said hello to the people that were at the same table; I didn't know anybody.
> I started talking to the people at my table, and there was a gentleman who literally ignored me. About ten years later [at a similar event], I saw him. "Hi, Mr. So-and-so," I said. "It's been a long time, but don't you remember the first time we met?" I told him the story and he said, "Did I really do that?" Yes, you did.

In the face of being ignored, diminished, or discounted, an inner drive was sustaining: "You have to believe that you can contribute and should be there. There is no reason why you shouldn't. I've always just worked on the assumption that I can, and therefore I will, even though I will sometimes be only grudgingly acknowledged or be labeled as difficult," one woman said. The leaders in our study were anchored in a sense of purpose that inspired them to get tough when they needed to. One CEO acknowledged that women couldn't count on being heard: "[I had] a realization that in some of the debates and arguments around the table, unless I really pushed my way forward and challenged and engaged, I would probably be sitting there quietly for a very long time." This determination to push past and navigate around barriers is even more critical for women of color, who face the additional disadvantage of being in the racial minority in the vast majority of professional settings. Several of our colleagues undertook a study of Black women who had achieved C-suite or other leadership roles and found that a key contributor to their success was agility in steering through and transforming the many obstacles they experienced over the course of their careers, often through making unconventional industry or function switches and exiting organizations where they couldn't grow.[24]

Before Every Successful Woman

As we continued to explore what women said about resilience, we saw that it wasn't only an intrinsic quality but also a product of the interplay between women and their environments. Resilience could either be cultivated or quashed, and the context mattered. As a senior vice president at an energy concern explained, "I found that I had to stand my ground, but it was hard to do when you're the most junior person in the room, and you're the only woman in the room." One late-career executive serving on the boards of several companies explained, "You have to find avenues that support that resilience" both at work and in one's personal relationships. And a finance executive made an impassioned case for prioritizing the right environment. More than just culture fit, a context where women can succeed is one where their confidence is fostered, she explained:

> Don't let yourself be surrounded by people who diminish your self-esteem. I left my first banking job for that reason. Life is short, and your self-confidence is the most important resource you've got; you have to nurture and protect it. If you find yourself in such a position, get out. If you can't change it and you don't see signs of improvement, take the risk and move on. It can be difficult and scary to leave a job today, in an environment where jobs are not as plentiful as they might have once been, but you must find opportunities where you're going to be nurtured. You want to be in an environment where people help you succeed, not places where they're going to tear you down.

The presence of female role models emerged as a crucial feature of resilience-building environments. Seeing even one woman in leadership in their company or industry could foster optimism. A visible woman leader who was respected and valued within the organization reassured that high performance would be rewarded. "I worked with a female boss, and she was very efficient; she was known in our bank as one of the very efficient managers. She had risen in her career very young in life, so she was a role model for me," the head of operations at a large bank told us. "I looked forward to emulating that kind of growth in my career, by just being as efficient and effective as her." Meanwhile, an energy executive emphasized the impact that seeing women succeeding at the top of her field had on her:

> During the five years I was at [my previous company], we had a female CEO. So that was an extraordinarily important period for me. That was an excellent, excellent experience for me, because I had a female CEO and also a board that was very supportive of her. I saw how important it was not just to have females in leadership roles but to have male leaders who completely support women in leadership roles.

Seeing women in supervisory and senior positions had made our interviewees aware of their own leadership potential, both directly and indirectly. A vice president at a multinational oil and gas company told us about the transformative influence of a female boss who believed in her potential: "One of my most inspiring managers was female. I remember her saying, 'You are so capable that someday I'll be reporting to you, or you'll go way past me.' And she was extremely capable herself and quite the high flyer. For her to say that, and have that very clear vote of confidence in me, was hugely inspiring." For another executive, having a female sponsor provided access to important networks:

> She didn't mentor you by telling you what to do. She mentored you by always giving you maximum exposure. For example, she had approached the chairman and said, "Are you okay if

[interviewee] comes to the board meeting and takes the minutes?" It was not just about giving you the skills, but it was about giving you the exposure to dealing with people at different levels in the organization and not feeling at all threatened by that.

Whether or not role models had been personal mentors or direct supervisors, their presence had made it possible for women to project themselves into leadership roles and, importantly, to believe that their company was a place where women could reach top positions. Just as important, we found, were men who chose to create opportunities for high-performing women and recognized their contributions, as recounted by one executive:

One of my first jobs at [my current company] was with the CIO here, who basically gave me my assignment, told me I was the best-qualified person he could possibly hope to find, and that he was going to get out of my way and let me make it happen. He was there for me when I needed him, but he basically said, "I know you can do it," and he stepped aside.

While female leaders had often been critical as role models, most of the women we studied had primarily reported to men; without male mentors and supporters, their careers would have foundered. Men's predominance in supervisory roles is a key feature of the context women experience, and male managers profoundly shape the extent to which their workplaces enable or undermine women's development. In Chapter 4, we will more deeply explore the role of men in addressing the underrepresentation of women in leadership, but our conversations with women executives already make clear that men can exert an enormous positive influence on women's advancement. Considering the fact that men still hold the majority of managerial and decision-making positions, companies need men to fully engage in the project of removing obstacles to women's advancement if they are ultimately to see their leadership ranks become more gender-balanced.

Yet, the very atypicality of our sample—female senior executives, many in male-dominated industries such as finance, energy, and mining—implies a lack of systemic commitment. The "survivors" we studied reached the top of the hierarchy through their own willingness to take on the work that comes with minority status but also through the men, and some women, in positions of power who opened doors that might otherwise have remained locked. In our final chapter we will turn toward the role of organizations in crafting less haphazard, more systematic leadership ladders. But first, we will look to the highest level of corporate power—the boardroom—and how women are agitating and strategizing for seats at that table.

LEADING WITH PURPOSE

Ana Paula Pessoa

When Ana Paula Pessoa was growing up in Brazil in the 1970s and early 1980s, the country's press was censored by a military regime that would ultimately fall around the time Pessoa moved to the United States to attend Stanford University. So perhaps it's fitting that years later she became an executive at the largest media company in South America. "I ended up working in the field that I felt was really important for democracy: a strong and free media," she reflects, looking back on eighteen years at Rio de Janeiro–based Grupo Globo. But even before launching her media career, Pessoa was motivated by an aspiration to better society, looking for ways to combine her love of math and economics with her desire to improve people's lives.

After earning her undergraduate degree, Pessoa went to work for the United Nations and the World Bank, managing projects while also pursuing graduate research in economic development. While she initially aimed to earn a PhD in development economics, her interests began to branch out in the early 1990s as she observed the rapid technological changes around her. Personal computers and other innovations were having, as she recalls, "an incredible impact on everyday life. The changes were profound, and they really interested me. I had this intuition about how important technology would be for individuals, not just companies and countries."

In 1993, Pessoa moved back to Brazil after nearly a decade away, joining Globo as a telecommunications manager. Transitioning to the rapidly evolving media industry was a natural step, allowing her to deploy her technical aptitude and have an impact on the social and economic changes unfolding in her home country. A sense of mission motivated Pessoa as she climbed the ranks at Globo:

> I worked hard and fearless, with an open heart and really confident that what I was doing was not selfishly for me personally, but for a very good cause. The promotions I received were ultimately because I thought the work was really interesting, and I was never afraid to ask "Can I do this?" I was never afraid of putting myself up for a job.

That sense of purpose and possibility helped Pessoa counter assumptions that threatened to slow her pace. Early on, one well-meaning boss thought she wouldn't be interested in a role based in Globo's São Paulo office, six hours away by car, but Pessoa was quick to set the record straight:

> I heard about a position in São Paulo I wasn't chosen for, and I went to [my manager] and I said, you know, I would move. And he was shocked because I was recently married. He said "Oh! I never realized you would be willing to move. I thought you wouldn't want to relocate to São Paulo." I explained to him it would not be a problem. It's an hourlong plane ride—I could commute on Monday and come home to Rio on Friday, that way spending the weekend together with my husband. And if I stay there longer than a few years, I continued, maybe he'll move to São Paulo too. I didn't get that specific job I'd been passed over for, and it took maybe another year for another position to open up, but by this time they knew I was open to it. I think this kind of situation occurs to a lot of women, because the corporate world assumes women will not or cannot relocate in order to embrace an opportunity. You have to speak up and say "I'll go!"

Pessoa spent almost two decades at Globo in business roles of increasing responsibility, ultimately becoming CFO for the publishing arm Infoglobo, responsible for all print media. In 2011 she made a second major career change, this time leaving the media industry to invest in technology startups, a pursuit combining her longtime interest in innovation with her financial expertise as well as harkening back to her undergraduate years in the heart of Silicon Valley. "I always had this interest in startups and integrating technology in business," she explains. "Although I was in finance, I felt that technology would be increasingly crucial and would permeate every single activity in the future." After selling Neemu, an e-commerce startup, Pessoa then spent eighteen months as CFO of the 2016 Rio de Janeiro summer Olympics, another "I'll go!" conversation having planted the seed for that opportunity, as she explains:

> I had mentioned to a friend that I would of course be interested in that role despite the fact that it wasn't open at the time. But when it did come up, it happened to be the right time in my life, so I was called in for an interview. Again, if you don't express and show your desires—not only at work, but in everything you do—no one will know how you feel about it.

After her stint with the Olympics, Pessoa returned to Brazil's tech sector as a partner at Kunumi, a newly launched artificial intelligence firm. Over the years she didn't feel at a disadvantage as a woman, although she did focus on establishing credibility and producing results: "Did I work more than the guys? Probably. Probably women do have to work more, though to be fair I was a workaholic from day one," she says. She was vocal about her own goals and what she thought was best for her team and company, making sure her voice did not go unheard: "In order to stand my ground I did feel like I needed to be harsher sometimes. Especially early on—I was very young, and I felt that I had to be tough to gain respect."

Determination to chart her own course was crucial, but senior colleagues—many of them men—also played a role in Pessoa's career trajectory. A belief in women's leadership potential on the part of her managers meant that Pessoa had meaningful opportunities to contribute:

> I always tried to work with bosses who would teach me, who would actually help me in my quest to learn. I've had male bosses my whole career, and I've learned a lot from them, and they've always been open about my particular skills and strengths. One emblematic boss who hired me as CFO had a male assistant, typically a role that women are in—that small detail showcased to me that he really didn't care about gender. He made me the CFO of the largest newspaper conglomerate in Brazil, and it was great. I was the only woman and the youngest director around the table.

When Pessoa had her second child, soon after taking on the CFO role, she wasn't marginalized but instead had the support of her CEO to continue leading the finance function. When she returned from maternity leave, the company was in the midst of a major restructuring. She recalls managing this time in her career and life with characteristic assurance:

> I was still breastfeeding, so I negotiated coming back early from my leave as long as I could continue breastfeeding. The restructuring took us three years, and during the first year I would pump for milk if I needed to. I would turn on my electric pump in meetings with lawyers, with bankers, at the directors' meeting, at the board, literally at any meeting. People still remember the noise it made after all these years!

Helping to lead the restructuring during this new phase of her life was important to Pessoa, not only because she wanted it to be successful. She knew that by normalizing motherhood at work, she could be a role model for other women at Globo and even beyond.

"I had understanding and supportive bosses, and I would frequently thank them," she explains, "and remind them that I was doing this for their daughters. Hopefully it would be easier for them in the future."

As her career progressed, Pessoa took the time to cultivate connections outside Globo. One year, she traveled across the United States visiting major newspapers as part of an effort to understand worldwide trends in the industry. Years later, an editor she had met on that trip spoke at a journalism conference in Brazil. Pessoa sought him out:

I went up to him and asked if he remembered me. He didn't, and so I refreshed his memory and suggested that my husband and I take him to dinner. He was attending the conference with his wife, and we showed them around town and spent a great afternoon together. This was in maybe 2007, and we remained in contact. Years later this editor was made a CEO, and he contacted me and said, "You really know the business—would you like to interview for our board?" I was no longer at Globo by that time, so I was free to pursue the opportunity. Maintaining those relationships is super important, but it needs to be real, a truthful connection needs to exist. It's important to network with women, with men, with everyone. Back in 2007, I was simply interested in the transformation he was implementing in the newsroom, bringing in digital, and it never crossed my mind that our interaction would result in a future fruitful collaboration. You just never know what will eventually come from those contacts. You can't be afraid of putting yourself out there. It was a huge conference, three hundred–plus people, and I was the one that approached this particular editor. Why not me?

That first board interview resulted in an appointment, and Pessoa soon found herself being recruited for other directorships. Today she sits on the boards of NewsCorp, the French construction firm

Vinci, Credit Suisse, and Suzano, Brazil's largest paper and pulp company. She also serves on the Global Advisory Council for Stanford University and the Brazil Consulting Board for the Nature Conservancy. As Pessoa's governance portfolio grew, she saw the benefits of diversity at the board level but at the same time observed the ways in which women remained shut out of the high-level roles that would make them viable candidates. Boards need to leverage various kinds of diversity to be effective, she argues. "Do you want everyone to be a finance expert? No. Boards face different issues. You want diversity. If you're a global company, you want geographic, skill, and gender diversity. It's good when there are backgrounds in legal, business, technology. Having all those perspectives makes a board stronger."

And yet, women across fields and industries fill up the leadership pipeline but don't achieve top roles from which boards tend to recruit. "A big example for me is the communications field," Pessoa points out. "There are a lot of women working on communications teams, across all companies. They're everywhere. Yet C-Suites are usually occupied by men. And you look at journalists. You have a lot of women," she says, "possibly more than 50 percent of many editing rooms, but how many are editors? Top editors? Editor in chief? There are few. Or partners at law firms. There might be lots of female partners, yes. But how many are the managing, number one, named partners at those firms?"

Pessoa was part of a wave of working women that further shifted the landscape for those who followed, and she is both gratified by how far women have come and dissatisfied with the current state of affairs. "I think a lot of us, women of our generation, had to be really tough all the time," she reflects. "Now I see younger women expressing their different perspectives in a much more powerful way." For women on the rise, there is still much to prove, but Pessoa's success dispels any notion that women were ill-suited for leadership or ill-equipped to be both parents and professionals. Today, she is passionate about the need to foster the ambitions of girls and women. "I think middle school is a turning point," she says. "It's a time when young women stop dreaming of being astronauts or whatever they want to be. We need to work really hard at allowing them to dream and continue dreaming, continue aiming for what they want, and we need to ensure they will be able to do it."

Today, Pessoa sees an opportunity to hasten the pace of change and dismantle the barriers that keep women from reaching the top. "I think #MeToo and everything with it is fabulous," she says. "My question is what's next? How do you move beyond it? We need to think about the whole system, when you look at enterprises— what happens to women, where and when do they start falling through the cracks? We need to push women all the way up so that the culture changes."

CHAPTER 3

CRACKS IN THE CEILING

Women on Corporate Boards

"Change comes from the top" is an often-repeated maxim. Leaders' priorities shape an organizational agenda, determine resource allocation, and send a message about the company's values to employees and other stakeholders. But what about change *at* the top? As we discussed in the previous chapter, women remain a minority among senior-level employees across industries. The women executives we studied had nimbly deployed a variety of strategies to avoid falling off an ever more precarious ladder as they climbed. Their presence challenges the overrepresentation of men in leadership. Yet women's inroads into high-level ranks have not dramatically shifted the imbalance at the very top of the corporate hierarchy.

In corporate boardrooms around the world, white men predominate. Over 98 percent of boards in the MSCI ACWI Index, which covers both developed and emerging economies, are majority male.[1] Between January 2019 and early 2020, over half of the 304 companies in the United States and Europe that had executed or announced an initial public offering had zero women on their boards.[2] A census of *Fortune* 500 boards found that 22.5 percent of seats were held by women, and just 4.6 percent by women of color. Their dramatic underrepresentation reflects a general overrepresentation of white directors; the same study found that men of color sat in less than 12 percent of *Fortune* 500 seats.[3] A review of the FTSE 100 found that more than a third of companies had no directors representing a racial or ethnic minority.[4] Women of color have been largely left out of even the limited gender diversity gains made thus far.

The Governance Gap

As we began writing this chapter, *Fortune* published a story about the General Motors board, which had just become majority female with six women and five men, making it one of eleven *Fortune* 500 companies with majority-female or gender-balanced boards. So exceptional are boards not dominated by men that the (not quite) dozen where women are at least equally represented amounts to a newsworthy trend.[5] But beyond this one-off story, interest in the demographic composition of boards is increasing. Over the past decade, the *New York Times*, the *Wall Street Journal*, and *Financial Times* have collectively published more than 260 stories about board diversity. Academic interest, reflected in research publications, has also been growing steadily since the mid-2000s, and business educators have taken up the charge.[6] Our own institution and other business schools offer executive education courses for women seeking board seats. Case studies about efforts to achieve board gender diversity proliferate, while search firms and consulting companies churn out reports and recommendations.

Are boards listening? Not everyone has been embracing the need to diversify. In 2019, well under half (38 percent) of directors agreed that board gender diversity was important, according to a survey of more than seven hundred public companies. Racial and ethnic diversity has even less overall support; just 25 percent of directors agreed that it is important.[7] In 2020 these numbers rose, with 47 percent of directors believing that gender diversity was very important and

34 percent saying the same about racial diversity—almost certainly a consequence of worldwide protests against racial injustice that arose in the summer of that year.[8] Renewed focus on inequality seems to be convincing more board members that it matters, but just how much emphasis boards will put on recruiting directors of color remains to be seen. To date, there have been fewer studies, news stories, and initiatives addressing the lack of board racial diversity, and progress toward gender diversity has primarily benefited white women. However, more than twenty Black directors joined the boards of publicly listed companies in September and October of 2020—more than the total for all of 2019.[9] The coming years will reveal whether that surge in racial diversity, which could boost the proportion of Black women in the boardroom, was a one-time phenomenon or the start of a trend.

Unless attitudes evolve, we are unlikely to see significant progress toward diversity of any kind. About a quarter of directors feel that a focus on diversity is leading to the nomination of unneeded or unqualified candidates, according to the same survey.[10] Other research has found that people perceive the appointment of a female board member to mean prioritization of social performance at the expense of shareholder interests.[11] (Evidence from countries that have implemented gender quotas has not borne out these fears. In Norway, women appointed to boards after a 40 percent quota took effect actually had stronger educational and professional backgrounds than women appointed prior to the law.[12]) Lingering skepticism about the importance of diversifying boards is likely one reason all the attention has yet to result in a sea change. Even new companies are stuck in an old mindset: Among two hundred venture-backed private companies, just 7 percent of board seats were held by women. On 60 percent of these boards there were no women at all.[13]

When asked about this slow and limited progress, current boards often point to a dearth of women in the roles considered natural antecedents to directorships. The United Kingdom's Hampton-Alexander committee heard this sentiment from board chairs it interviewed; one common refrain was "there just aren't enough senior women" to fill available seats.[14] Yet boards tend to return to the same predominantly white and male candidate pools when they search for new members. Just 25 percent of boards that added a new director in 2018 elected someone who had not previously served on a public company board.[15] There is also evidence that when women do start gaining access to directorships, the opportunity is restricted to a handful of token women or strategically contained so that men still dominate individual boards. A 2019 analysis of the top two hundred companies in Australia found that an overall increase in board gender diversity was driven by just eight women who served on multiple boards.[16] A series of studies of the S&P 500 found that a disproportionate number of boards have two female directors; once there are two women directors, boards are statistically less likely to appoint any additional women—an apparent ceiling the researchers termed "twokenism."[17]

No matter how many women executives are capable of serving, if boards remain insular there is little opportunity for them to step forward in large numbers. "It's sometimes easy to find excuses why a woman doesn't fit on a board," said Bill George, who has served on the boards of Goldman Sachs, ExxonMobil, and the Target Corporation, among others. George has seen firsthand the tendency for directorship opportunities to circulate within closed networks: "I've heard so many times, 'Oh, I know a great guy from the club.' Selection has to be done through a wider range of people over a period of time, and much more professionally, and you have to have a lot of women in that mix, and people of color. You're not serving the company if you have an old boys' club with all the same voices." Likewise, Cindy Fornelli, former head of the Center for Audit Quality, pointed out in an interview that companies aren't going to source a diversity of candidates if they keep relying on the proverbial usual suspects: "We hear this argument that there is a supply issue with diverse candidates. There are plenty of diverse candidates, but it does require folks to go outside their individual networks, and particularly smaller companies who may have only recruited their friends are going to have to go other places, like a Women Corporate Directors' event. We hear it a lot—'There aren't any women, or any people of color.' Well, not if you only look at your normal haunts."

Even large corporations with more structured and formal board processes can experience this feedback loop if no real effort is made to expand the pool. A small subgroup will typically oversee the process of identifying new directors, and when these nominating committees do not include any women, the likelihood of the new director being female plummets.[18] Henrietta Holsman Fore, a former director at General Mills and other public companies, pointed out that disrupting networks is key to bringing in new members who are different from the typical director:

> The committee is a subset of the whole board, and the board itself is already small. It just does not lend itself to surfacing more women's names. The more that boards become diverse, the better the informal networks become. If you can get more diversity on the nominating committee, then the informal networks begin to become much broader, and more candidates are seen and evaluated.

Window Dressing or Culture Renovation?

Why should boards—or for that matter shareholders, consumers, legislators, and the public—care that female directors are scarce? In his 2020 letter to shareholders, famed investor Warren Buffett called out the continued underrepresentation of women in the boardroom. While the year marked the one-hundredth anniversary of the Nineteenth Amendment "guarantee[ing] American women the right to have their voices heard in a voting booth," he observed, "their attaining similar status in a board room remains a work in progress." Buffett went on to emphasize the importance of board independence, noting that rubber-stamping CEO decisions can be all too tempting and that groupthink often charts the course. Can disrupting the homogenous makeup of a board help it govern more effectively? Scholar Rosabeth

Moss Kanter argues that it most certainly can: "Lack of diversity can lead to a kind of crony capitalism in which insiders favor other insiders, surround themselves with people who look and think like them and rarely hear other points of view," she explained in a 2020 op-ed.[19] Directors need to be inquisitive, independent, and willing to ask hard questions—all of which can be hard to do in a clubby context where everyone looks like you. (We should note that Buffett resisted a shareholder proposal that would have formally required his own company to diversify candidate slates by race and gender when conducting searches for directors and CEOs, although he affirmed support for its ultimate goal.)[20]

Of course, board members are stewards acting on behalf of everyone who holds shares in a company and in so doing hopes to make money. Might greater gender diversity not only help guard against mismanagement but also lead to stronger financial performance? Although the so-called business case for diversity claims that it will lead to better returns, evidence for a causal link is inconclusive. Some studies have found a positive effect of more women on boards, while others have found it to inhibit performance, and still others have found no effect at all. The performance implications of racial and ethnic diversity on boards have been studied far less but with similarly unsettled results.[21] All such explorations of the relationship between board composition and performance confront the challenge of many unobservable and unknown factors that likely influence both board makeup and financial outcomes, making that relationship exceedingly difficult to measure.

An emphasis on adding women to add profits, we would argue, does not actually help boards become more diverse and inclusive. In fact, it is preventing a richer and more meaningful discussion about the benefits that diversity truly can confer and the reasons it remains so difficult to cultivate. Lip service about the "value of diversity" is not translating into widespread change, and too little attention is paid to why. One recent study of directors' views on gender and race in the boardroom found that while nearly all endorsed diversity in the abstract, most could not clearly articulate the reasons for that support, falling back on minor anecdotes about contributions by white women or people of color that were rarely about high-level strategy or other domains of board decision-making.[22] All the attention the business case has garnered doesn't seem to be leading to a clear understanding about how boards can leverage a more diverse group of directors. Boards would be better served by asking a more sophisticated question: What prevents us from fostering diversity and making the most of it?

Benefits do emerge under certain circumstances that are highly relevant to corporate governance. For instance, when groups must wrestle with complex tasks and decisions or harness the collective thinking of a group to problem-solve and generate ideas, gender diversity is a boon.[23] When a company's strategy focuses on innovation, performance does improve with more women in leadership.[24] There is also compelling evidence that both racial and gender diversity spur teams to think more creatively, consider alternative viewpoints, and become less prone to groupthink.[25] But it is vital to understand that these positive effects are not inevitable. Boards, like any group of individuals tasked with a common purpose, must know *how* to reap the benefits of having a variety of voices in the room. Contributions from those who speak differently—literally or figuratively—can all too easily be lost or reduced in impact and importance. Approaching diversity not as a superficial add-on but rather as a primary input can generate real learning. With this kind of approach, differences are viewed as sources of deep knowledge and insight, and people in both the majority and the minority believe their perspectives are respected and valued.[26] But when diversity is accepted begrudgingly or is viewed as morally correct but unrelated to the "real work," it can't be leveraged to benefit the group's problem-solving, creativity, or decision-making. The best-case scenario might be that of the directors described above who endorsed diversity but couldn't think of a way it actually enhanced their boards' primary tasks. More troublingly, this kind of surface-level support can bolster stereotypes that are ultimately unhelpful and even undermining to racial or gender equality. In 2010, French luxury goods conglomerate LVMH responded to a proposed gender quota by appointing former first lady Bernadette Chirac and citing her regular attendance at fashion shows as her key qualification.[27]

If boards aren't fully embracing the diversity they already have, directors in the minority are less integrated and less able to exert influence. They are also less likely to be in roles with the most formal power, such as chair or lead director. Even as the overall proportion of women on boards has edged up, there has been little to no change in the extent to which female directors are in leadership positions. According to a 2019 analysis, the vast majority of board chairs are men.[28] Among the five hundred largest (by revenue) public companies in the United States, the percentage of women lead directors, board chairs, and CEO chairs increased by less than 1 percent (to 7.5 percent) between 2015 and 2019.[29]

Even when their qualifications and experience are identical or superior to that of their fellow directors, white women and people of color are less likely to be in key leadership roles such as chair, lead director, and committee chair.[30] These leadership opportunities can be powerful, as reflected in the experience of Monique Leroux, a Canadian banking executive. In 2008 she was elected president and board chair of the Desjardins Group, the leading bank in Quebec, and seized the opportunity to address the lack of women in leadership at the institution: "I decided to put diversity on the agenda very strongly internally, because we were essentially not diverse at all. We had less than 20 percent women in senior ranks and I said, it's not acceptable. So, I put a target. We agreed as a board on a target of at least 30 percent, though the goal was 40 percent. Without targets that are widely communicated, you cannot make real progress."

Appointing white women or people of color as directors but effectively sidelining them may actually impede further progress toward diversity; being overlooked for influential roles makes women and minority directors more likely to depart their boards.[31] Marginalization can also take more subtle forms. In a study we conducted, women directors described being treated as outsiders, a dynamic that their male peers seemed oblivious to. More than half of male directors in the study did not believe that women faced hurdles based on their gender, yet women's experiences told a very different story. They recounted having their contributions ignored or dismissed in meetings, being excluded from informal gatherings and outings, and having their expertise questioned or their perspective treated as intrusive.[32] Sadly, this insight isn't new. More than seventy years ago, Wilma Soss founded the Federation of Women Shareholders to advocate for the representation of women in corporate governance; in 1954, she told the *New Yorker* that "one woman on these big boards isn't enough. What can one woman do against thirty men?"[33]

Today's corporate boards are not so large, but the principle holds. Phyllis Campbell, a director at Alaska Air Group, told us about her past experience serving on a range of boards and noted how easily women's contributions could be minimized: "When I was one of only two women, our voices would usually get drowned out." Indeed, research has shown that sole women speak up less often than women in more gender-balanced groups and that women are seen more favorably in professional settings in which there are at least two of them in a group.[34] One study identified a clear tipping point in board dynamics when female directors numbered three or more. Women described being stereotyped or excluded when they were the sole woman or even one of two, but they exerted more influence and felt more comfortable and effective in raising questions when there were at least two other women on the board. These dynamics were observed not only by women directors themselves but also by CEOs who saw the pattern play out in the boardroom.[35] In this light, the implicit "twokenism" we referenced above is a new barrier erected before the women who actually make it into the boardroom.

Isabelle Marcoux, chair of the board of Transcontinental, a publicly traded media company headquartered in Canada, affirmed the importance of critical mass: "When you're three, you're part of a group and you're no longer tagged as the 'woman's voice.' So, I really, really believe in numbers. To me, three is the minimum; boards should have at least three women, and four or five is even better because then you get a more diverse group of women." And the more women there are, the more likely it may be that the board will move further toward gender parity. A lone woman advocating for greater diversity can have an impact, particularly if she is board chair or head of the nominating committee, but a chorus of voices is even harder to ignore, as Herta von Stiegel, head of a clean-energy developer and director at several large European corporations, explained: "When it got to the point where I was able to really have a very direct influence on board composition either as chair or on the nominations committee, I strongly pushed for diversity. And not just gender diversity but diversity in terms of ethnic and cultural background as well as race, although I have not been as successful with respect to the latter. The healthiest environment that I've experienced is truly a diverse environment where you have at least 40 percent women."

Pressure from All Sides

In an ever more complex global economy, wasting the talent and insight of women, whether they are excluded from meaningful debate among directors or excluded from the boardroom altogether, surely can't be a strategic advantage. But not only does the homogeneity of boards look like a potential handicap for companies, it is also becoming increasingly untenable as multiple stakeholders criticize the predominance of white men in corporate governance and demand, through public pressure as well as legislation, that companies act to diversify their boardrooms. Over the past fifteen years, governments around the world have stepped in to mandate greater representation of women. These efforts have been concentrated in Europe but also extend to Israel, Malaysia, and India, where boards of large or publicly listed firms must include women, and to Quebec, Kenya, and the

United Arab Emirates, where state-owned companies are required to have female directors. In 2018, California passed legislation requiring companies headquartered in the state to include women on their boards, and the state of Washington followed suit in 2020.[36] Also in 2020 the European Union announced that it would revisit a proposal, tabled in 2012, to mandate a 40 percent quota for women on the boards of companies in its member states.[37]

These kinds of legislative quotas are varied in both kind and effect. Some are "hard" and carry sanctions that impede or block a company's operations. In Norway, companies that fail to meet a 40 percent quota can be delisted from the stock exchange, and in other European countries, director appointments can be voided and companies can be fined for noncompliance. But some quotas are nonbinding; companies might be named and shamed but face no sanctions. Spain's 40 percent quota sets incentives whereby companies that comply may receive preference in the award of government contracts but face no fines or other measures for failure to meet the quota.[38] Other countries, such as Australia and the United States, have opted for an even lighter touch, with consortia of business and government leaders advocating, with some success, targets for women's representation.

In 2011, a government-commissioned review committee examining gender on UK company boards recommended a voluntary target of filling 25 percent of FTSE 100 board seats with women by 2015, a proportion that would double women's share of seats. Calling on regulatory bodies, executive search firms, and companies themselves to rally around the effort, the committee urged all stakeholders to remove barriers to appointing women. Concurrently, a group of female executives formed the 30% Club to advocate for increased representation. Together, the club and the committee, known as the Davies Review, leveraged the media to bring attention to companies' action (or inaction) and conducted personal outreach to board chairs and other powerful stakeholders. The target was missed in 2015, but by the following year 26 percent of FTSE 100 seats were held by women.[39] By 2020, the proportion hit 33 percent.[40]

There has been little appetite among officials in the United States for establishing quotas, with the California and Washington state mandates being major exceptions. In 2019, Illinois passed a bill requiring companies headquartered in the state to have at least one woman, an African American, and a Latinx director on their boards, but the requirement was ultimately dropped; instead, Illinois companies must publish the race and gender composition of their boards and executive management teams on their websites.[41] A disclosure approach has been in place at the federal level since 2010 via a Securities and Exchange Commission (SEC) rule compelling companies to explain whether and how nominating committees consider diversity when appointing new directors. While an analysis of *Fortune* 500 boards covering the years 1996 to 2015 identified an upward trend in the proportion of women after 2010, for most companies the increase had already begun prior to the SEC rule, making it unclear that the rule meaningfully changed boards' approach. Meanwhile, a multicountry study has found that targets and quotas are more effective than disclosure requirements.[42]

The SEC approach allows companies themselves to define "diversity" and to specify how they believe it can be furthered. One effect of this more expansive and malleable concept could be to encourage companies to consider multiple dimensions of diversity at once. As noted above, boards are extremely homogenous when it comes to race: Men of color lag white women in representation, and women of color hold a tiny fraction of directorships, yet gender diversity alone has long dominated the conversation. That emphasis has meant that the challenges faced by women of color are obscured or overlooked. Unfortunately, the open-to-interpretation definition of diversity can easily become overly broad. Research on the SEC rule's effects has found that companies actually tend not to cite gender *or* racial diversity in their disclosures but instead discuss candidates' prior experience and expertise as forms of diversity, an approach that has clearly not led to major change when it comes to boards' demographic composition.[43] Similarly, only about half of the board diversity policies at FTSE 250 companies specifically mention racial and ethnic diversity, and the vast majority set no measurable objectives around it.[44]

In the absence of public policy, other US stakeholders have attempted to exert influence and pressure. Major investment firms and pension funds have asked companies in which they invest to disclose the gender and/or racial makeup of their boards and describe their strategy for advancing diversity. Several, including BlackRock, State Street Global Advisors, and the California Public Employees' Retirement System, have withheld votes or voted against director candidates to protest companies' lack of progress on board diversity.[45] In 2020, Goldman Sachs announced that it would not underwrite the initial public offerings of US and European companies with all-male boards.[46] As this book went to press, the Nasdaq stock exchange filed a proposal that would require listed companies to have on their boards at least one woman and one director from an underrepresented minority or who identifies as LGBTQ+.[47]

Shareholder proposals pressuring companies to increase race and gender diversity are increasingly popular. One firm alone, Trillium Asset Management, put forward more than fifty diversity-related proposals between 2016 and early 2019.[48] We analyzed shareholder proposals in the S&P 1500 from 1997 to 2018 and found more than 330 related to diversity. In addition, we found that proposals aimed at increasing diversity averaged 8 percent more "yes" votes than other proposals. Reflecting this interest from shareholders, diversity has become a frequent topic in companies' securities filings. Analyzing proxy statements filed with the SEC, we found a more than 10 percent jump in the number of statements that discussed diversity between 2009 and 2010 and a steady uptick in the decade since. In 2018, over 20 percent of proxies included some mention of diversity. The trend is also garnering widespread public attention outside the business press and the C-suite. In 2018, Amazon received a wave of backlash from its own employees after initially rejecting a shareholder proposal that it implement a "Rooney Rule" requiring board slates to include women and minority candidates. Not long after the outcry was picked up in the media, the company reversed course and said that the board's nominating committee would indeed adopt such a policy.[49]

All this attention may have helped spur some recent gains. 2017 saw the largest-yet single jump in the appointment of women to boards, when 38 percent of *Fortune* 500 director appointments went to women (up from 27 percent in 2016). Women's share of appointments climbed slightly higher, to 40 percent, in 2018.[50] The California mandate, which was covered widely in the US media, led to the appointment of 511 women to board seats at companies headquartered in the state, many of which had previously never had a female director. Yet we should once again note that white women dominated this shift toward more gender diversity, making up 78 percent of these new directors.[51] (In 2020, California expanded its diversity mandate to include quotas for racial and ethnic diversity on boards.[52])

The Power of Corporate Sisterhood

Despite more conversation, it isn't clear that the push from investors and the public is fostering a sense of urgency on the part of current directors, especially those in the majority. A study we conducted with over five thousand directors at companies headquartered in more than sixty countries revealed that men were apt to attribute the continued underrepresentation of women to a lack of qualified female candidates, an explanation pointed to by far fewer of their female peers (more than a third of men versus 7 percent of women). Rather than this supply-side rationale, women directors cited the persistence of male-dominated networks and said that despite all the talk, diversity is not a priority when it comes to recruiting new members.[53] In another study we conducted with male and female directors based mostly in the United States, almost 30 percent of men cited a lack of experience and knowledge as an impediment to women's access to board seats, yet just 4 percent of women directors agreed.[54] And the traditional view that the ideal director has CEO experience, an approach that dramatically limits the pool of women candidates, persists. In 2018, current and former CEOs made up 60 percent of all appointees to *Fortune* 500 boards, an all-time high. "It's clear," one search firm pointed out, "that companies aren't consistently casting their nets widely."[55] Boards have yet to undergo a paradigm shift in how they think about, leverage, and value diversity.

Michele Hooper, whose profile appears after this chapter, is impatient with the notion that a lack of candidates is the major impediment to board diversity. "This whole argument that we can't find qualified candidates is just so much hooey. Our markets, customers, and employees are becoming more diverse. There are well-qualified diverse people available for our boards. We have to expand the pools in which we search for those candidates. We need to seek skills and experiences regardless of sex or ethnicity." Fatima Al Jaber, who has served on the boards of several companies headquartered in the United Arab Emirates and was the first woman elected to the board of directors of the Abu Dhabi Chamber of Commerce, argues that even in the Persian Gulf region, where women are less represented in the labor force compared to many other parts of the world, "We're qualified. We have the experience, and we have the right candidates. But the problem is we need the door to open." And women executives are trying to make their way through the narrow openings that currently exist. Numerous academic institutions and nonprofit centers offer formal training, mentoring programs, and access to headhunting firms, all with the aim of preparing women to navigate board search channels and step into directorships with the skills to be effective. Efforts to make female candidates more visible to companies and search firms proliferate. Initiatives such as the 30% Club and 2020 Women on Boards focus dialogue and attention on the underrepresentation of women on boards and advocate for accelerating the pace of change.

The Women on Boards program at our own institution has seen runaway enthusiasm, igniting a network of past participants committed not just to their own board service but to one another's success. When the program launched in 2016, seats filled up at a faster rate than usual for the school's executive education courses, and demand has continued apace. To date, more than four hundred women from around the world have been through the program, and interest exceeds capacity each year. Beginning with the inaugural cohort, participants began holding monthly conference calls after the course ended, to keep the momentum going by trading referrals, advice, and professional connections. An active social media network is a forum for still more strategic support, as well as a way for participants to remain rooted in a global community of female leaders. The women who have thus far secured board seats are working to pay it forward to their fellow participants and create a movement that extends far beyond their time on campus.[56]

This ever-expanding HBS-based network builds on a precedent set more than two decades ago by another organized effort to get more women onto boards, Women Corporate Directors (WCD). The evolution of WCD offers a kind of case study in why such groups continue to be necessary as well as some measure of optimism about their effects. Founded in 2001, WCD was at first simply a forum for women already on boards. They rarely encountered fellow female directors.[57] In an interview, WCD founder Susan Stautberg explained how the need for such a group became clear to her:

> I was on a board, and I was seeing how hard it was to get more women onto boards. I also saw that women were constantly trying to get together informally to talk about how to be effective in the boardroom. How do you ask the difficult questions? Where do I go when I want to know more about a certain topic? And how to handle the gender issues that did come up. What do you do when the CEO puts his hand on your knee? The women who were on boards at the time didn't really have any place to turn.

A friend of Stautberg's, Edie Weiner, was one of those women, having resigned from a board where her expertise was questioned and her advice unheeded. "I couldn't get the guys to listen to me," Weiner, head of a strategy consulting firm, told us. "The CEO was really not interested in anything I had to tell him." Weiner had already served on other boards quite successfully but felt disheartened and frustrated at encountering such retrograde bias in the twenty-first century. "I called up Susan and said, I know the next group of women that you're going to put together. Female directors need to be able to talk to each other."

Over the next two decades, WCD grew from a handful of women who gathered at Stautberg's New York apartment to many hundreds of women at chapters in more than forty countries. It wasn't long before the directors assembled around Stautberg's dining room table and later at conferences in various US cities were talking about the women missing from their ranks, as founding member Elaine Eisenman described:

> It started off in the beginning as a dinner group that provided mutual support, education, and experience-sharing about how to best contribute as the only woman on our respective boards, more than anything else. We were fellow travelers in the same room, sharing stories about navigating the foreign land of the boardroom. But it also became a political force to say there should be more women on boards. As time went on and slowly but surely more women joined boards, it started to morph beyond simply the support and sharing function, recognizing that there's more women who sit on boards—asking why aren't there even more of us? There's extraordinary talent out there, and the need for diversity is critical, especially in terms of today's turbulent marketplace. You can't have singular vision for growth and impact.

When another founding member, finance executive Alison Winter, moved to Chicago, she started a local chapter that was soon joined by chapters in Boston, Atlanta, and Washington, D.C. By 2004, the demand was clear. Women on boards were hungry for opportunities to network with one another, sharpen their skills, and pave the way for more female directors. Stautberg approached the professional service firm KPMG to sponsor the organization, and WCD began hosting regular conferences for its growing membership. Chicago-based member Joan Steel explained that WCD events both enhanced the skills women could bring to boards and disrupted the closed networks that tended to keep them out of the running for open seats:

> We learn about cutting-edge, best-in-class governance practices on public and private boards from around the world. This is important to our education and growth as directors. There are also networking opportunities with other women who are on boards or who are in the C-suite seeking to expand or refresh their boards or who know of opportunities. It's the access to potential board opportunities, networking resources, educational resources and friendships that underscore the value of WCD. WCD has helped move the dial on placing women on boards. For companies who say they can't find qualified female directors or search firms seeking to widen their candidate field, WCD is a reservoir of talented, capable, and experienced women directors to be tapped. Whatever director requirements you have—if you're a search professional, if you're a corporate CEO, if you're the chair of nomination & governance—we can provide access to our members, the best and the brightest female directors.

Getting more women "into the flow," as founder Stautberg calls it, of opportunities in governance means taking advantage of every avenue of influence. "For instance, we are doing more and more events where we bring in private equity firms and have them meet with women," Stautberg told us, "because private equity firms are very much putting men on the boards of their companies." WCD hasn't shied away from stronger persuasive tactics either. In 2016 as the group prepared for a conference in Chile, Stautberg took a call from the executive vice president of the Santiago Stock Exchange. He invited the WCD leadership to ring the opening bell, marking the first time a woman would do so. But Stautberg wasn't satisfied with the symbolic weight such a gesture would carry, not when the board of the exchange counted zero women members. She recalled explaining to the chairman, "I can't do that. The stock exchange board is eleven white men. When you elect women on the board of the stock exchange, we'll come ring the bell." The executive vice president called Stautberg the next day and promised to appoint a woman. In 2017 WCD held its Chile conference, and a local member was appointed to the Chilean exchange board as its first female director.[58]

As the organization passed the fifteen-year mark, Stautberg handed the reins to Susan Keating, who became WCD's second CEO. Just as Keating prepared to take over in the fall of 2017, the #MeToo movement took off. Asked about the group's mission in light of this cultural shift, Keating saw an opportunity: "This is a big reckoning for many companies right now. I believe WCD can be part of the solution. We can ensure these problems don't continue to be institutionalized and happen in the future. The solution lies with good governance, and board diversity is part of that. We need to ensure that companies have the right culture, processes, procedures, reporting and oversight." Indeed, the #MeToo movement has made it increasingly clear that any attempts to tackle persistent gender disparities will require top leaders—who remain mostly men—to do the hard work of identifying and addressing all the ways that gender inequalities are enabled and perpetuated throughout the structures and cultures they oversee.

For its part, WCD has been clear about the value of engaging men since its early days. Stautberg noted that men's participation has been critical to the impact achieved so far:

In the early days around my dining room table, we were often bringing in male CEOs, male board members and just talking about various issues in the boardroom and then also asking what we could do better. What do you think we can do to get more women on boards? You get them relaxed and get some ideas. And you know, men are competitive, so then it becomes, "next time we have a board opportunity, I'll let you know." They don't want to be left behind. But it was also having them spend some time with women executives and see that these are competent people. Today, we do it with our chapters. Take the San Francisco chapter. Once a year, they hold a cocktail reception, and every female director who joins has to invite a male director, and ideally, they are inviting male directors who are on nominating committees. The chapter puts together a brochure of everyone's bio which they give to everyone. And they have this cocktail party and just generally get to know each other. The men do come because other men are going to be there. And the chapter has been getting women onto boards every single time afterward, because the guys come and they see these really bright people, they have the bio, and it really works.

Hundreds of women have secured board seats through the WCD network, but CEO Keating knows there is still much work ahead:

I think some companies are leading the way. Others are recognizing the importance of board diversity, but we have a long way to go. There is some resistance. Any time you're going against an institutional, cultural norm, there can be resistance. So how do we break through that? We take leaders that are advocates for diversity and making headway with their boards to advance diversity and give them a platform.

Changing the status quo is never easy, but when people in power act as allies and advocates, they can accelerate momentum. In the next chapter, we'll look at the role that men, inside and outside the boardroom, can play in advancing gender equity.

PAVING THE WAY
AND PAYING IT FORWARD

Michele Hooper

Michele Hooper grew up in a large family in small-town Pennsylvania, the studious child of a homemaker mother and a father who worked in the local coal mine. "I was the one with, as my dad would say, my face stuck in a book. I just loved reading and loved learning," she recalls. "And I got that from my parents. My mother, while she was a housewife, was very creative—she cooked, she was a tailor, she painted. She was always very interested in education—in sixth grade I was selected to learn Russian. I recall going home each day teaching my mom the Russian-language lessons I had learned. And my Dad would quiz me about current events. He would come home from a swing shift and have me read aloud that day's newspaper, and he would pose questions about what I was reading. This love of learning and curiosity has been a part of me since I can remember."

While Hooper was an exceptional student, it wasn't clear to her what kind of working life might be available: "I didn't have anyone in my family that had gone on to higher education. My family was poor (although I didn't think so at the time), so I didn't know business or have any professional role models." If not for a University of Pennsylvania initiative to recruit rural students, she might have set her sights far lower than her ultimate career path, as she explains: "Even though I was in advanced placement and took all these college courses, my high school guidance counselor advised me to be either a nurse or a teacher, which is what they counseled young Black achievers to do at the time." But fortuitously, the university's Small Communities Talent Search was reaching out to rural parts of Pennsylvania to identify capable young people who would otherwise not be encouraged to apply to the state's most prestigious university, and Hooper soon found herself on the University of Pennsylvania campus, fascinated by courses such as economics and corporate law. After graduating, she applied to the business school at the University of Chicago and secured "a lot of scholarships and grants and very few loans" to attend.

Soon after earning her MBA, Hooper began her career as a financial analyst at the health care corporation Baxter International before moving into strategy and industry analysis. In 1988 she was tapped to lead the company's Canadian subsidiary, a critical move. "I was one of the first women to be moved from a staff role into a senior line role," she remembers. Baxter Canada "was a microcosm of the company—I oversaw manufacturing, distribution, a unionized plant, all of that. And being a thirty-eight-year-old African American woman in that job gave me a slightly higher profile." Hooper's visibility soon resulted in offers to join various corporate boards, although she wasn't at first seeking such opportunities, as she remembers:

> Very few women were on boards in the 1980s. I mentor women today, and they ask "how do I position myself to get on a board?" Times have really changed. For me, it was not a goal, but it was something I was encouraged to do. My mentor felt it would be very helpful for me as a leader in the business, because part of what you gain from being on a board is knowledge and expertise you bring back to your own organization.

Hooper's mentor, Baxter's then-CEO, helped her evaluate the board offers she received, but more importantly, he actively sponsored her career advancement, a benefit that, as much research has demonstrated, is less available to women, especially women of color, than men: "He put me into the Canadian operation. He felt I had the abilities to move forward against, quite frankly, a lot of naysaying white, male, senior-level executives in the organization. He made sure I had a door that was open. I had to walk through it and be successful, but he made sure it opened."

In 1989 Hooper joined the board of the Dayton-Hudson Corporation, now Target. It was an ideal introduction to governance, as she concludes in retrospect:

I didn't realize it at the time, but Dayton-Hudson was very advanced when it came to governance. A lot of the good-governance regulations that came up with the Sarbanes-Oxley Act were things Dayton had been doing for years, so I came up in a foundation of governance that was very, very strong. And my fellow directors were experienced CEOs, so dissecting the issues in the boardroom was like getting another degree. It was an incredible opportunity to grow as an executive.

Although she was the only woman and only person of color as well as the youngest director on the Dayton board, Hooper found her minority status undaunting. "I've always been the only one, my whole life, starting from grade school," she explains. "I grew up in a very small coal-mining town and was one of the brighter kids in the school, so I've always dealt with being the other. You have to figure out how to get things done. I focused on bringing my A+ game to the boardroom. They've elected me to this board, so I am their equal." Hooper believes this conviction enabled her to succeed:

I was brought up to believe that I am as good as anybody else. If you come in with an attitude that you belong, you just keep powering through. I don't recall being marginalized, although women always have an issue of making sure their voice is heard.

Sometimes guys talk over you; it still happens. You just have to keep making your point, and if somebody makes a point I already made I will say "Didn't I just say that?" I've always done that. That's the only way as a Black female you can make sure that you get heard. Your role can also help. I was chair of the audit committee, I was on the CEO succession committee, so I was taken seriously as a peer. But I also had to have the attitude and the confidence that I was their peer, that I had something to contribute.

After four years running Canadian operations at Baxter, Hooper moved to Caremark, a unit that had just spun off from the company. While building Caremark's new international business, she pursued additional board service opportunities. "I wasn't restricted by Caremark to serving on only one board, as executives sometimes are, so I actually served on a couple of boards while leading our international unit. And when did I sleep? Who knows! But I have served on a number of boards in leadership roles." By the early 2000s, Hooper found herself exploring a full-time career in corporate governance. "Caremark got sold off," she explains, "and I went on to two small private companies but ultimately left both and tried to decide what to do next with my life." Governance turned out to be a natural fit for Hooper. "I have held just about every board role there is. I was lead director for several companies. I've chaired audit committees for twenty-plus years. I've chaired nominating and governance committees. I've done CEO searches. I've sort of run the table, in terms of what you can do in governance." As her career progressed, she became increasingly involved in governance leadership, serving on the board of the National Association of Corporate Directors (NACD) for a decade, leading the Chicago chapter of the NACD, and consulting on and teaching corporate governance to current and future directors.

In 2003, Hooper cofounded the Directors' Council. "I started the firm with some women director colleagues, and we wanted to focus on diversity issues in the boardroom. A lot of people would come to us and ask for ideas about how to increase gender diversity, and we thought, well, this is a business." The Directors' Council helps boards identify and recruit white women and people of color to join boards and also provides mentoring and training for candidates. Although the council elevates both racial and gender diversity, the former—to Hooper's disappointment—has received far less attention from companies and the business press. "The discussion about gender has been at the forefront for a really long time," she notes:

> I think the focus is not going to be on people of color and diverse ethnicities unless there are champions. Right now, it seems like a lot of the oxygen in the room is being sucked up by gender equity, which is important but not the only issue. I keep telling my peers—and anyone that will listen, quite frankly—that we are moving toward a more multicultural society. Our customers, our employees, our constituents, our stakeholders are becoming more and more ethnically diverse. I went to an event recently, and the stage was full of white men and the audience was full of white men and white women. Where are we in the broader conversation of ethnic and racial diversity? When you look specifically at women of color in the boardroom, for example, it is less than 4 percent. That's ridiculous when you look at demographics. There are talented, experienced people of color who deserve to be mentored and trained to join the senior executive ranks and to be able to also take a seat at the boardroom table. There has to be a better path; there is a larger conversation to be had.

Hooper points out that people of color don't receive the same degree of grooming and development throughout their careers to move into senior levels as their white peers, resulting in a more limited pool of board candidates. "Senior executives are not doing a good job of identifying, retaining, and reaching down into their organizations and pulling talented people forward who are different from them. It's the whole supply chain. We are doing a better, but not sufficient, job with white women." Despite this underlying problem, she believes there are immediate steps boards can take to diversify, including requiring diverse candidate slates. Diverse slates, she argues, "allow boards and management teams to see a range of individuals who are qualified, so it debunks the notion that we just can't find qualified candidates."

However, she notes that boards must be genuinely open to candidates who aren't already in their (largely homogenous) net-works: "I used to do board searches, and I would bring in a slate of people and the response would be 'Do we know any of these people? Do my fellow board members know these candidates? And it's like no, you don't know them, that's why you brought me in! That's why you do reference checking." In addition to sourcing and considering a range of candidates, Hooper also views boards as benefiting from more rigorous evaluation approaches: "We need to figure out our version of the blind orchestral audition, how we can take conscious and unconscious biases out. We could review résumés without identifiers, just as a first step, so you're selecting from a pool of résumés, looking just at qualifications before you get to the face-to-face interview." The final piece of the puzzle, Hooper argues, is the investing community:

> I do think there is a role for investors to play that could be quite meaningful and effective. I look at some of the other governance issues that have been dealt with because boards have got beaten up, so to speak, by investors. There are things like the annual election of directors that I would never have thought would happen when I first went on boards twenty-eight years ago. It happened because there was a very focused and consistent argument by investors. I am hoping we get to the point where investors say that if you don't have diversity, including multicul-

tural diversity, on your board, we will vote against you. That will get directors' attention.

In 2017, Hooper was named "Director of the Year" by the NACD in recognition of her profound impact on the field of corporate governance. Former Medtronic CEO and Harvard Business School senior fellow Bill George served with Hooper on the Target Corporation board in the early 2000s and recalled her as "a powerful force on that board." Having followed Hooper's career in the years since, George pointed out that she has continued to step up at key times: "She's not just a board member—she's taken on leadership roles, chairing committees, being a lead director. Very time-consuming, very important roles. She has such a broad range of experience, and she's improved board governance, not just in terms of diversity."

Asked about the role of organizations such as the NACD in diversifying boards, Hooper is hopeful about the power of training and education. "Many organizations do outreach through conferences and other venues to try to get more women and people of color who are at the cusp of moving into a director role to understand what it's like to be on a board. We try to get these individuals ready to be interviewed to go on a board and ready to participate as a new director." Equipping underrepresented candidates to not only be seen as viable possibilities but also be truly successful as directors, Hooper believes, will help shift the balance of power in boardrooms more fundamentally. "It's important not only to get on a board, but then to get into leadership positions on the board," she explains. "Leadership is where you make the most impact. And when women are on the board in a leadership role, you are modeling for male colleagues women's ability to lead—which then allows men to be more comfortable bringing other women onto management teams as well as other boards of which they are part."

Reflecting on her own role in normalizing the presence of women and of racial minorities in the boardroom, Hooper sees her success as inextricably linked to the larger project of breaking down barriers:

> I absolutely think of myself as a role model and a mentor, and I always have. I've always been one of the very few African Americans—much less African American women—in any role. I've felt an obligation to succeed because of that. I feel I have a responsibility to do well so that my success will help others to follow in my footsteps and go beyond. I stand on the shoulders of a lot of people, and there are a lot of people who will stand on my shoulders and go even further.

PART TWO

CLEARING THE PATH TO GENDER EQUALITY AT WORK

CHAPTER 4

ALLIES ON THE SIDELINES

The Role of Men

In the midst of writing this book, we began to hear speculations about the aftermath of the #MeToo movement. Some of the prominent men brought down by revelations of sexual misconduct and assault were making tentative professional comebacks, even as journalists continued to break new stories about companywide cultures of sexual harassment.[1] We also heard about changes effected by the movement, such as startup investors adding "#MeToo clauses" to their deals, requiring entrepreneurs to disclose whether they've been accused of harassment, and executive contracts that now allow companies to deny severance pay and other benefits to bigwigs terminated for sexual misconduct.[2] Many firms set up new mechanisms for reporting harassment and new measures for preventing retaliation, internalizing the movement's outcry against silence. Companies pledged to be leaders in preventing and punishing discriminatory behavior. The status of women in the workplace had taken on renewed importance and urgency.

Yet even as we saw massively increased awareness translate into organizational change, we also began to hear worried musings from women and men in a variety of industries. Speculation that the attention to men as perpetrators of harassment would create a climate of fear among them abounded. An anxious question followed: Would men start to limit their interactions with female colleagues—withdraw their mentorship, their advice, their professional friendship? Some preliminary studies suggested that men did reduce their interactions with and their support for their women colleagues as the #MeToo movement unfolded.[3] More research is needed to understand the nature of these reactions—at least one study found greater #MeToo backlash in workplaces with hypermasculine cultures, which also produce more harassment in the first place—and we need to know more about the underlying factors that drive them.[4] It's not clear yet whether those men who pulled back from their female colleagues are typical or if the reaction is concentrated among those predisposed to devalue or exclude women.

At an individual level, men who are loath to work closely with women can of course have a damaging effect on the careers of their female colleagues. But men who are apathetic about gender equality also, without necessarily meaning to, stymie women's advancement. Today we are at something of a crossroads. Women's representation in leadership roles across sectors and industries has remained virtually unchanged since the 1990s. Will men shrink from grappling with the complex and persistent conditions that perpetuate this state of affairs, or will they respond to the demand, surfaced powerfully in the #MeToo moment, that they actively work to dismantle discrimination? In the fight to create workplace cultures where women can succeed, will men retreat to the sidelines or join the battle?

Gender Equality Is a Men's Issue

Men have never been entirely absent from the struggle to expand economic access and professional opportunity for women. The first *Harvard Business Review* article to examine biases toward women in managerial roles, 1965's "Are Women Executives People?," was green-lit and coauthored by then-editor Stephen Greyser. Around the same time the Society of Women Engineers formed the Men's Auxiliary, composed of the husbands and partners of Society of Women Engineers members, to raise money to support the organization.[5] In 1984, the Speaker of the US House of Representatives, the governors of New York and Ohio, and New York City's mayor—all men—spoke out in favor of naming a woman to the Democratic Party's presidential slate; candidate Walter Mondale ultimately tapped Geraldine Ferraro as his vice president, the first woman ever to run on a major party ticket.[6] These examples help illustrate why men's advocacy is critical: Men are in positions of power, authority, and influence. In 1984 men held the governor's office in all but one US state, the mayor's office in most major US cities, and more than 95 percent of congressional seats. Ferraro's access to a prominent leadership role was the product not only of decades of activism and agitation by women but also powerful men's endorsement of those demands, a practice that continues to be important today. In 2020, Democratic presidential candidate Joseph Biden made a pledge to select a woman as his vice-presidential nominee and ultimately shared electoral victory with running mate Kamala Harris, the first woman and first person of color to be elected vice president.

In 2019, National Institutes of Health director Francis Collins issued a public call to "end the tradition of all-male panels" at science conferences, pledging to look at whether and how event organizers had worked to create diverse agendas and decline speaking engagements where inclusivity was not reflected in the program. In an interview with the *New York Times* about the statement, Collins noted that the #MeToo movement had impacted biomedicine and heightened his sense of urgency about creating environments where women scientists experience equal opportunity and treatment. Princeton neuroscientist Yael Niv, whose website BiasWatchNeuro.com tracks speaker gender at neuroscience conferences, explained to the *New York Times* why Collins's statement was so important: "People really want him at a conference—he brings the crowds. So if he says, 'I'm not coming to your conference to give the keynote speech because I don't see adequate representation,' that is huge."[7]

Niv went on to point out that Collins's influence runs along two dimensions: "It's great to have someone who's a leading figure and a man" take this stance. Collins's role leading one of the field's most important and respected organizations matters. As Niv notes, Collins "brings the crowds" as a famous scientist. But even more specifically, Collins is a man advocating for greater representation of women, and scholars who study diversity advocacy have found that men's efforts to combat sexism or support gender inclusion are often seen as more legitimate and viewed more favorably than women's are. Men can sidestep some of the backlash that women receive; one series of studies found that women who push for more gender balance in hiring and promotion are perceived as less competent, while their male peers who advocate for gender-parity experience no such penalty.[8] Men's voices are critical because of, not in spite of, their gender. When men speak up against gender disparities or gender discrimination, they not only become visible as allies who can be counted on to support industry or company initiatives to advance parity; they also foster awareness and acceptance about gender inequity as a shared problem, not a special interest. Collins's pledge highlights both of these benefits: Conferences that want to secure him as a speaker are incentivized to change their practices to include more women, and at the same time his public statement frames the underrepresentation of women as a problem for the field. Indeed, the impact of that framing was felt almost immediately, as the head of the Wellcome Trust, a prominent global health nonprofit, tweeted that he and his colleagues would also decline invitations to events that don't prioritize gender diversity among speakers.

We interviewed a number of men who have been advocates for women's advancement in their own companies and beyond, including Doug Conant, former CEO of Campbell Soup, who saw female talent—and diversity more broadly—as central to his turnaround strategy for the struggling company upon taking the reins in 2001. "We had to craft an employee value proposition that worked for everybody," he explained. Conant knew that employee perception of inclusion and equity was low and that the company needed to demonstrate an investment in its twenty thousand–strong workforce. Early in his tenure, the company started its first employee resource groups, beginning with Women of Campbell: "All we had to do was sanction the first event and it went from something like twelve women to, I'm going to say, five thousand women in about a year, all around the world. All we had to do was open the door and be supportive of the concept of women helping a company perform better."

Conant approached cultivating women leaders as an individual responsibility too. Denise Morrison succeeded Conant as CEO in 2011, the first woman to hold Campbell Soup's top post; Conant had mentored Morrison for a number of years before Campbell's board began looking at its CEO succession needs. He recalled, "I hired Denise Morrison in a staff role as our first chief global customer officer, but then I got her into a profit-and-loss role, and she had a chance to show that she could run line businesses for six or seven years before the board had to have a discussion about my successor. At that point she had a clear track record of contribution and experience." Boards often bemoan the paucity of women in the CEO pipeline, but Conant's example shows that this needn't be the case—if men in powerful roles today open the door for women to step in tomorrow.

Not only is men's participation necessary to change the practices and norms that limit women's advancement, but men themselves also stand to gain from disrupting the status quo. The gender hierarchy that disadvantages women creates pitfalls for men, who are penalized if they don't adhere to an idealized and rigid standard of male behavior. For men, showing vulnerability and empathy, being warm and agreeable, and expressing emotions (other than anger) have all been shown to elicit criticism. Even though these characteristics and behaviors are known to create greater trust and effectiveness within companies (indeed, executive coaches often work with clients to improve and enhance these exact traits), men who enact them are viewed as less competent and likable.[9]

Deviating from the norm is perhaps most difficult and consequential when it comes to men's role in caregiving. Even as men's careers can be boosted by gender inequities within companies, they pay a price when it comes to life beyond work. In the early 1990s, *Harvard Business Review* suggested that men's expectations for work and family might be changing, noting that "the Corporate America originally designed by men doesn't work anymore for most of us," with a new generation of men looking to be more involved fathers and more equal partners.[10] Yet nearly thirty years later, men still find themselves locked into an outmoded set of expectations that call on them to diminish and limit their commitment to caregiving and parenting. In 2015, the *New York Times* reported that despite having more egalitarian beliefs about gender roles than prior generations, professional millennial men were largely living the lives of their fathers and grandfathers: working long hours and doing little childcare.[11]

This fact should come as no surprise given the way many companies approach men's parenting responsibilities: at best as an oddity that renders them suspect or at worst as a lark not to be taken seriously. Although parental leave is a standard benefit at many large employers, men take leave at dramatically lower rates than women. In 2018, the Society for Human Resource Management reported that 36 percent of men who had access to leave took the total available time off, compared to 66 percent of women.[12] In 2019, JPMorgan Chase agreed to pay a $5 million settlement in a class-action suit initiated by a male employee who was prevented from taking advantage of the bank's sixteen-week leave for primary caregivers. The employee, a fraud investigator in Ohio, was told he could only qualify for the leave if he demonstrated that his wife couldn't be the child's primary caregiver. It was inconceivable to his managers that he might choose such a role, and in their view the bank's parental leave benefit wasn't intended to support men in doing so but instead was really aimed at women, even if it was on paper gender-neutral.[13] In other cases, such expectations become explicit and are wielded against men who don't toe the line. One former employee of Jones Day, one of the largest law firms in the United States, alleged in a 2019 suit that the firm's parental leave policies discriminated against fathers and that the firm's partners encouraged harmful gender stereotypes. According to the complaint, one prominent male partner mocked a male associate for taking leave and asked, "What would a man do on parental leave—watch his wife unload the dishwasher?"[14] Other similar suits against CNN and the US Transportation Department brought by male caregivers who were denied leave or retaliated against for taking it are a reminder that policies and cultures that treat men and women differently not only put a ceiling on women's careers but also constrain men's choices.[15] And bias toward men who prioritize parenting isn't confined to stodgy, traditional workplaces either; in 2020, a lawsuit filed by a former SoulCycle employee alleged that the company's CEO chastised an executive about his upcoming leave, scoffing that "paternity leave is for pussies."[16]

Men on the Bench

If men's full participation in combating gender-based disparities is not only necessary but also ultimately beneficial to both men and women, why don't we see more of it? Men may struggle to step out of line with traditional expectations, buy into zero-sum thinking about women's gains as men's losses, or feel uncertain about their place in the conversation about gender inequality—or all three. When men act unconventionally in relation to work and family, they can risk career and reputational consequences. As a state senator, Barack Obama was harangued by a fellow legislator when he missed a vote due to his toddler daughter's illness: "To use your child as an excuse for not going to work also shows poorly on the individual's character," his fellow senator Donne Trotter told the press.[17] These kinds of criticisms—whether explicit or unspoken—discourage men from bucking the work-above-all expectation. One finance professional told a Bloomberg reporter that men who attempt to take all the parental leave offered by their employers "are practically asking to get fired."[18] In a 2016 survey, a third of men said that taking parental leave could jeopardize their position, and less than half said that their employers fostered an environment in which men feel comfortable taking parental leave.[19] Researchers have found that when work-family policies such as parental leave are in place, men are less likely to use them if they believe that their male peers subscribe to traditional beliefs about men's roles.[20] Men may fear the stigma that comes along with prioritizing caregiving and quietly accept a social script that discourages more egalitarian partnerships.

Men may be reluctant to swim against the tide of conventional expectations out of a fear of backlash or a belief that their peers and colleagues prefer the status quo, but they may also see the playing field as more level than women report it to be. A 2019 IBM study found that most male executives did not believe they would have had a more challenging career path as women; 80 percent said they would have been at least as likely to be promoted to a top leadership role had they been female.[21] Various other studies have demonstrated that men see gender as less of a barrier than women. Even when final conclusions differ, a consistent gap emerges across this research wherein men see women as having more opportunity than women say they actually experience. In one study, men were more likely than women to say that opportunities and promotions are doled out according to fair criteria.[22] A Pew Research Center poll found that 56 percent of men believe that obstacles to women's advancement are largely a thing of the past; meanwhile, 63 percent of women think that "significant obstacles" to women's paths remain.[23] A similar question in yet another survey yielded the same result, with 58 percent of men agreeing that obstacles for women are largely gone.[24] And in a 2020 Gallup poll, 42 percent of US men claimed that equality in the workplace has been achieved—double the proportion of women who agreed.[25]

If men tend to see structural barriers as minimal to nonexistent, is it any wonder that they feel little incentive to advocate for women? Indeed, recent academic research has found that men's lower support for workplace diversity initiatives is tied directly to the fact that men are less likely than women to believe that gender discrimination is the cause of unequal outcomes.[26] Apprehension about the loss of status or power may be particularly relevant for men who are skeptical of the role of gender biases in the workplace, and zero-sum thinking about women's advancement as a threat to their own standing is likely to produce resistance to the kinds of policies and practices intended to counterbalance or mitigate discrimination.[27] We have conducted research on men's views after the #MeToo movement, and the results suggest that renewed attention to gender inequality at work is sometimes viewed through a zero-sum lens: In a survey of Harvard Business School (HBS) alumni, 12 percent of male graduates felt that men have lost status in the workplace as women have gained status. While clearly a minority viewpoint, it becomes disconcerting when added to the 27 percent of men who chose to "neither agree nor disagree" with the assertion that men have lost status as women have made gains. That is, 40 percent of men were, at the very least, uncertain about whether women's advancement is harmful to men. And a 2020 Pew study of gender equality found that over a quarter of American men felt that women's gains have come at men's expense.[28]

However, even men who don't worry that women's gains result in men's losses, who see gender discrimination as a real and continued problem and wholeheartedly believe it should be rectified, don't always take up an active role. In fact, a belief that gender bias is real and persistent can sometimes, paradoxically, make it harder for men to speak up about it. Our research suggests that many men are well aware of gender inequities at work. As one young man from our study of recent college graduates said, "As far as how I'm treated in the workplace, I feel like I'm favored as a male." In a 2019 survey published in the HBS student newspaper, male MBAs ranked the severity of gender inequality at 6 on a 7-point scale, where 6 indicated "a very large problem."[29] And in our study of HBS alumni, more than 40 percent of men said they believed gender had been an advantage to their careers.[30] If the thousands of men represented by these statistics—not to mention their like-minded peers—were outspoken advocates for gender equality, change could accelerate.

Why are only some of them speaking up? "Even for men who want to engage, there's a natural question of whether we should be the people taking the lead on trying to solve these problems or whether we should be living the values of equity and stepping back so women can lead instead," explained 2019 MBA grad Matt Piltch, who worked on a number of gender equity initiatives during his time in business school. Accustomed to speaking with both male and female peers about issues of gender discrimination and inequality, Piltch observed that some men struggled with finding their place: "If a person believes women should be empowered to solve these problems, there's a little bit of tension" that can be felt by men who want to support gender equity. This sense of unease is well known to social psychologists who study men's sense of "psychological standing" when it comes to being advocates for women. Ironically, while men's support for equity initiatives often lends legitimacy, as we noted above, men themselves may feel that their voice isn't an appropriate part of the chorus. The question Piltch identified ("Should I be the one?") reflects a hesitation that correlates with reduced action. One series of studies looking at men's participation in workplace gender-parity initiatives found that men were indeed less engaged in such programs than women, and their lower participation was driven by feelings that speaking up about gender issues wasn't their place, even if they believed that promoting gender parity was important. But more crucially, the research revealed that men's sense of psychological standing could be shifted simply by talking about their stake in gender equality and highlighting the importance of men's role in such initiatives. When companies and individuals frame the work of increasing gender equity as a collective imperative, men are empowered to take part.[31]

Getting onto the Field

Advocates for women are well aware that mobilizing men by increasing their sense of standing is critical. The United Nations HeForShe campaign invites "men and people of all genders to stand in solidarity with women," and Lean In Together, a program of Sheryl Sandberg's gender equity nonprofit, declares that "when men lean in for equality, they win—and so does everyone else." Catalyst, a think tank focused on gender in corporate America, offers to companies a program called Men Advocating for Real Change, a suite of offerings to develop men as advocates and allies for women's advancement. Piltch participated in the Manbassadors program at HBS, a group of male students who pledge to "take meaningful action against gender bias, discrimination, and violence against women" and to be "active participant[s] in the gender equity conversation at HBS and beyond." (See the epilogue for more about the Manbassadors and their influence on the school.) Piltch's classmate Kyle Emory, who led the Manbassadors during the 2018–2019 academic year, emphasized the promise embedded in that language: "We're asking them to act—not necessarily through huge, sweeping changes but just by being thoughtful in their conversations and the way in which they engage with other classmates. By doing a little bit, we can make a little bit of a change. But as more people do a little, the bigger the change will be." Emory knows that even incremental changes can be daunting but necessary: "I do think that everyone should try to push themselves a little further than what they're comfortable doing. That's what I did in this role [with the Manbassadors]. At first, I was uncomfortable because I'm not someone who's typically outspoken, but pushing myself really helped me better understand the importance of men engaging in more conversations around gender equity."

At HBS, the Manbassadors have a clear role and a place in the campus conversation about gender. The group, though led by men, is sponsored by the Women's Student Association (WSA). Emory had female classmates who collaborated with him on programming and activities, which lent validity to his own leadership and the group's role as a collective of allies. Within the MBA community, the WSA and the Manbassadors endorse and promote the idea that men belong in the fight for gender equity, but without this kind of consensus, men's engagement can falter. Organizational psychologist Adam Grant has written about how advocating for causes that don't directly benefit us can create fears of backlash. Men's anxiety about their place within the movement to advance women's opportunities can stem from a belief that their efforts may be met with suspicion or dismissal. Grant cites research on negative reactions toward male advocates but also describes hearing from readers critical of his own articles on women in leadership. "What business do you have writing about women?" they asked.[32] But emphasizing the role of men in gender-parity efforts doesn't mean succumbing to what researchers Brad Johnson and David Smith term the "pedestal effect," whereby men are lavishly praised for the most minor gestures of solidarity or support. Rather, they write, men simply need to know that their voice matters: "Evidence reveals that gender-parity efforts are most effective when men believe they have a dignified and important role to play. . . . The motivation for this role is often tied to personal examples and a sense of fairness and justice."[33] Men don't need to be given medals for confronting bias or supporting women in their lives, but men do need to know that such actions are meaningful and impactful and to see greater gender parity as a collective benefit and social good, not a narrow special interest.

As Johnson and Smith point out, men's values and lived experiences are often the motivation for taking an active part in gender-equity efforts. A strong sense of fair play was the biggest predictor of men's engagement in gender initiatives, according to one in-depth study. Moreover, the stronger men's sense of fair play, the more likely they themselves had experienced being excluded or marginalized. "Their commitment to fairness ideals was rooted in very personal and emotional experiences," the authors wrote.[34] This connection between personal stories and personal values is borne out in our research as well. Manbassador leader Emory described his own inspiration in very personal terms: "My motivation really comes from my mom. She has faced many difficulties in her career both as a veteran and doctor but has always found creative ways to overcome them and has gone on to do momentous things."

Experiencing the discomfort and discrimination that come with being in the minority has informed the leadership of a number of men we've interviewed. One South Asian CEO noted that "there have been a hundred times when I have felt different from other people in the room or in the business." Even white men, such as one CEO from the rural southern US who found himself at a Washington, D.C., law firm early in his career, sometimes experience being outsiders and carry forward an awareness about how hard that can be. In an in-depth qualitative study of two dozen CEOs from around the world, we found that male leaders who championed gender diversity and inclusion often had witnessed the women in their lives experience discrimination or be denied opportunities based on their sex. "When I see that women do not have the same opportunities as men," one said, "it touches me a in personal way. I think it's some kind of refusal related to my sisters or to my daughters."[35] Similarly, former Campbell Soup CEO Doug Conant told us that his interest in being an advocate for gender parity intensified when he considered how gender bias might impact his own daughter's trajectory. At an event focused on women in the workplace, a female colleague asked Conant, "Don't you think your daughter deserves the kind of opportunities we're talking about? Shouldn't she get a fair shot?" Conant recalled how the moment triggered a new feeling of urgency: "I had intellectually thought about it— of course, the concept of gender equality makes sense—but all of a sudden it was my daughter. It really forced me to take it even more personally, and it heightened my commitment. This was back in maybe 2007, and I've become even more passionate on the subject in the last decade."

Connecting these kinds of individual experiences to the broader phenomenon of gender inequality incentivized the men we interviewed to use their power and influence to institute programs and policies aimed at increasing opportunities for women in their organizations. Economist Paul Gompers has found something similar in his research on the venture capital industry: The higher the proportion of daughters among the children of a firm's senior partners, the more likely they are to hire a female investor. The same study also found that firms that brought on female partners through this "daughter effect" saw greater overall returns and more profitable exits compared to other firms.[36] As discussed elsewhere in this book, a direct link between gender diversity and financial performance is not always identifiable, but the male leaders we interviewed for this chapter did see combating gender discrimination as both a moral imperative and a common-sense business approach. In the words of John Tracy, chairman and former CEO of Dot Foods, "It's the right thing to do and it's consistent with our values, but the second thing is that it's really practical. From a business perspective, why in the world would you want to go out and only recruit from a portion of the talent pool? It makes no sense."

Changing the Game

Dot Foods's Tracy understood that as a leader, he could educate and inspire his employees about why gender inclusion mattered. Increasingly, businesses and business executives are being called on for moral leadership on the most pressing problems faced by society, but advancing gender parity requires more than a mission statement. CEOs and business owners shape both culture and policy; although practices such as hiring and evaluation are executed throughout the hierarchy, leaders at the highest levels set expectations. Both Tracy and Conant spoke not only about instituting new talent management practices but also about how they strove to inspire employees to internalize the goals of those initiatives. Tracy told us that when Dot Foods began to focus on improving gender as well as other forms of diversity in the company, he made a point of explaining and promoting the efforts across the organization. When he spoke at the company's annual nationwide meeting, he visualized the problem of biased recruiting by presenting a slide with "a huge population of people that overwhelm the slide" in which he would pinpoint a small circle and ask, "Why in the world would we want to just recruit from this portion?" At a growing company the answer was obvious, and Tracy tied diversity to business needs: "It was a pretty easy sell to say this makes ridiculously logical sense, and we need to get better at it. We need to become more inclusive in order to become more diverse, and we need to modify all kinds of things in our business to make that happen." As a white man at the head of the company, Tracy knew that championing Dot Foods's commitment to hiring, developing, and promoting people who didn't look like him or other members of the current senior management was a core component of his leadership role.

Likewise, Duchossois Group chairman and CEO Craig Duchossois understood that cultivating female leaders meant more than simply hiring women; when the company brought in JoAnna Garcia Sohovich as new head of the Chamberlain Group, its operating company, Duchossois knew that he had an obligation to position her for success. "Any CEO that brings in talented women has a responsibility to make sure they receive the proper mentoring on both the professional as well as cultural side of the organization. I worked to ensure that she had solid mentoring from others on our board besides me." And the company's focus on female leadership sets the stage for growing the pipeline to leadership, as Duchossois was gratified to see: "Our largest manufacturing operation is in Mexico. At JoAnna's first plant visit, she gave a presentation to a group of our high-potential female associates. And afterward, a young woman came up and said, 'I can't tell you how proud I am that you're running the company. Does this mean I now have a higher ladder to climb?' And of course, the answer was 'Yes!'"

It's not only CEOs and executives who can be change agents; men at every career stage have opportunities to break down barriers and catalyze new ways of thinking and working. Managers needn't oversee dozens or hundreds of employees to push back against gender bias, and one such action can create ripple effects. We spoke to one man in midcareer who told us about wanting to make sure a junior colleague's path wasn't derailed by biased feedback:

> I was coaching a female associate who seriously underperformed in her first year and was being moved to a back-office role. To be clear, she had performance gaps, and the move wasn't unwarranted. However, the written commentary in her review felt a bit heavy-handed, and the comments had some gender and also cultural bias embedded. It was a lot to unpack, but I did feel compelled to try to help or offset a bit by being more positive and pointing out that just because "some dude" wrote it in a review doesn't mean it's 100 percent true or fair. He's your boss because he's good at investing, not coaching. It just didn't feel like an entirely fair assessment, and I didn't want her to walk away from this associate experience thinking she was hopelessly incompetent.

Mindful of the way subtle biases could be influencing how the associate was treated, he helped her distinguish job-relevant and actionable feedback from the kind of vague criticism about likability and fit that is often grounded in bias and is nearly impossible for an employee to act on. As a raft of studies as well as stories from women across industries have made clear, women receive less, and less effective, guidance than their male peers. Concerns about women's lack of access to mentors and sponsors becoming more entrenched through backlash to #MeToo are reflected in media reports of men avoiding female colleagues.[37] Whether spurred by a genuinely felt anxiety or merely a convenient rationale for a preexisting preference, when men withdraw from the women they work with, they limit opportunities for their coworkers to learn important business information, hear about projects they could pursue, and increase their visibility. Because men make up the majority of high-level decision makers, it is especially critical that they choose to develop and sponsor women, as Nicole Grogan, chief people officer at a West Coast investment firm, passionately argued:

> There aren't enough women in leadership roles that women can just rely on other women. Women coming up in the organization need to rely on men too for their careers to be accelerated or developed. And I sense that there is a little more hesitance or sensitivity now, with men not wanting to do anything that could be perceived as inappropriate or showing too much attention to women. And that's exactly the wrong thing. You've got to put yourself in the place of discomfort, and if you're uncertain about what's appropriate, talk to somebody you trust about how to navigate these relationships, but please don't disengage. This is not the time to pull back.

How men relate to female colleagues, especially subordinates and peers, has enormous implications for women's experiences at work, but what has received comparatively less attention is how men's interactions with other men can advance—or impede—gender equity. By interrupting moments of bias or bigotry, men can foster, day by day, more gender-equal cultures. Even minor instances of discrimination or harassment add up, and when men call them out, they delegitimize the attitudes and behaviors that marginalize their female colleagues. But there is a gap between men's acknowledgment that sexism is wrong and their comfort with confronting it. In a 2019 study conducted by Promundo, an international consortium advocating for gender equality, most women (59 percent) did not agree that "men are doing everything they can to advance gender equality in the workplace." Focus groups revealed that women were skeptical about men's willingness to challenge sexist behavior. While a majority of women felt that men would be good listeners to women about discriminatory experiences, they weren't confident that men would step up and confront other men.[38] Another study, focused on workplaces in Australia, found that the number-one action that women said was important for male allies to do, "calling out instances of gender discrimination," was ranked near the bottom in importance by men and was far from the top activity (seventh of sixteen activities) that men actually engaged in to support gender parity.[39] In a study conducted in Mexico with male employees at three multinational corporations, the vast majority (86 percent) felt personally committed to addressing sexist incidents at work, but less than a third actually felt comfortable speaking up in the moment.[40]

This gap between conviction and action is especially troubling because men's voices can have a powerful impact on decisions and practices. We spoke to Santiago Ocejo, who earned an MBA in 2014 and subsequently cofounded a social enterprise providing health care at low-cost clinics in Mexico City. When Ocejo came to learn that a director at the startup had instituted a policy prohibiting women from working evening shifts, he knew he had to speak up about the problematic nature of basing staffing decisions on gender:

> I think it was well-intentioned; we operated in high-risk locations, and it was saying "we don't want you to be exposed to dangerous situations." But even though he was well-intentioned, I realized that we were kind of institutionalizing discrimination against women. So, there was a huge internal debate that probably lasted for a couple of months. Instead of just changing the policy unilaterally, I opened it up to a larger debate, and we did end up changing it. My feeling was, let women decide what is or is not safe for them. We can acknowledge and accommodate the safety concerns, but we should not close doors because of gender.

Another time, Ocejo had to address a technology vendor that was using "humorous" stereotypical images of women to illustrate a process manual: "I had to say, 'I know you did this for fun, but it's not acceptable. I'm the client, and if you worked for me this wouldn't be acceptable either.'" Moreover, Ocejo didn't limit his advocacy to settings in which he had formal authority. He also challenged peers on issues of sexism and bias, as with one friend who expressed reluctance to hire an attractive woman, despite her qualifications, out of worry that working with her would somehow undermine his marriage: "I was like, come on, dude, you're basically discriminating because of some personal situation, and you need to sort that out yourself instead of discriminating against women based on their appearance."

Redefining the Goal

Men in the millennial generation to which Ocejo belongs are changing our expectations around what men can and should do about gender inequality. One recent study of finance professionals found that entry-level men were the group most concerned about unequal gender representation at their firms, and in another survey across twenty-one countries, men under forty were the most willing to undergo bias-reduction training and were more accommodating of coworkers with flexible schedules.[41] Our own research on HBS alumni found that millennial men were much more likely than older alumni to have assumed, upon graduation, that they would share childcare and housework with their spouses.[42] In *Unfinished Business: Men Women Work Family*, the follow-up book to her viral *Atlantic* article, Anne-Marie Slaughter argues that "the next phase of the women's movement is a men's movement." Until it is not seen as exceptional at best and strange at worst for men to be primary caregivers, gendered divisions of labor at home will continue to disadvantage women at work. A recent study of one large unionized workplace where pay and promotions are highly regulated found that women earned eighty-nine cents for every dollar paid to their male counterparts, a difference that was entirely attributable to women taking less advantage of lucrative overtime opportunities and taking more unpaid time off. Why were women not maximizing their earnings? The researchers found that women had less flexibility to pick up additional shifts or change their schedules on short notice, meaning they couldn't take advantage of opportunities to work extra hours. Even when men also had children, they were more likely than women to work overtime.[43] If this kind of earnings disparity couldn't be overcome even when compensation policies are formalized and clear, is it any wonder that it often blossoms in white-collar settings where managers have greater discretion to set pay and distribute assignments?

There is mounting evidence that men themselves are chafing at restrictive expectations that they prioritize breadwinning at the expense of caregiving. Slaughter recounts the backlash against a diaper ad that depicted fathers as incompetent and hapless. One father started a Change.org petition taking the brand to task for demeaning dads' parenting, and the brand's Facebook page was flooded with complaints. Not long afterward the company pulled the commercial and issued a public apology.[44] Despite continuing to face fairly rigid expectations about what fatherhood means (most Americans view fathers' financial role as more central than caregiving), fathers today are spending more time with their children than any previous generation and feeling similar levels of stress as mothers about balancing work and family.[45]

Expectations for men to treat parenthood as less important than work can come directly from employers, both explicitly and indirectly. In the Jones Day lawsuit mentioned above, a young associate was fired days after he raised the issue of the firm's lesser leave time for new fathers, although his performance had been highly rated.[46] While the pressure on women to prioritize caregiving is intense, so too is the expectation that fathers will focus on work; according to the Boston College Center for Work and Family, the vast majority of US fathers want to spend more time with their children than they currently do and would prefer an egalitarian partnership with 50/50 child-rearing— yet three-quarters of dads returned to work less than a week after birth or adoption, and 96 percent were back at work within two weeks. As the center's 2014 report pointed out, "This failure of men to be active co-parents in the first few months of the children's lives sets a pattern in motion that is difficult to change. . . . The father is immediately cast in the role of a supporting actor."[47] Research on dual-career families has found that many couples fall into these traditional roles without consciously intending to and find themselves dissatisfied both at work and at home, with neither spouse feeling as though they are fulfilled as parents or professionals. In the absence of open discussion about career prioritization and parenting roles, couples struggle to find a balance that meets both partners' needs, defaulting to social pressures, reinforced by the messages they receive in the workplace, for men to have a more limited role at home.[48]

There are high-profile dads taking a more conscious approach in their own families and advocating for a change to the policies and norms that make them such outliers. Reddit cofounder Alexis Ohanian took four months of leave after the birth of his first child, which he contrasted, in a 2019 *New York Times* op-ed, with the single vacation day his father used when Ohanian himself was born thirty-four years earlier. Rather than fault his dad or any other father who spends limited time at home, Ohanian cited the stigma around caregiving that makes many men reluctant to put their professional role on hold for even a few weeks. And while Ohanian emphasized the need for public policies that enable more men to choose to take parental leave, he looked to his status as a public figure as a vehicle for change. Ohanian offered up to readers his own story as a way to legitimize their desire to take advantage of leave time: "I took my full 16 weeks and I'm still ambitious and care about my career," he writes. "Talk to your bosses and tell them I sent you."[49]

The fact that a lack of managerial support, not a lack of on-paper leave, can be the biggest obstacle to men's caregiving is a reminder about the power of organizational culture. Even countries with government-sponsored leave policies do not always see equal uptake of benefits. In South Korea, where fathers can ostensibly take advantage of one of the world's most generous leaves (fifty-two weeks), just 5 percent of workers who took leave in 2015 were men. A survey by a major Korean employment website revealed that the number-one reason men chose not to take leave was company pressure.[50] But companies can apply positive pressure too. Boston-based analytics startup Humanyze mandates that dads take the full twelve weeks of leave the company provides to new parents. Like Ohanian, Humanyze's (male) CEO penned an op-ed, his aimed at other company leaders with the power to set not only formal policy but also expectations about what high-performing employees do. When he and a cofounder both went on leave at the same time, "the company thrived, the world didn't collapse, and we were able to spend time with our new children," he wrote. "It was an easy call to make that leave should be mandatory for the rest of the company."[51]

Enabling men to more fully show up in their lives outside of work is critical to advancing women's opportunities in the workplace. Without a change to men's roles, women's careers will continue to be constrained by outsize burdens outside the office. Japan offers a case in point. Despite Prime Minister Shinzo Abe's much-touted "womenomics" initiative to boost women's participation and standing in the labor force, Japanese women's careers continue to be hindered because they still shoulder the vast majority of household labor. While more women are in the workforce today than were at the time of the initiative's launch in 2013, half of new female workers are in part-time jobs, and women hold just 13 percent of managerial positions.[52] The extreme hours endemic to Japanese work culture have changed but little, and most men continue to adhere to expectations that they will devote virtually all their time to work and work-based socializing. Men in dual-career families spend fewer than five hours a week on household labor, compared to twenty-five hours spent by their wives, who are also working fifty or more hours each week. "Theoretically, it sounds ideal to have me work fewer hours and Yoshiko work more," one father of three told the *New York Times*. "But realistically, it is not feasible," given the goals he is expected to meet.[53] There are some nascent but limited signs that more men are willing to challenge these norms; in January 2020, the country's environment minister announced that he would take two weeks of paternity leave, spread out over a three-month period, after the birth of his first child, an announcement that garnered international news coverage and social media fanfare.[54]

Even without children in the picture, the expectation that the man's career is primary in a dual-career heterosexual partnership means that men who go against the grain face friction. One example from our own research: David Rawlinson was offered a promotion leading the London-based online business for his *Fortune* 500 employer soon after his wife Nadia Rawlinson began a new job leading human resources for the US arm of a multibillion-dollar Japanese ecommerce firm. David was eager to take on the new opportunity, but the couple had just relocated to San Francisco for his wife's role. Accepting the offer on the condition that he could stay based in San Francisco, David found that it took numerous discussions with his new colleagues to assure them of his commitment to and excitement about the job; most of his peers were men in more traditional marriages whose careers had always taken precedence, and they were discomfited by the request. Ultimately the company supported his need for an egalitarian balance, and the couple established a routine that enabled both of them to thrive in their careers and model how men can pursue a high-powered path without subscribing to outmoded gender norms.

The real-life examples of Rawlinson, Ohanian, and Humanyze CEO Ben Waber remind us that the choices men make can break down barriers for women in their own lives as well as present an example for men at their companies and beyond. The everyday actions of leaders at all levels send important messages about what leadership is, who belongs in positions of power, and who is committed to changing the game. In our final chapter, we will dig into the ways every manager can recognize and combat the barriers that prevent women in their companies from advancing. Everyone—from CEOs to frontline managers, men as well as women—who hires, trains, and evaluates employees can use our framework to upgrade how they source, develop, and retain talent. We need change agents of every gender, and they belong everywhere, not just in the C-suite or the halls of Congress but also in the cubicles, on the shop floors, and roaming the open-plan offices where day-to-day business gets done. But first, Chapter 5 will take a final look at the structures and systems that create unequal outcomes and how they might be transformed.

CHAMPIONING GENDER EQUALITY IN THE MEDIA

Ros Atkins

R os Atkins began paying attention to gender disparities as a teenager growing up in southwest England, long before he entered the professional workplace.[55] "When I was sixteen or seventeen, my mum, who was a voracious consumer of feminist literature, bought a copy of *The Beauty Myth* by Naomi Wolf, and I found it something that I was interested to read. While I don't agree with all the narratives in the book, it opened my eyes to the relationship between the media and the experience of gender inequality for women. It planted a seed." This seed grew as Atkins pursued his undergraduate degree. "I studied history at university, and I started to choose essay and paper topics that were connected to gender. And for a short while I also worked on an eating disorders help line. I made various decisions that were connected to my interest in gender and that has just stayed with me." Firmly established, that interest would ultimately spur Atkins to plant a change initiative in his chosen field of journalism, one that would blossom at his own media organization and far beyond.

After graduating from Cambridge, Atkins launched his career in South Africa, reporting for the *Sunday Independent* and also working as a disc jockey and policy researcher. Not long after returning to the United Kingdom, he joined the BBC as a radio news producer. It was 2001, and while there was widespread cultural awareness about gender gaps, they remained pronounced in the media and across society more generally. Atkins soon noticed the imbalance at his new employer, one of England's most treasured public institutions and a leading source of news and information around the world. "I was twenty-seven, suddenly working in this huge organization, and I wasn't just observing what was happening in the media with reference to gender, I was now part of that media in a way I hadn't been before. Very quickly I became aware that the programming I was involved in making and the programming all around me was much more likely to skew male than female." Atkins wanted to make a change, but, as he recalls today,

> I didn't have enough understanding of the organization to really do very much. In one instance, early on in my BBC career, I wrote to my editor and said, "Look, of all the regular guests on our show, the vast majority are men," and I didn't get a reply. I bumped into him a few days later and asked if he had seen my email, and he said, "I did, and I didn't like your tone." It was an interesting lesson that I could notice these things and feel motivated, but that in itself was not necessarily enough to deliver any change.

For some time, Atkins continued to raise the issue of women's underrepresentation in BBC programming with various colleagues, all the while building his own career. He started occasionally filling in on *World Have Your Say*, a program on BBC radio, and by 2006 was one of the show's main presenters. In 2014, Atkins created and began anchoring a new nightly television broadcast, *Outside Source*, which he helms today. As he advanced, he continued to try to ignite interest in gender-parity initiatives. Some of these attempts were more positively received than his first but still didn't yield much action. "I was far from the only person to be mindful of these issues," he explains. "When I was a radio presenter on BBC World Service, I had a very close relationship with my editor, and I asked him if we could start counting the numbers of male and female guests, and he said 'I don't think we need to. We're thinking about it all the time.' He absolutely agreed it was an important point; he just wasn't convinced about the approach I was suggesting, which was to actually measure it every day."

Yet as time went on, Atkins became more and more convinced that rigorous measurement was exactly what was needed to make progress. By 2016, with a prominent presenting role and the enhanced influence that came with it, he felt compelled to try analyzing his own show. "I was aware that my program had more men on it than women," he recalls, "and I started to think quite deeply about why this was happening and why we weren't making more progress when the goal of having fair representation of women was so widely accepted." The disjuncture between aspiration and results was, he observed, a general problem and a puzzling one. "We had accepted the goal but at the same time accepted that it wasn't possible. A phrase popped into my mind one day on the bus going to work, which is that we were in *a constant state of trying*, where the trying becomes an end in itself." The notion that the goal was unattainable kept people resigned to the status quo and dampened any urgency that might be harnessed for action. "It creates a narrative that claims 'we are trying and doing better,' and the goal actually becomes secondary."

But Atkins knew that his colleagues did care about gender balance, and he believed that if he got them to pay closer attention to just how imbalanced the content was, they could—and would—move beyond that state of constant trying. "If you could prove that it was possible [to increase the proportion of women], then you would very much change that dynamic," he explains. "But we just had no ability to gauge what we were doing." Toward the end of 2016, Atkins traveled to Silicon Valley and, after speaking with experts at companies such as Google and Facebook, left with even greater certainty that collecting and tracking the numbers was the right approach. "I left with an overwhelming sense that data was being used in very profound ways to drive ongoing cultural change in those workplaces. And I ultimately combined these two ideas—one, that data has the power to drive cultural change, and two, that you aren't going to deliver this change unless you prove that it's possible."

By this time, Atkins was no longer a junior producer finding his way but now was a fifteen-year BBC veteran and a respected journalist. As he puts it, "I had enough influence over my own program's production team to say, 'Hey, can we give this a go?'" It wasn't an edict. As Atkins is quick to point out, "News anchors are not managers. We have soft power but not hard power in terms of budgets and line management." Rather than an order from on high, it was an appeal to peers, whom he knew shared his desire to pursue gender parity. Looking back, it seems to Atkins that this collegial approach, powered by influence rather than mandate, was not only sufficient but perhaps ideal.

> Maybe, someone without hard power coming to you with an idea and suggesting "Why don't you try this?" is less intense than someone very senior coming to you and saying "We need you to do this." I've worked in parts of the BBC where management were keen to implement some change or modernization, and you would spend a lot of time trying to persuade people to do things that they really didn't want to do. I found it a largely unproductive exercise, which often didn't end up with people changing their behavior and did end up with them being a little frustrated with you. More unhappiness and not a great deal of progress.

Knowing all too well these pitfalls, Atkins approached his conversations with colleagues as opportunities to help, not occasions to impress. "I'd do a big presentation for a group of editors, and you could see on their faces that they're expecting the hard sell, for me to say 'Who's going to start next month?' And instead I just say, 'It's been interesting for us. If you're interested, let us know. No problem if it doesn't work for you.' That pressure point which they're anticipating never arrives."

To test his theory that a data-driven approach would spark a shift in the gender ratio, Atkins first approached the producers and editors of his own program, *Outside Source*. "I simply made the case to my team that we should try it, and between us we resolved to do it," he explains. Calling it the 50:50 Project, he proposed tracking, on a monthly basis, the number of male and female contributors (i.e., reporters, analysts, experts—anyone who was on the program to report or analyze the news). The makeup of contributors was not only integral to a program's voice but was also a journalistic choice, and Atkins knew he needed to propose a way of examining gender balance that spoke to his colleagues' sphere of influence and scope of work. *Outside Source* forged ahead. "For the first six months," Atkins recalls, "we didn't really talk to any other program or any other editors. It was only after we had proved that it worked, and that was several months in, that I started to have conversations with managers and editors. I waited until I had something credible to underpin the conversation."

Compelling results soon emerged. *Outside Source* first began its tally in January 2017 and by April had increased the proportion of women contributors from 39 percent to 51 percent. Atkins's theory had been proved: Tracking the data had spurred them to tap more women to appear on the show and, consequently, achieve gender balance. "If you're sensitive to something and you notice it and you feel it, you're much, much more likely to act to resolve that issue," he explains. "50:50 has really been a gargantuan exercise in sensitization. The numbers sensitize you to what is happening, and you feel disappointment if you aren't doing as well as you'd like, and your motivation to do better is considerably higher."

If his own program was any indication, Atkins knew that when others became sensitized in this way, they too were likely to create more balanced content. However, he was well aware that all newsrooms juggle a number of important priorities and that his colleagues were already overloaded with work. How could he convince them that adding another task, even if quite straightforward, to their ever-growing lists was worthwhile? He knew he'd have to make a strong case, and he also felt that he needed to demonstrate the seriousness of his own commitment. "I was asking a lot of them to join, to add to their daily commitments, and I felt the least I could do was meet them halfway and say if you invest in this, I'll match you. I promise I'll support you every step of the way, and I'll make sure your work on this is noticed."

Atkins also thought hard about the potential objections he might hear:

I wrote down all the questions that I could imagine my most skeptical colleagues asking and wrote down what my answers would be. I needed to make sure that those answers were seriously credible, so I asked a couple of senior female colleagues to meet with me, and we reviewed all the concerns I thought would come up. For instance, there is some hostility toward quotas in the UK media, so it had to be clear that while 50 percent women was an aspiration, it wasn't a quota. And I also knew that people would say "I'd love to do this, but I haven't got time," so I had to be able to demonstrate that monitoring even a quite complicated program would take less than two minutes. The list went on, and we made sure we had very clear, solid answers to all the reasons not to try it—because my theory was that if people tried it, they would realize that it wasn't that much work and that it was not about compromising the quality of their journalism. Indeed, it's arguably about making their journalism better.

By the middle of 2017 five new programs had joined 50:50, and by year's end another dozen had signed on. The pace picked up as Atkins continued to meet with other teams and word spread about the project. "In autumn 2017," he recalls, "I landed three or four really high-profile flagship BBC news programs, and it gave my conversations with other programs much more credibility, and we went from ten programs to sixty programs quite quickly. That was one tipping point." More than eighty teams had joined by early 2018. In February of that year Atkins was invited to meet with the head of the BBC, Director-General Tony Hall; that conversation further accelerated the momentum. "The BBC is a huge organization," Atkins explains. "It wouldn't be normal, even for someone like me who's reasonably senior in the newsroom, to encounter the director-general. I think it was the second time I'd ever met him. A couple of weeks later, he referenced 50:50 in a speech, and that was like throwing a match on the fire. The fact that he had endorsed it, that he was saying 'I know about this effort, and I want it to thrive,' was incredibly powerful." The project picked up considerable steam from there. In April the BBC press office issued the "50:50 Challenge," exhorting programs to join. The *Daily Telegraph*, one of the largest-circulation daily newspapers in the country, put the challenge on its front page. The attention "transformed everything," Atkins remembers. The success that *Outside Source* had first achieved was soon replicated. In April 2019, 57 percent of all participating teams had reached a ratio of 50 percent women contributors; among teams that had been following the approach for at least a year, 74 percent had reached gender parity—compared to just 27 percent of teams that were at parity before joining.[56]

From Atkins's perspective, the success of 50:50 is a testament to the power of a group of committed individuals, most of whom just needed a way to activate their desire to close gender gaps. "What I've heard from a lot of colleagues is that they weren't sure how to talk about these issues," he says. "They weren't sure how to measure their progress toward greater gender equality. They weren't sure if management was really serious about reaching 50 percent women. And suddenly this project says to them, 'Yes, we care. This is how we're going to do it, and if you want to get involved go for it.' That tapped into a passion a lot of my colleagues already had and just gave it some shape."

As the next decade began, the shape of 50:50 continued to expand. By early 2020 not only had more than six hundred BBC teams joined, but over sixty other organizations in twenty countries had also signed on.[57] In just a few short years, it had clearly grown far beyond Atkins's network. Speaking in January 2020, he recounted a recent example of how the project had taken on a life of its own: "On Monday, there was an event in Salford, just outside Manchester, about diversifying the BBC's contacts for that newsroom, and I was looking at all these photos of people at the event, and they were all tweeting 'I've had a brilliant day at this 50:50 event.' And with the exception of two people, I didn't know any of them. That's when it becomes very powerful, when you lose control in the best way possible and it becomes a vehicle for something much bigger than you could ever create yourself."

The 50:50 Project became so big, in fact, that Atkins could no longer run it on his own. Two BBC colleagues joined Atkins to manage the program, and the BBC also invested in technology capabilities, building a dashboard for teams to input their data and track their own and others' progress. Yet even as 50:50 became more robust and operated at a much larger scale, Atkins continued to lead with a personal touch, driven by his conviction that a genuine person-to-person appeal was key to building real commitment. "Because I'm a man, it's entirely inappropriate for me to walk into an editorial meeting with a group of people I don't particularly know, made up of men and women, and start by being anything other than very humble when talking about this issue," he points out. "There's nothing strident about it. There are no lectures being made. Every time a new team joins, it means a huge amount that they're willing to invest their time and faith."

The 50:50 Project was clearly successful on the metric of member-ship. But did the efforts that programs undertook make a real difference to news consumers and to the public more broadly? To find out, the BBC conducted a nationally representative survey, which revealed that 39 percent of respondents noticed more women being featured by the BBC. Thirty-two percent of female respon-dents saw the greater representation as an improvement.[58] More-over, Atkins argues that gender balance is critical to high performance: "Journalism is about understanding the world, explaining it and analyzing it to the people who are consuming your work. You can't possibly do that effectively if you don't speak to the entire world. If you're only speaking to a section of the world or you're disproportionately hearing from one part of the world, that is sure to undermine your ability to fairly and accurately report and analyze what's happening around you."

Atkins is proud of the impact that the 50:50 Project has had on the BBC and on the conversation about gender in the media, although he is not one to don rose-colored glasses. "My entire approach to this project, and it remains my entire approach," he says, "is that it not succeeding is by far the most likely outcome, because gender inequality in media content has existed since media has existed." Yet 50:50 has been part of a movement that just may eradicate it. Looking back over the last few years, Atkins can see a real change of pace: "If I compare the prominence of the issue of gender equality today to three and half years ago when I started 50:50, a lot has changed. The conversations around how to make progress as quickly as we can have become easier with every month that goes by. There is an urgency not just within the BBC but within the media, and it would be a great surprise to me if that urgency doesn't continue to increase."

CHAPTER 5

BECOMING A GLASS-SHATTERING ORGANIZATION

A Systemic Approach to Closing Gender Gaps

Companies today are well aware of a pervasive gender imbalance in leadership, and the vast majority see this phenomenon reflected in their own executive ranks. In the words of one (male) C-level executive at JPMorgan Chase, "The more senior the group, the fewer women there are. And yet, if you look at some of the younger groups—people that are right out of college and a little further along in their careers—there's a more balanced representation. We're losing very high-quality talent, and there's no reason we should have this much asymmetry as we progress."[1] Such a statement could have come from nearly any company leader, given the persistent underrepresentation of women in managerial and executive roles across sectors and industries. In Part 1 of this book, we examined gender barriers from the perspective of the women who contend with them—identifying and exploring the expectations, biases, and judgments that steer women off the leadership track and slow their ascent. Throughout, we've also heard the voices of women who have overcome these obstacles reflecting on how they did so and what changes they believe are most needed today, decades after the removal of many formal barriers. To begin Part 2, we turned our attention to how men might—and must—take up the fight for gender parity. Thanks in part to the generosity of our interviewees, we learned how individual men are advocating for and enacting change. We hope their stories motivate others to do the same, but we also recognize that broader, more systemic efforts are needed, which is why this chapter shifts our focus to the organizational level. It is only when companies mobilize to assess, update, and improve their managerial practices—not in piecemeal fashion but systematically and thoroughly—that the patterns explored earlier in this volume will begin to shift and break down.

Fundamentally, eliminating gender disparities at work is about more effective talent management. Talent acquisition, engagement, and retention are critical for any company—be it a *Fortune* 100 corporation or an early-stage startup. Indeed, "attracting and retaining top talent" was ranked among the top three concerns of boards in a survey we conducted with over five thousand company directors across sixty countries.[2] Talent management is also complex and multifaceted; it requires both an overarching vision from the top about how to best meet the company's needs as well as day-to-day execution by managers at all levels, typically in the midst of other pressing obligations. And yet, a study conducted by the Canada–United States Council for Advancement of Women Entrepreneurs & Business Leaders found that less than half of companies had actually articulated a plan to advance women to senior leadership.[3] Another survey of more than a thousand companies in fifty-four countries found that less than half of organizations reported having a plan to advance gender equality, even though 80 percent said that it was important.[4] Despite broad acknowledgment of gender gaps, many companies have not translated interest into action in the form of structural and cultural changes. As a result, the systems that organizations use to hire, train, and retain employees continue to perpetuate an uneven playing field even as CEOs espouse a sincere belief in advancing women's opportunities.

The formal processes that make up people management are influenced by gender biases that we all hold, often without even being aware of them, as well as by structural features of the workplace that hinder women's careers. The unintentional nature of these barriers has been described by management scholars as a second-generation form of gender disadvantage; unlike overt first-generation barriers such as sex-segregated job listings, second-generation gender bias is more subtle and therefore harder to identify and eliminate. When managers' unconscious biases influence how they assess performance, second-generation bias is at work, as it is when seemingly gender-neutral practices, such as assignment rotations, create uneven opportunities for men and women.[5] We dug deep into the research on talent management and talked to women from companies around the world who came to Harvard Business School to attend various executive education programs in order to understand when and how barriers to women's advancement occur today and how they can be deconstructed or altogether prevented. Each step presents an opportunity to ensure that talented women are not unnecessarily stalled in their career progress or compelled to leave their companies for better prospects elsewhere.

Ultimately, this chapter presents a unifying framework for identifying the systemic patterns that can lead to this kind of talent drain. The good news is that these patterns are not set in stone; companies can eliminate or mitigate the inputs that create them. Those in positions of more power can create greater change, but there are steps even midlevel managers can take to improve systems. (In Chapter 6, we will discuss in depth the role that individual managers can play even when their sphere of influence is small in scope.) Organizations that tackle these flaws and leaks in the system gain a real advantage over competitors that accept a status quo, which leaves women underdeveloped and derailed from the leadership track. As Dot Foods chairman John Tracy pointed out in Chapter 4, focusing on only part of the talent pool—white men who have an easier time navigating the workplace—deprives your company of the skills and insights of the many people who don't fit that narrow mold. Some exceptional women will break through, hammering an individual opening in the glass ceiling. But that piecemeal progress will get you only so far—despite holes and chinks, the ceiling stays intact. Shattering it would be far more effective. To find out how to become a glass-shattering organization, read on.

Attracting Candidates

Before you even have an applicant pool, your organization might be inadvertently weeding out women. Consider how managers tend to source candidates. Is it by tapping personal networks for recommendations? While this approach has the benefit of drawing on trustworthy information, it's likely that those sources lack variation not only by gender but also by race, educational background, age, and other characteristics. All of us tend to be drawn to people who share key aspects of our identities. This principle, called homophily, has been well documented by researchers and, more pertinently, has been shown to shape business decisions, sometimes with inadvertently discriminatory effects.[6] In one study of MBA students forming teams to launch microbusinesses, students were 25 percent more likely to partner with others who shared their gender or ethnicity.[7] Among white-collar professionals looking for work after a layoff, gender-segregated professional networks result in women getting lower-paying job leads compared to men who have similar professional backgrounds.[8]

An executive at LinkedIn described how homogeneity was perpetuated there: a pattern of hiring too quickly, "not giving ourselves enough time to look more deeply," and seeing the first candidate—who typically looked like existing team members—as the right candidate.[9] One woman we interviewed put it this way: "What I see happening time and time again is people defaulting to their immediate network when they're hiring, especially the more senior the position." We spoke to Francis Collins, director of the National Institutes of Health (NIH), about efforts to diversify the leadership ranks of the NIH's twenty-seven centers and institutes, which required a new approach to recruiting: "Of the last six [center directors] I recruited, five of them were women. In at least some of those instances, I don't think it would have turned out that way if we had done the search in the usual crank-turning way of asking 'who do we know that's good' and reaching out to them. It took some additional steps to make sure we weren't missing people who weren't on those short lists, which were mostly populated with men." Key to that process was Hannah Valantine, the NIH's chief officer for scientific workforce diversity, a position created by Collins in 2014: "[Valantine] has been engaged in virtually every search committee process, making sure that we are finding out about candidates that would add to our diversity. And I always spend a fair amount of time with committees, highlighting for them how crucial it is to do that kind of exceptional outreach and not just taking the easy way out, which is often just a call to men."

Many employers routinely expose job opportunities to thousands of potential applicants through various search engines and sites. Online job postings are particularly important for roles lower in the hierarchy—perhaps the kinds of jobs that new NIH center directors themselves are trying to fill. Although such advertisements help make opportunities more widely known, what they say can discourage qualified women. One study of Canada's top two employment websites found that numerous jobs were presented in highly gendered language, with occupations where men predominate described with terms connoting masculine stereotypes (e.g., *competitive, dominant*) and those where women predominate with traditionally feminine terms (e.g., *support, understand, interpersonal*). These ads were not merely reflecting the reality of male- and female-dominated jobs, they were creating it: Women were systematically less interested in applying to roles couched in masculine language, even when they believed that they had the skills to actually *do* the job.[10] Other research has confirmed that women are less likely to apply for a job if the ideal candidate is described with traditionally masculine characteristics.[11]

One company that develops software for writing job ads has found a strong correlation between masculine- or feminine-typed phrases and the likelihood of a man or woman being hired into the role, using data from its own clients. In cases where a man was ultimately hired, the job's original posting had nearly double the number of masculine-typed phrases. Describing this discovery, the company founder noted the downstream effects of a skewed pool: "The language you use changes who applies to your job, and you're much more likely to hire a woman . . . if your pipeline has several women to consider."[12]

In addition, highly qualified women may opt out of applying when descriptions are either scant and unclear or extreme in the other direction—over the top in describing the perfect candidate. A series of studies conducted in both the lab and the field discovered that clearly stated job requirements made qualified women more likely to apply. Men's likelihood to apply wasn't affected by clarifying the requirements, meaning that the applicant pool became larger and more gender-diverse.[13] Meanwhile, a different study analyzed data from Uber's corporate job advertisements to understand gender differences in technical job applications. When postings were stripped of language about exceptional expertise (e.g., by listing "coding skills" rather than "excellent coding skills") as well as optional "nice to have" qualifications, the gender gap closed. Women holding advanced degrees became just as likely to apply as men with the same qualifications, where earlier fewer qualified women were throwing their hats in the ring.[14]

The Bottom Line about Attracting Candidates

Common approaches to sourcing candidates as well as overt and subtle messages in job postings can artificially depress the number of qualified women who appear in an applicant pool.

What managers can do:

- Track the proportion of male and female candidates and compare results to the average for your industry as well as to your internal aspirations for diversity.

- Harness networks to increase rather than thwart diversity. Research in multiple settings has found that both white women and racial minorities tend to refer applicants of their same race and gender, which suggests that companies can use targeted referrals to increase the diversity of applicant pools.[15]

- Assess the language used to advertise jobs and identify where it may suggest that women candidates are less desirable. Technology can aid in this kind of analysis, systematically flagging terms that connote gendered characteristics or stereotypes. But a technological solution isn't a replacement for managerial reflection; if the ideal candidate is assumed (explicitly or implicitly) to be male, the job description will likely reflect those assumptions.

Hiring

Once the process of reviewing applicants is underway, gender biases have numerous opportunities to impact the hiring process, beginning at the earliest stage. In multiple studies across a range of industries and sectors, researchers have examined the effects of indicating the gender, race or ethnicity, and sexual orientation on résumés where all other factors are the same, finding that those from historically disadvantaged groups (e.g., white women, men and women of color, gay men) are less likely to called for interviews by employers.[16] One firm that we studied started tracking the gender ratio of applications received, candidates interviewed, and offers extended in order to surface where gender biases could be weeding out female candidates. The country head where this practice was instituted recalled that "these metrics initiated a healthy dialogue that helped changed behaviors. . . . We could positively highlight managers that were making conscious efforts to create a diverse team and understand the rationale of those managers who were having difficulty hiring women and address those areas where possible."[17] This kind of acknowledgment that barriers exist is a critical first step. Particularly in male-dominated fields, denying the existence of gender bias is correlated with a lower likelihood to hire women. By contrast, recognizing that women face obstacles seems to help interviewers assess candidates impartially.[18]

Exactly why might the résumés of equally or better-qualified women be set aside in favor of men's? There are several drivers of this kind of discrimination, which is often not deliberate. Managers may not evaluate men and women candidates using the same standards; one study looking at the traditionally male-dominated role of police chief found that reviewers actually redefined job criteria to benefit male over female applicants.[19] Women's résumés are also held to a higher standard: One study found that women economists received less credit for coauthored papers than did their male peers, resulting in lower promotion rates for women.[20] And beliefs about women as generally less skilled than men in certain areas can diminish the likelihood of female candidates being hired for jobs that require those skills, even when the qualifications of the actual applicant are in fact strong.[21] And finally, the résumés of childbearing-age women may also be evaluated less favorably because of a belief that mothers are less committed to their jobs than men or women without children; when applicants' parental status is known, mothers are less likely to receive a callback from a potential employer, even when their résumés are identical to those of male applicants or women without children.[22] This pattern occurs even when applicants come from top-tier educational backgrounds.[23]

Ensuring gender diversity among the people reviewing résumés and conducting interviews can help disrupt the tendency of interviewers to look more favorably on male applicants, particularly if interviewers are empowered to point out instances where biased assumptions are made about female candidates. As one executive we spoke to explained, "When I'm looking at a selection, where we get a list of names for jobs, I look at it very differently than someone else does. Because I'm a minority, I'm involved in diversity and inclusion. But I think that our men aren't equipped to look at it through that lens."

As far back as the 1980s, diversifying interview panels brought advantages to a large Wall Street investment firm; more gender-diverse interview panels and an avowed commitment to developing talented women resulted in a dramatic rise (more than quintuple) in the firm's share of high performing female research analysts.[24] Gender-diverse interview panels send a message to applicants. In the words of the Asia Pacific region president of a global health care company, the presence of women became "a self-fulfilling prophecy: Women were attracted because they saw more women interviewing them; you build a reputation of being a good and fair employer."[25]

However, not all obstacles are mitigated through greater interviewer diversity. A common pitfall is conducting interviews without a standardized format and rubric. When individual applicants are assessed in a one-off informal manner, they may not be held to the same set of standards. By contrast, in a formal process wherein job criteria are explicitly brought to bear as reviewers consider an entire slate of candidates, reviewers are more likely to focus on job requirements.[26] Multiple studies have demonstrated that unstructured interviews are ripe for unintended discrimination; the less clarity about how and on what basis to assess candidates, the more likely interviewers are to view potential employees through the lens of gender and other stereotypes. (Plus, it should be noted that unstructured interviews are not very effective for assessment qua assessment: A meta-analysis of eighty-five years of research on hiring found that they are significantly worse than structured interviews at predicting actual job performance.[27])

We spoke to one executive who was told that she didn't receive a job offer partly because her husband "also had a job," which made the hiring committee unsure "if you would stay if your husband went elsewhere," as she was told. Ironically, as she explained, "if they would have asked, I would have told them that my husband generally follows me. They would never have questioned this of a man." Consciously or unconsciously, interviews may fall back on assumptions about women's lower commitment or lower competence. The latter is a particular risk in highly technical fields where men predominate. Removing information about candidate gender, through blind auditions and anonymized résumés, has been shown to increase the proportion of women who advance in an application process, effectively obviating the need to counteract bias by removing it from the process at the outset.[28] Of course, as candidates proceed to speak and meet with hiring managers, it's no longer possible for evaluators to remove gender from the equation, but they can still take steps to minimize its impact. We spoke to the head of a large information technology organization that had implemented an interview rubric that equally weighted technical skills, leadership skills, and alignment with the organization's values. After implementation the number of women hired increased, as interviewers were reminded and guided to take a holistic view of candidates and not overweight technical skills—an area where women may be perceived as weaker. The US Federal Reserve made a similar shift in its hiring process for research assistants, emphasizing candidates' aptitude for collaboration and teamwork and discouraging reviewers from filtering primarily on factors such as the relative prestige of applicants' academic backgrounds. After these and other updates, the proportion of women hires increased by 5 percent over four years.[29] And the merchant banking division at Goldman Sachs saw an uptick in female hires when recruiters stopped assessing whether candidates were "aggressive" and instead asked a set of questions more focused on intellectual curiosity and candidates' ability to articulate their points of view.[30]

The Bottom Line about Hiring

Biases on the part of interviewers and decision makers, particularly when coupled with lack of structure in the interview process, result in fewer offers made to women.

What managers can do:

- Consider anonymizing résumés during initial screening.

- Diversify interview panels.

- Educate interviewers and evaluators about commonly held gender biases and encourage self-reflection as well as conversation about whether biases are coloring views about candidates.

- Don't make evaluations and decisions on a rolling basis. Instead, judge a slate of candidates together, comparing each applicant against an agreed-upon set of job criteria.

Integration

You've progressed through finding, vetting, and hiring a candidate, so you now have a brand-new employee. Is she going to succeed? She likely won't if she is positioned as an outlier or token rather than effectively integrated. When an employee isn't fully integrated into her team or department, she is not privy to informal conversations that build trust, and she lacks access to important information that flows outside official communication channels. She may be seen as less important to the team or even as less capable of taking on key assignments. When women are poorly integrated, they miss out on forming and benefiting from relationships with their colleagues. We directly observed such a phenomenon while studying the investment banking industry. Women stock analysts faced barriers in forming the kinds of relationships critical for success in the industry; their male colleagues, who made up the majority, were simply less willing to spend time with them. One male analyst described his reluctance to form bonds with women in his firm: "So many female analysts are no longer with the firm, so it feels like that mentorship was for nothing. Many female analysts leave because it is just hard to succeed in this business; many leave for personal reasons. I still mentor, but I can understand people that prefer mentoring men."[31] This sentiment was not unusual. Prior research on Wall Street had found that a quarter of women missed out on opportunities to work on accounts and deals because their male managers preferred junior men.[32]

Patterns of exclusion result in a lack of access to important information and influential people. Poor integration has real career consequences, as a senior health care executive described: "When boards or senior leadership bring high-performing women of color into companies, they often don't give them the right level of subtlety and counsel in terms of integrating and onboarding. I think it's a real high-wire act from a cultural assessment perspective, because likability is so profound—it sometimes is more about 'who do I want to be stuck with at an airport?' than anything else." As her example so vividly points out, limited integration results in limited career advancement even if the employee is highly capable. An exemplary story was recounted by another executive we spoke to:

> [A major sporting event] took place in our area last year. My boss and I had been spending [the past] six to nine months talking about how I could have a bigger role with clients. My company was hosting a major event, bringing clients in. And I was not invited; I was not asked to attend—as a senior leader of the company—this client event. And why not? I think part of it is that these guys always hang out together, and it's easy and it's fun. And I'm the anomaly. It's funny, because if you had asked me if I had access to the inner circle, I would have said yeah—I meet with these guys all the time. But it's always in a professional setting, rarely in a social setting, whereas these guys socialize together all the time.

It's well known that deals and decisions are very often primed, if not made, outside the office and that some of the most common settings for such conversations are seen as masculine. Female board members and executives have told us about being instructed to take up golf, lest they find themselves left out of the real power structure.[33] These kinds of social interactions are so powerful precisely because they combine work with leisure, fostering deeper feelings of connection and closeness between colleagues that can lead to greater trust, cooperation, and mutual support in the professional realm.[34]

The good news is that companies don't have to accept the inevitability of such occurrences; they can put in place systems to encourage more cross-gender, as well as cross-race, contact, which has been shown to foster greater diversity in management. Studying more than eight hundred organizations over a twenty-two-year span, researchers saw that when companies implemented collaborative work approaches, such as cross-training programs and self-directed teams with members based in different functions, the percentage of women in management rose, although the effect was stronger for white women than women of color.[35] Meanwhile, research on cross-race relationships has found that white executives who mentor African American employees play a crucial role in confronting and countering biased views about their protégés.[36] To ensure that women of color fully benefit from efforts to foster strong employee relationships, companies must recognize that race influences what women experience at work and support meaningful collaboration and connection across multiple lines of difference.

The Bottom Line about Integration

When employees are, even unintentionally, excluded from socializing and relationship-building interactions, they lack access to information and people who can support their success. In a self-perpetuating cycle, their outlier status can then be taken as evidence that they are not cut out for the team or the company. Women who aren't integrated may leave or fail to progress to higher-level roles. Either way, their leadership potential is lost.

What managers can do:

- Create and implement opportunities for people to work toward shared goals in mixed-gender and mixed-race groups, and set genuine collaboration as an expectation for such teams.

- Ensure that new employees aren't left out of social activities where important connections are made.

- Set the tone for a post-#MeToo era by making clear that isolating female colleagues is not acceptable.

Development

Professional development is multifaceted; principal components include formal training (which might take place internally or through offsite opportunities such as executive education programs), hands-on experience through opportunities such as job rotations and developmental assignments, and relationships with role models, mentors, and sponsors. Career growth requires taking on new and more complex work, but the stretch assignments that enable employees to push themselves to new levels of competence and enhance their reputations remain most accessible to white men. In one study conducted with a pharmaceutical company, researchers found that senior managers funneled challenging projects to men more than women, even when controlling for workers' age, education, job tenure, performance, and perceived ambition.[37] In academia, women are less likely to be invited to give talks—important résumé boosters—than men, even though women are no more likely to decline a speaking invitation.[38] Another study across multiple industries found that men received more challenging assignments than did women, even though men and women expressed equal desire for such assignments. This discrepancy was driven not by acrimony toward women on the part of their managers but rather by beliefs that women needed to be protected or sheltered from difficult experiences.[39] One executive we spoke to observed this dynamic firsthand at various client companies:

> [Women] said, they won't give me the top roles, the ones that earn the most, or the ability to present in this forum, or to travel overseas, because they assume that as a woman I have family responsibilities that would interfere with my ability to produce, that I do not necessarily want to travel, or that I need a break.

The problem is that they make decisions for you based on their assumptions of what you want. Not what you want, but what they assume you may want. It is a paternalistic attitude.

When assignments that offer visibility and growth are not equally accessible to men and women, work itself becomes gendered, with lower-status projects and roles seen as the province of female employees. Even within jobs "task segregation" occurs, with women expected to handle less rewarding work, compared to male peers doing the same job.[40] Women are also more likely to be asked to volunteer for duties that do not advance their standing or skills, so-called office housework that adds little to their résumés.[41] Moreover, when they decline to perform such tasks that won't be beneficial for their careers, they are viewed negatively.[42]

Many of our baseline assumptions about what kinds of work are most valuable systematically disadvantage women. As one executive who held both marketing and sales roles early in her career told us, "When women dominate or become a larger percentage of a function, the function becomes less valued. That's actually why I chose to leave marketing at one company—I was concerned it was becoming the proverbial pink ghetto." In today's large global companies, serving in sales and/or operations roles and taking international postings are seen as prerequisites for leadership, and women are less likely to do either. While these expectations have long been common practice, it isn't clear that they are actually necessary to prepare someone for a senior role. Behind-the-scenes work that women are more likely to perform, such as managing a crisis, is often undervalued but may be just as relevant for developing the capability to lead at higher levels.[43] Too often, we default to what's familiar instead of identifying what's important.

The path to career growth isn't always explicitly laid out. In most white-collar industries, employees are expected to manage their own careers and proactively aim for the next step. Opportunities to advance tend to flow through people, be they direct managers or other senior colleagues. Allies in leadership positions play a defining role: steering key assignments to junior colleagues, including them in high-level meetings, or keeping their names in the mix for promotions. Yet even those women identified as high-potential by their companies are on average less likely to receive such sponsorship than their male peers, and women of color are at the greatest disadvantage.[44] In one survey of more than seventy thousand workers, 10 percent fewer Black than white women reported that their managers had advocated for an opportunity for them, and Latinas were also less likely than white women to report that their managers did so.[45]

In a longitudinal study we're involved in, 42 percent of women in mid- and late-career stages had not had access to mentors and sponsors, either informally or through a standardized program. Moreover, a third of those who lacked informal, organically developed mentoring relationships said the absence was very or extremely detrimental to their career trajectory. That perception seems to be objectively true, as our study also found that women who had the benefit of mentors and sponsors were more likely to be in senior management. We spoke to a firm that had designed and instituted a sponsorship program targeted at midlevel women and racial minorities, not only providing them with access to senior leaders but also educating sponsors themselves about the critical role they play in developing talent. "We always say the most important decisions made about your career usually happen in a room that you're not in," explained the chair of the firm's diversity committee in an interview. "We also know that men tend to find sponsors more organically, and it's typically harder for women and minorities. In any organization it's so important to have someone who is sponsoring you, who's advocating for you."

The Bottom Line about Development

Women tend to have reduced access to the key factors for professional growth because they are provided fewer opportunities for formal and informal development and/or they have fewer and less robust relationships with colleagues who can facilitate their upward movement.

Without the experience and visibility needed to demonstrate their ability to perform at higher levels, they plateau or seek opportunities to advance elsewhere.

What managers can do:

- Assess the process by which projects and teams are staffed and create objective criteria if none are codified.

- Track who receives developmental opportunities such as skip-level promotions, job rotations, and training programs and analyze the data for patterns by gender and race.

- Institute programs to increase access to mentors and sponsors. Women who participated in a mentoring program sponsored by the American Economic Association obtained higher rates of publication and grants than those who didn't, holding all other factors constant.[46]

Performance Assessment

Gauging whether an employee is contributing at, below, or above expected levels is a core managerial function, and regular performance assessments shape the paths of most professionals. Although this process typically has some level of formality—evaluation rubrics, calibration meetings, review periods—the judgment of managers ultimately determines how assessment tools are applied. And thus, managers' conscious and unconscious beliefs about how women should or do act exert enormous influence on the outcome. As one executive we spoke to put it, "I did not understand how much likability was going to be this big, unquantified thing that matters so much more than performance in some cases. I think for women it kills you if you're not likable." In addition, assessment processes are informed and undergirded by shared assumptions about what success looks like and what it means to be a top employee. Such assumptions are not necessarily grounded in what serves the company's overall health but may instead be based on standards that reward exaggerated forms of masculinity such as aggression and hypercompetitiveness. Researchers have termed this set of assumptions a "workplace masculinity contest." These contests come to shape organizational cultures, particularly when "winning" is seen as the basis for professional rewards.[47] When the masculinity contest is endorsed, high performance becomes conflated with seeking individual status and coming out ahead in cut-throat competitions. Not only are these behaviors often counterproductive in team-based and collaborative work, but they are also seen as more natural and appropriate for white heterosexual men to display (think "boys will be boys"). When women—or racial or sexual minority men—play by the rules of the masculinity contest, they may experience backlash or simply be seen as "weaker" competition.

More broadly, the well-known double bind shapes how women's job performance is viewed and leads to backlash in all kinds of organizational contexts, even those that don't have a strong masculinity contest component. Archetypal leader characteristics such as authority, decisiveness, and directness have traditionally been coded as masculine. Thus, when women exhibit strong leadership, they violate feminine gender expectations and may be characterized as difficult to work with or temperamental. But when women act in accordance with gender expectations, they are often seen as less capable and effective.[48] For instance, researchers have found that expressions of anger are taken as signs of lower competence in women but not in men.[49] And when women in leadership positions speak more than their male peers, they are seen as less competent, while views of male leaders' competence are unchanged regardless of how much or how often they speak.[50] A study of students at the US Naval Academy found that even when male and female students had the same grade point average and company military ranking, performance evaluations of women included more negative characterizations (e.g., terms such as *frivolous, inept, passive,* and *scattered*).[51]

Women's performance may not be evaluated objectively or against the same standard as that of their male peers. When our colleagues Frances Frei and Anne Morriss asked a group of senior leaders at a government agency to identify men and women they considered equivalent performers and then circulated the performance reviews of everyone on that list, the senior leaders were dismayed to find that the reviews did not convey that the men and women in the group were performing equally well.[52] Experimental research has shown that women's performance on tasks is held to a more stringent standard than men's, with women having to demonstrate higher performance to achieve the same rating as men with lower performance.[53] A study conducted at a legal firm documented this phenomenon in the real world: Although male and female lawyers received equally positive comments in their performance evaluations, men were given higher numerical ratings.[54] Other research finds double standards in the evaluation process; whereas a female employee is seen as having "analysis paralysis," a male colleague is described as being thoughtful and thorough.[55] Even among academics already at the top of their fields, women need to put in more time and effort to reach parity with men.[56]

In addition, accomplished women may be perceived, consciously or not, as threatening, which can suppress ratings of their actual performance. One set of studies found that women with college degrees received lower assessments than women with high school diplomas, even when objective performance (and all other factors) were held constant; the same pattern held true when the study varied the relative prestige and success of the companies where the women previously worked, with women who had worked at higher-status companies being rated more poorly than women previously employed at less successful organizations.[57] And even if bias isn't present when managers evaluate the output and accomplishments of their reports, prior discrimination may have artificially depressed women's performance relative to their ability. A study of stockbrokers across two large firms revealed that women's lower sales were the result of systematically receiving lower-quality accounts.[58]

Many companies have implemented training to make people aware of these kinds of biases, which are often not consciously held. Research on implicit, or unconscious, bias has established that stereotypes based on gender, race, and other social identities influence our perceptions and interactions regardless of our conscious beliefs about, for instance, women's capacity to lead.[59] Educating employees about unconscious bias has the potential to encourage them to reflect on ways that bias might influence their decision-making and be vigilant about preventing biased behaviors. But how such programs are framed and communicated determines how effective they are. Simply making people aware of the prevalence of unconscious bias can actually make them more likely to express bias. However, when training includes messaging about *overcoming* biases, it is successful at reducing biased expressions and making employees more willing to work with people who challenge assumptions about how certain groups should act—such as a woman who argues vigorously for her own promotion.[60]

In addition to educating employees about biases that may subtly influence judgment, companies can take steps to de-bias the evaluation process itself by focusing attention on objectively measurable qualities and eliminating reliance on gut feelings about who the top employees are. When we default to advancing those workers who "seem like" stars, we can easily overlook hard data that tell a different story. For instance, recent research has found that women tend to promote their accomplishments to a lesser extent than men with the same performance. Relying on employees' self-assessments to inform ratings, this study suggests, will lead to women's performance being under-recognized relative to its actual value.[61] Organizations can also analyze the outputs in their evaluation processes to identify where more objectivity is needed. For instance, researchers looking at technology and professional service firms found that the performance feedback women received was less tied to specific business outcomes regardless of whether the feedback was praise or constructive criticism. That lack of specificity meant that women had less clarity about the factors contributing to strong performance and less insight into what they needed to do to advance.[62] The feedback women receive may even be less accurate; one study found that evaluators were less candid and truthful with women about their performance.[63]

Finally, the way that companies interpret feedback can be shaped by inadvertent bias. One large Silicon Valley company discovered that men received greater rewards for take-charge behaviors such as leading change or making innovative contributions. When men and women had an equal amount of such take-charge language in their evaluations, the men received higher numeric ratings. In response, the company designed a checklist system to ensure that all employees were judged against the same objective criteria and rewarded equally for the same level of contribution and impact.[64]

The Bottom Line about Performance Assessment

Having a formal performance assessment system does not guarantee outcomes based on merit. The design and implementation of assessment processes determines whether employees are evaluated fairly and accurately and, in turn, whether women's rankings and associated rewards are commensurate with performance.

What managers can do:

- Educate everyone about how bias might influence their perceptions of others and emphasize a shared interest in overcoming such biases.

- Create and ensure the use of rubrics that measure objective characteristics of performance; don't rely on subjective assessments; tie feedback to specific business goals and outcomes.

- Review evaluations across teams or departments to identify any systematic differences between men's and women's evaluations, especially in references to personality characteristics.

Compensation and Promotion

One of the surveys we conducted for this book sampled female executives from around the globe, representing a cross-section of industries. Almost three-quarters of them agreed that when it comes to compensation, gender biases disadvantage women "a great deal." Despite companies' best intentions to base compensation on objective factors, pay for performance is often a misnomer. A field study examining the evaluations and compensation of over eight thousand employees at a large service-sector organization discovered that women and racial minorities whose evaluation scores were equal to white men's received smaller raises.[65] Similarly, research on middle and senior managers at a multinational financial services firm found that the performance ratings of promoted men were lower than those of promoted women.[66]

The gender pay gap has long been one of the most talked-about challenges facing women at work, and in recent years discussion has accelerated with investigations and lawsuits faced by high-profile organizations such as Google, Walmart, Nike, and Microsoft and even the Boston Symphony Orchestra.[67] Companies also face increasing public pressure to disclose pay disparities between men and women, and some countries, including England and France, have begun requiring companies to report gender pay differentials. In early 2019, a US federal judge blocked the Donald Trump administration's attempt to suspend an Equal Employment Opportunity Commission (EEOC) rule designed to help the agency collect pay data by gender and race.[68] (The EEOC later discontinued the data collection.)[69] In 2020, the California legislature considered a bill to require large employers to submit to the state data on gender, race, and compensation.[70] Dialogue on the topic has expanded to include not only "adjusted" pay gaps, which control for things such as job title and tenure and thus appear when men and women are being paid unequally for the same job, but also companies' "median" pay gaps, which simply report the overall difference between what men and women make and thus reflect the fact that women are often concentrated at lower levels. In 2019, Citigroup reported that while its adjusted pay gap was very small, women at the bank earned 29 percent less than men, a result of its senior ranks being male-dominated.[71] In the face of increasing regulation and attention, how can companies ensure that women are promoted and compensated fairly?

Gender-based compensation disparities often start before an employee is hired. When the terms and parameters of a salary negotiation are unclear, women consistently end up with lower starting salaries than men, even when controlling for factors that should predict salary, such as job function and geographic location.[72] Simply making explicit that a salary offer is negotiable eliminates the differential between men's and women's likelihood to try to negotiate.[73] Ambiguity might reside in something as fundamental as the appropriate salary range for a position, as in this example described by one of the executives we interviewed:

> I was evaluating where people are, I had the actual numbers, and I realized that this woman who is [considered] top talent is making 30 percent less than the average. I go to Human Resources and say this is not possible, we need to put her at parity and even above, because she's much better [than her peers]. And they said, we can't do a 30 percent increase. They said, when we hired her we gave her a very good increase from her previous salary. She had a lag when we brought her in. We gave a 30 percent increase, which was great for her at that point, but even with that 30 percent increase she was still 30 percent below the average that was mostly male.

The candidate in this example didn't know that the job she was offered was worth significantly more to the company than the rate she accepted and wasn't equipped to negotiate effectively for a salary commensurate with that value. (And as this story illustrates, trying to redress the gap at a later date can be difficult or even impossible.) But companies can even the playing field by providing clear information. An online recruiting platform for engineers completely eliminated the gender salary gap for new hires simply by providing the median salary for the position. Prior to this change, women asked for lower salaries than men to the tune of more than $4,000. When candidates saw the median data, the salary requests equalized.[74]

While prior salary can depress the offer a female candidate receives, changing jobs can also be an opportunity to boost one's compensation. In a cross-industry study, we found that when women executives moved to new jobs, they were able to attain higher salaries and narrow the pay gap with male executives in comparable roles.[75] While it's encouraging to see women command fairer compensation, job switching is often a strategy borne out of frustration with stymied internal growth. The few women who have managed to make it to senior ranks, well aware that many companies are keen to address gender imbalance in leadership, are able to parlay that interest into a better deal, but the underlying systemic pattern of women's limited advancement continues. One woman we spoke to found that she was only able to move up to a higher pay grade when her organization learned she was considering an exit:

We have different levels of executives: There's first, second, and third level. I couldn't get past the first level; I got rejected something like six times for the second level. Well, I started getting courted by another sector, and I did some interviews. I don't know what happened, but I got jumped [to the next level] after I was flown out to interview externally. I think a lot of the men in my situation would have announced "Hey, I'm going to leave." But I didn't. I just went and did the process to leave because I didn't feel entitled to that promotion. And I always was the first at any level. I was the first Latina at my level, which was sad—it was 2016!

Many internal promotion processes require or encourage people to self-nominate. While self-nomination empowers employees to pursue advancement, gendered social norms can disadvantage women. Women experience backlash when they are perceived as self-promotional, so the self-nomination process can hold pitfalls that don't impact their male peers. Like negotiating for a salary offer, advocating for increased compensation can trigger this backlash, and consequently, qualified women may be reluctant to put themselves forward for promotion. As has been covered in the media, Google implemented interventions to counter this gendered social cost, including automatically prompting all employees who met promotion criteria to nominate themselves and having senior woman speak publicly about the importance of self-promotion, signaling that it was normal and expected.[76] But more importantly for managers, the tendency to assume that the most vocal employees are the most productive can prevent managers from accurately viewing the contributions of aspiring and potential leaders, as one executive we spoke to explained:

There is bias toward people who self-promote regularly, thus becoming the ones who are fresh in people's minds when they're talking about succession planning or new opportunities. Those self-promoters are always advancing far faster, and at least in my experience they tend to be men who are totally confident and really make it a part of their day job. And most women wait for somebody to notice, wait until they earn the recognition, or wait until their annual performance review to say "I'm proud of these five things that I did" rather than making it a daily part of their life. It is even a subtle thing, before a meeting starts: "Oh, by the way, I had dinner with so-and-so the other night." Sharing what they're doing, how they're out networking, what kind of work they're doing. Even hitting forward on emails from clients or colleagues that are praising them. Men make it part of their job, and do it immediately without hesitation. And [as a result] we're missing actually gathering data and objective facts about whether or not that person is performing well in their job, and making tremendous contributions—or they just think that they are.

The further up a company's hierarchy, the less defined the promotion process often is. With fewer roles at each level, employees looking to break into senior management must find ways to heighten their visibility and demonstrate their value outside of formal reviews. Women may find themselves with fewer natural opportunities to do so, as another executive experienced:

> You hit a certain level of seniority so you are squarely in middle management, and you are trying to figure out how to break through to the next level. As I've educated myself in the subtle ways that gender bias comes about, I do think that there was that, to the extent there were probably opportunities I wasn't considered for. And I think it's because I wasn't in the inner circle. The best example of that I can give is when we traveled. I had the occasion to travel on the [company] jet, and it's the four seats and one extra—I'm always in the one extra, so I'm not in the conversation. Little things like that; it's very subtle.

The difficulty that women have breaking through to the top levels of leadership has for decades been described as the glass ceiling—invisible but impervious. If and when women do rise to an organization's senior ranks, they face new hurdles, and their prior strategies for managing gender bias may be inadequate or even counterproductive. And there is evidence that implicit ceilings make it harder for more than one woman to sit in the C-suite, as was found in a study of the S&P 1500: The presence of one woman on a company's top management team actually reduced the likelihood that the team had additional female members.[77] When women ascend *almost* to the top, their gender becomes more and more noticeable in male-dominated senior ranks, and more subjective criteria about their fit come to the fore. (See Chapter 2 for how women wrestle with this barrier and what strategies seem to help some overcome it.)

Researchers have also identified a phenomenon known as the glass cliff, wherein women are more likely to be appointed to senior roles at underperforming companies.[78] Although the glass cliff effect does not appear to hold true across all contexts, insofar as it points to the relative precarity of many women leaders' positions it can serve to reinforce notions about men's greater suitability for leadership. One of the executives we interviewed vividly described how such problematic leadership opportunities undermine both white women and men and women of color: "Invariably, we put extremely talented women and minorities into horrible roles because it's the open position that no one else's protégé will take. It's 'Let's bring in a high-performing minority, because you know we're working on diversity.' But now that person is going to flame out in two years because they can't possibly survive this horrific job. It happens all the time."

The Bottom Line about Compensation and Promotion

Women's compensation and level can be artificially depressed by gender biases within both formal and informal processes for raises and promotions.

What managers can do:

- Make negotiation parameters clear.

- Establish standards for compensation tied to the market rather than a candidates' previous salary.

- Systematically review the outcomes of promotion and pay decisions by race and gender.

- Make nomination processes transparent and triggered by objective achievements.

- Look for patterns in who is being promoted into troubled or precarious roles.

Retention

Not only does the pipeline narrow when women get stuck at lower levels of the hierarchy, but employee exits also shrink the supply of potential female leaders. Over ten years ago Deloitte considered sunsetting its Women's Initiative, but the firm's leadership reconsidered after looking at the data on educational and workforce trends, which revealed that women were earning the majority of accounting degrees and generally exceeding men in educational attainment. Realizing that underinvesting in women employees was hardly a strategic move, the firm decided instead to deepen its efforts. As Cathy Benko, who took over leadership of the Women's Initiative, realized, "We don't have trouble attracting women—they are 51–52% of our hires. What is hard is retaining them."[79] What drives turnover among women? The data do not suggest that they are inherently less committed to their jobs. One study of managerial, administrative, and professional employees at a large service firm found no evidence that women systematically quit at higher rates than men; rather, both male and female employees who were underpaid, relative to the average salary for their position, were likely to leave.[80]

Barriers and limitations on advancement have been shown to influence women's departures. For example, one study conducted across the public and private sectors found that differences in women's and men's intentions to quit disappeared when job satisfaction, specifically as related to opportunities for promotion, was considered. Women were significantly less satisfied with their promotion opportunities; thus, what looked like a gender difference was actually a gap between employees who believed they could grow at their current organization and those who felt stuck.[81] In the health care industry, women's job departures are likewise influenced by their perception of the career opportunities both inside and outside the organization.[82] Studies of up-or-out professions such as consulting and law have found that the presence of senior women decreased the likelihood of departure for their women subordinates: seeing women in leadership roles implies that career advancement is viable, thus encouraging junior women to remain.[83] When there are more women in positions of power, sexual harassment, another drain on the retention of women, also declines.[84] Organizational cultures in which harassment flourishes tend to be ones that excuse or ignore bad behavior on the part of high flyers and star performers, sending the message to women that their well-being is less important than keeping rainmakers happy—a message received not only by those actually victimized but also by bystanders who read the writing on the wall when it comes to their own value.[85]

Another widely held belief asserts that child-rearing is the primary driver of women's job departures. Some of our own research has found that both men and women believe that "prioritizing family over work" explains women's lagged career advancement.[86] Yet studies of professional women who have ratcheted back their careers have found that it is actually the loss of status and opportunity that comes with becoming a mother that pushes women to step off the leadership track and sometimes out of the workforce altogether. In fact, there is a documented "motherhood penalty" that results in fewer opportunities and lower wages for women with children, driven by assumptions that they are less committed to work than women who are not parents or than men, including fathers.[87] Research on highly educated women who left the workforce finds that they believed they were unable to advance at their organizations, based on experiences of being passed over for key assignments or otherwise diminished in standing, ultimately an experience better described as being "pushed out" than "opting out."[88]

One of the women we interviewed described just such an experience:

The moment I said was pregnant my team was restructured, and two of the three people that I had reporting to me were put at my same level. And I was taken from a team of thirty people to a team of six people. It was a demotion. It was not that my salary was reduced, but my responsibilities were. I was not asked. Even though there were policies for flexibility at the global level, once you brought it down to the local level, it was up to your boss to actually decide if they wanted to give you flexibility or not. I said, look, I'm going to work, there is a flex policy here, and I'm going to take it. And they were like yeah, but only if your boss lets you and if it's feasible for your position. We do that for assistant positions but not for senior positions. At that point, I already had sixteen years of work experience, and I was top talent. I [had been] sent to an MBA program which they had paid for.

As this example reveals, the stigma surrounding flexibility and other family accommodation policies can derail women's careers. In organizational cultures where extreme dedication to work is prized and superstars are those who respond to email at all hours and overdeliver to clients, taking advantage of policies that promote work-life balance carries a professional cost. Women working flexible schedules tend to be seen as less committed and less motivated to advance their careers than women working a standard schedule, even when their actual performance is identical.[89]

Some forward-thinking companies have sought to avoid the derailment of women's careers by reframing flexibility as a business and organizational tool. This approach, known as work redesign, focuses on understanding how to enable employees to do their best work as well as questioning assumptions about when and where that work must be done. One such program, called the Results Only Work Environment (ROWE) was implemented at Best Buy in 2004, not as a work-life balance program or a gender equity effort but instead as a business innovation. ROWE specified that employees should be "free to do whatever they want, whenever they want, as long as the work gets done." To implement ROWE, training sessions were held to critically examine traditional work practices and develop effective new processes for accomplishing work. Employees reported improvements to their overall well-being and their work quality, and Best Buy saw reduced turnover during the program, which was discontinued in 2013 at the behest of a new CEO.[90] In 2016, Canada's national housing agency, the Canada Mortgage and Housing Corporation, implemented ROWE and saw increases in employee engagement and reported work-life balance.[91]

The Bottom Line about Retention

Women are more likely to leave jobs when they believe their opportunities are limited. A sense of limited growth may come from seeing few women in leadership, or it may be spurred by how women themselves are treated.

What managers can do:

- Collect data on attrition and retention by gender and race.

- Make the consequences for sexual harassment meaningful and concrete, regardless of the perpetrator's role or performance.

- Assess when face time is truly needed for business reasons, and allow employees flexibility when their work can be done asynchronously and/or remotely.

- Audit your internal communications about flexibility policies and other work-life benefits to ensure they frame work-life needs as relevant for all employees and as tools for better work.

Review and Reflect

Understanding the barriers embedded at each of the above stages and acting to mitigate them is a cyclical process. Putting new practices in place and training managers are not onetime solutions; rather, any measures to combat gender-based inequities should be seen as tools that need continuous assessment and improvement, just like many other business processes. Speaking to *Business Insider* in 2018, the chief people officer at Salesforce described the company's annual compensation analysis: "You're going to have to run the audit every single year. That's one thing I aligned with [CEO] Marc [Benioff] very early on, that this was not a one and done thing." Salesforce has seen positive results from its commitment to diagnosing and closing gender pay gaps: since implementing the annual audit in 2016, employee agreement with the statement "People here are paid fairly for the work they do" rose by 12 percent to reach over 90 percent. The company has also seen the overall number of women employees and the proportion of women in leadership roles rise.[92] And yet across the United States and Canada, less than 40 percent of companies analyze pay by gender, according to a 2018 study.[93]

Collecting and analyzing data at each stage of the people management process, from the diversity of your applicant pool to attrition rates by gender and other demographic characteristics, allows companies to make informed decisions. In 2017, a large tech company began publishing an "attrition index" that looked at leave rates by gender and race. The index revealed that in the United States, Black and Latinx employees were leaving faster than the average rate. In response, the company created a program in which "retention case managers" were empowered to connect employees with career resources, from training opportunities to affinity groups.[94] Yet despite the usefulness of such data, reflected in the adage "you can't manage what you don't measure," a recent survey of chief diversity officers in S&P 500 companies found that only 35 percent of CDOs had access to employee demographic data.[95]

With a foundation of assessment in place, managers must incorporate tools and approaches to preventing bias into how they lead their teams day to day. Without doing so, companies will not move talented women up through their ranks. Yes, tone at the top matters, but without translating messaging into practical action, it remains lip service, as one executive pointed out:

A phenomenon I've seen is super-senior men talking a lot about gender equity, racial equality, and the power of diversity, and at the very lowest levels of the company hiring classes that are full of women and men of color, and then this gauntlet in between and a lot of mediocrity standing in the way of talented, capable employees. That frozen middle. I spend a lot of time working with women and minorities in director-level roles in my company, because you may have a lot of VP-level, old status quo white guys who just are like, I don't care what they say at the top, this is how we do things here. And it can be really challenging to hit that [layer], and then before you know it, [white women and racial minorities] are opting out. [There is] an unwillingness among senior guys—the EVP, C-suite level—to truly take on their middle-layer VPs, because they want loyalty and focus on operating results, so they don't challenge the behavior.

The chief product officer at one firm that implemented a wide-ranging gender equity program described initial resistance and how it dissipated as senior leaders emphasized the strategic importance of the work: "When you talked about wanting to make certain that we've got a fair number of female managing directors, the instant response was 'Oh, so you're going to lower your standards for women?' And now that we've been doing this for four or five years, you just don't hear that anymore. We have made it very clear that it was about casting a wider net. It was about eliminating unconscious bias."

To ensure that any pronouncements about the value of gender diversity are reflected in your department or company's day-to-day management, there must be a commitment to continuous review on the part of all managers. In our interviews with women executives, we heard repeatedly that efforts to bring more women into leadership founder when they are exclusively designed and administered by human resource departments. As one executive pointed out, examining patterns in compensation sheds light on how a company defines success: "When it comes to those individuals that we promote, that have the highest compensation, and looking at the traits [we say we value], where would those individuals fall? Are these the traits that [their managers] have valued? Is there a difference between what senior management thinks about what should be rewarded, versus what lower-level managers are looking for and getting?"

More than forty years ago, scholar Rosabeth Moss Kanter published *Men and Women of the Corporation*, a groundbreaking study of gender in the workplace. Many of the barriers Kanter identified remain present today and involve, as described in this chapter, an interplay between structural factors and individual actors. Despite the persistence of these obstacles, Kanter remains hopeful, as do we. Speaking at the first annual Gender & Work Research Symposium at Harvard Business School, she emphasized the need to continue explicating how organizational processes and managers work together to either perpetuate or mitigate gender disparities: "If we understand these interacting elements, we can intervene and change them. Change is always possible. That is what leaders do."[96]

What Women Executives Say

We surveyed over 150 executives who had recently attended executive education programs for women leaders, gathering their observations about each of the talent management processes described in this chapter. These executives, who were based in companies across North and South America, Europe, Asia, Africa, Australia, and New Zealand, represented a range of industries spanning the public and private sectors. They had jobs with significant responsibility; most were in profit-and-loss holding roles in large companies. And they were experienced; three-quarters had been in their careers for over twenty years.

Their perceptions were not identical, but they were consistent; across the board a strong majority agreed that individual biases and structural barriers disadvantage women at each stage of talent acquisition and management. Women executives see an especially uneven playing field when it comes to compensation and promotion, with 89 percent of our survey respondents agreeing that women are at least somewhat disadvantaged in those processes. (In fact, 71 percent said that women face "a great deal" of disadvantage in pay and promotion [Table 5-1].)

The size of respondents' employers did not consistently predict the extent to which women saw bias in each management process, suggesting that larger (or smaller) companies are not necessarily better equipped to implement equitable processes. Younger respondents sometimes, but not always, perceived less bias than women who started their careers a decade or more earlier. While we know that progress in gender equity has been made, women continue to report that biases and barriers hinder their own and others' advancement.

Almost 90 percent said that auditing management processes to identify gender differences was "essential" or "important," and an

TABLE 5-1

Extent to which biases and barriers disadvantage women in organizational processes

	Recruitment	Hiring	Integration	Development	Performance management	Compensation and promotion
A great deal	31%	48%	34%	36%	46%	71%
Somewhat	45%	36%	31%	38%	26%	18%
Slightly	15%	12%	12%	18%	12%	7%
Not sure	2%	2%	3%	3%	3%	3%
Not at all	6%	3%	19%	5%	14%	2%

even higher proportion believe that companies in their respective fields and industries should incorporate a gender lens into employee engagement efforts, specifically by analyzing gender differences in attrition and other key metrics, creating policies or practices aimed at engaging and retaining women, or both. Two-thirds of our respondents don't believe that companies are currently doing enough to engage and retain women.

The Glass-Shattering Framework

Management process	The problem	Question to ask	Recommendations
Attraction	You lack women candidates, relative to your expectations and/or industry norms.	Are aspects of your recruitment turning away qualified women?	• Seek candidates outside managers' individual networks, which may be homogenous. • Assess the language used to describe jobs and your company.
Hiring	Women candidates do not make it through to the offer stage at the same rate as men.	Are aspects of your hiring process eliminating women whose qualifications and potential meet and exceed those of male candidates?	• Educate managers about gender biases and how they might influence hiring decisions. • Anonymize résumés. • Diversify interview panels. • Evaluate a slate of candidates as a group, against a set of defined criteria.
Integration	Women seem to be "on the outskirts" of their teams and departments.	Are new hires forming the relationships that enable them to contribute optimally and thrive professionally?	• Create opportunities for people to work toward shared goals with people who are different from them. • Discourage exclusionary social activities, and make sure women are not treated as outliers or extraneous team members.
Development	Women are not building out their skills and experience at rates similar to male peers.	Do employees have access to training, stretch assignments, and other components of development, irrespective of gender?	• Assess how training opportunities and developmental opportunities are assigned, and implement objective criteria. • Increase women's access to mentors and sponsors.

Management process	The problem	Question to ask	Recommendations
Performance assessment	Women's performance ratings are lower than those of male peers and/or lower than expected based on hiring assumptions.	Are your evaluation processes and their implementation influenced by gender biases?	• Educate managers about gender biases and how they might influence evaluation decisions. • Assess the criteria used to rate performance, and eliminate ambiguous, vague, and malleable standards.
Promotion and compensation	Women receive lower compensation than male peers and/or are promoted at lower rates.	Are your processes for determining compensation and making promotion decisions influenced by gender biases?	• Make parameters for salary offers and increases clear and transparent. • Review the outcomes of promotion and compensation processes by race, gender, and other identity characteristics.
Retention	Women are leaving your company at rates higher than men and/or your expectations.	Do women believe they can advance at your company, and are they rewarded for strong performance?	• Track attrition and retention by gender. • Combat flexibility stigma by focusing on measurable aspects of performance. • Don't turn a blind eye to high performers who harass.

SETTLING FOR EQUALITY

Qualcomm

I n 2015, seven women employed in technical and engineering jobs at Qualcomm sued the San Diego–based chipmaker on behalf of its female employees, claiming that the company's pay and promotion practices systematically discriminated against women. The women made a formal complaint with the EEOC and the California Department of Fair Employment and Housing, but before the suit was brought to court, Qualcomm agreed to pay $19.5 million and institute a series of measures aimed at rectifying the discriminatory practices brought to light by the action. Although the company claimed to have "strong defenses" to the allegations of unequal treatment, it agreed to overhaul its approach to employee development, compensation, and work flexibility, in its words "mak[ing] meaningful enhancements to our internal programs and processes."[97] A telecommunications giant known for being on the leading edge of mobile technology, Qualcomm agreed to hire independent experts to implement reforms—when it came to designing an equitable workplace, the company was behind the curve.

Qualcomm isn't unusual. The EEOC receives roughly a thousand complaints a year alleging violations of the Equal Pay Act, and discrimination complaints are filed at the state and local levels too.[98] While there are no centralized data on gender discrimination lawsuits brought to court, anyone casually following the news in recent years has likely heard about suits filed against Twitter, Google, Facebook, the Walt Disney Company, Microsoft, Oracle, KPMG, Kleiner Perkins, and Goldman Sachs, to name a few. While explicit discrimination, including sexual harassment, is sometimes alleged, today's cases often focus on what researchers have termed "second-generation bias," a subtler set of patterns and practices that disadvantage women but can go unnoticed, so thoroughly baked into organizational cultures and structures that they seem natural or neutral.

The plaintiffs in Qualcomm's case pointed to both overt and second-generation discrimination. Men received higher base salaries than women in similar roles, a clear case of gender-based discrimination, but women were also kept off the leadership track through indirect and implicit means. The company's promotion process, which relied on managers—the majority of whom were men—to sanction employees' pursuit of advancement, was one such mechanism. Rather than systematically make employees aware of paths for professional development and growth, managers meted out desirable assignments, training opportunities, and promotions in the absence of standard criteria. Statistical analyses carried out in negotiations between Qualcomm and the firm representing the class of over three thousand women employees found differences in promotion rates between equally qualified men and women. Compounding these barriers, the plaintiffs claimed, was a culture that disproportionately rewarded long hours and constant availability, creating in effect a second-class status for employees with significant caregiving responsibilities, primarily women, and those who took pregnancy leave. Employees who could or would be on call 24/7 were rewarded regardless of their productivity or performance, while those working reduced hours or flex-time schedules saw their ratings prorated—effectively reduced—without regard to their output. In addition, women claimed that the way Qualcomm set pay rates for jobs placed too little emphasis on the core skills and responsibilities entailed, resulting in pay gaps between jobs of similar nature; while not an explicit practice of paying women lower wages for the same work, the company's approach nonetheless resulted in differential pay by gender.[99] One of the lawyers for the women described these problems as revealing a gap between Qualcomm's rhetorical endorsement of gender equity and the conditions for women actually in place at the company: "The abstract commitment to workplace equality for women will never become a reality without tangible commitments to transparency and guaranteed freedom from reprisal. Without those and other concrete structural changes, lofty promises for diversity and equality go unfulfilled."[100]

Qualcomm's legal team and the lawyers representing female employees never debated these claims of discrimination in court. Instead, they went straight to generating structural changes, spending months analyzing company data and records to come up with an agreement about how women were impacted by Qualcomm's management practices and what rectifying measures should be taken. By the middle of 2016, both sides had agreed to a settlement that included monetary damages and an overhaul of many of the company's managerial practices. The company agreed to implement women's leadership development initiatives to address disparities in access to promotions brought on by the informal "tap on the shoulder" system and to strengthen support for flex work and parental leave, such that utilizing those benefits would not sideline women's careers. The company also agreed to collect and analyze data on employee evaluations, promotions, and compensation in order to identify gender gaps and to improve the internal process by which employees could raise complaints about discrimination.[101]

Through the settlement, current and former employees who had been disadvantaged not only were able to recoup a nominal fraction of wages lost (at about $4,000 per employee, the awards were essentially symbolic) but also to effect organizational changes with the potential to positively impact women at the company for years to come. More than just an avenue of redress, the Qualcomm settlement was future-focused and if implemented with full commitment will make the company's path to leadership more gender-equitable. It's not a quick fix, and time will tell if the company's pipeline to leadership becomes gender-balanced. One early sign of progress is a modest jump in the proportion of women in technical roles, from 14.3 percent the year the lawsuit was filed to 16.4 percent in 2019.[102] By institutionalizing the programs and practices outlined in the settlement and sustaining a commitment to gender equity, Qualcomm has the opportunity to become a leader not only in wireless technology but also in retaining and advancing women.

CHAPTER 6

DAY-TO-DAY PARITY

How to Manage for Gender Equity and Inclusion

The talent management processes explored in Chapter 5 make up a complex, multifaceted, and interdependent system. Individual managers, especially those at the middle and frontline levels, don't always have the authority to initiate some of the systemic changes we recommend. Even managers higher up in the hierarchy are typically limited in how much they can alter or influence practices outside their function or geographic scope. What if you're not a CEO or managing partner who can overhaul how your organization handles hiring or implement a new performance review system? Are your hands tied when it comes to breaking down gender barriers? Far from it. People-management processes are interpreted and implemented by individual managers, and there is often room to do things differently and more equitably within existing structures. Moreover, even the most forward-thinking programs initiated from on high will fail if individual managers implement them ineffectively. A case in point is JPMorgan Chase's career reentry program, launched in 2013 to create avenues into the firm for women candidates whose time out of the paid workforce might have otherwise caused their qualifications and competence to be undervalued. Executive endorsement was just one part of the equation. As the head of diversity for the unit that piloted the program explained, managers were just as important:

> We wanted to make sure we were positioning these women for success, and we wanted to make sure that the manager was going to be a willing participant in the process. . . . We wanted managers that were going to take a more coaching-and-development perspective during the conversations [with the participant]. We wanted somebody who was going to buy into the philosophy of the program, [who] want their participants to be well networked, [who] want them to be well developed, [who] want them to have solid understanding of not just their sub-specific line of business, or part of the business, but the broader context of the business as well.[1]

Improving the systems that shrink the pipeline of potential women leaders takes time, precisely because of the interplay between organizational processes and the people utilizing them. Without managers committed to taking everyday actions to break down common barriers—such as access to mentors, development opportunities, and integration into the company as a whole—the reentry program would do little to grow the number of women moving up at the firm. (Indeed, this kind of managerial support is necessary for anyone's career growth.) Research backs up the idea that managers are the not-so-secret weapon in the battle to break down inequality at work. An analysis of numerous studies finds that well-intentioned training and policies consistently fall short when it comes to producing and maintaining greater diversity. But engaged managers who feel responsible for improving diversity, equity, and inclusion create results. Companies that encourage managers to act as change agents through activities such as mentoring and participating in diversity task forces ultimately see more white women and men and women of color advance.[2]

As a manager, the culture you foster on your team and the approach you take to developing and engaging individual employees can enable women to deliver the results they are truly capable of, which contributes to not only their success but also your own. Inclusive management has the potential to be your competitive advantage especially as workers, particularly those who are underrepresented in leadership, become more and more aware of how important it is to their success. Working for a boss who doesn't practice inclusion is simply a nonstarter for many capable professionals. As one woman whose thirty-year career has included stints at consumer products companies, start-ups, and large professional service firms, put it, "I advise people to find out if a place/management [team] is inclusive. It will make *all* the difference; it might be the *only* thing that matters about where one builds a career."

We wanted to better understand what inclusive management really looked like from the perspective of women themselves, so we surveyed a group of about 130 women who had taken executive education courses designed for female leaders. We gathered a wealth of data both quantitative and qualitative, including numerous examples of what a *lack* of inclusive management meant. The women we surveyed are connected to our institution and know us from the classroom, so their candor was not surprising, but we are grateful that they were willing to trust us with the unvarnished truth. They told us about leaving jobs and companies they loved but where they were treated dismissively or denied opportunities to grow. They moved on, but the experiences took a toll. As one woman explained, "My tendency is to just become disengaged. Noninclusive behavior also hurts your soul. When I didn't feel I could be as present as my male counterparts, I felt very tired and unworthy."

Inequitable management doesn't happen only in male-dominated industries or in regions with greater overall gender inequality, and it isn't perpetuated only by men. The women we surveyed were working in public and private companies, nonprofits, family businesses, and government agencies. The vast majority were at least two decades into their careers, and over 40 percent were more than thirty years along. They came from a highly diverse range of industries, from manufacturing to health care to advertising to finance, and they hailed from North America, Europe, Latin America, Asia, Africa, Australia, and the Middle East. Experiences of being dismissed, undermined, or actively excluded came up many times in our survey, underscoring the fact that no industry, region, or type of company is free of barriers to women's careers. Nor did we find that noninclusive management is characteristic of one gender. Most of the women executives we surveyed have had noninclusive male *and* female managers (see Figure 6-1).

We did find some gender differences when it comes to the nature of noninclusive management. When female managers were not inclusive, the problem was often hoarding—being unwilling to give credit or power to subordinates and taking a zero-sum approach to management wherein others' success was seen as threatening their own. As a result, the women who had such experiences with female managers felt undermined and unable to see a clear path to advancement. We know from research going back to the 1970s that these kinds of so-called queen bee behaviors result from organizational cultures that

FIGURE 6-1

Survey of women executives

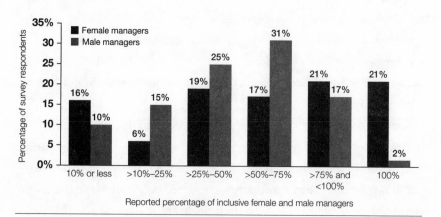

Reported percentage of inclusive female and male managers

devalue women's contributions; to succeed in such environments, women distance themselves from their gender and from other women in order to be seen as competent.[3] Thus, we weren't surprised to see that the women executives in our survey had had far fewer female bosses over the years; the average number across an entire career was just two, compared to an average of nine male bosses. Though investigating the drivers of noninclusive behavior is beyond the scope of our survey, the data suggest that this dynamic was at play in many of the organizations where our respondents had worked.

By contrast, we heard about a wider array of exclusionary behaviors from male managers. They favored male subordinates, bestowing on them more opportunities and larger rewards than women with the same track record. They also excluded women from social events and even pushed them out of work teams, gravitating toward other (typically white) men for both personal and professional networking. As one respondent described, "I took over from a man who systematically downgraded all of the jobs on his direct team held by women and then removed all women from his leadership team. After that, he hired only white men to replace them." This experience was echoed by another woman: "One male manager fired/downsized and marginalized the three most senior women in [our] division." There were also some instances of sexual harassment, demeaning and dismissive comments, and overtly sexist views from male managers. (While we heard about both men and women who held biased attitudes—such as one female manager "who expected me to make less than a male at a lower level because I did not have a family"—even noninclusive female managers didn't belittle the capabilities of women as a whole or suggest that women's contributions were inherently less valuable, for obvious reasons.)

These examples of exclusion and bias illustrate much of what we have explored throughout this book. But we weren't interested simply in confirming the continued prevalence of these barriers—by now, we hope that readers better understand where, how, and why they persist today. We wanted to gather data about the managerial styles and practices that illuminate a different path. What are the everyday actions that make a critical difference? We know that they matter: nearly three-quarters of the women we surveyed (who, remember, had attained senior leadership) said that inclusive management had positively impacted their careers.

Below we detail five key attributes of inclusive management and explain the underlying behaviors and practices that enable managers to develop these capabilities. Inclusive management isn't feel-good fluff. It requires self-reflection, awareness of the drivers of workplace disadvantage, and a commitment to changing the conditions, including your own habits and assumptions, that perpetuate it. Granted, your actions can't always fix problems in the systems at your organization, but you can mitigate and push back against them. For example, you might not be able to change the fact that your company lacks an objective rubric for staffing important projects or for putting employees up for promotion, but you can be sure to use standard and job-specific criteria when it comes to your own decisions. In so doing, not only can you ensure that the people you work with are being treated fairly, but you can also model inclusive management for others. Especially in the absence of policies and procedures, normalizing inclusive and equitable approaches is powerful. Being a change agent doesn't require being a CEO; you can help break down those barriers that maintain the status quo.

Dozens of the women in our survey said they'd left jobs, companies, and even industries because their managers weren't up to par on inclusion. The women went on to grow and lead but at a cost to themselves and to the organizations they left. As one woman explained, "Looking back on my career, I left noninclusive leaders for new companies. It probably helped me in the long run because it forced me to change [jobs], but on the other hand, I don't think it helped the companies they worked for, because those companies lost talent, and the current talent is also underutilized and not offering their best."

Motivating and enabling your team to deliver its best work is central to any managerial role. By focusing on fairness, you can remove obstacles to performance and unleash employees to thrive in their roles. Call it your inclusive advantage.

Inclusive Managers *Develop an Objective Lens for Recruiting and Rewarding Employees*

We won't argue that deliberate discrimination plays no part in perpetuating gender inequality in the workplace. Certainly, the #MeToo movement quickly disillusioned anyone inclined to think otherwise. However, we don't believe that most managers set out to create barriers to women's advancement. Indeed, over many years of teaching and studying managers at various levels in a wide range of industries and sectors from all over the world, we have consistently heard a desire to do the opposite: foster a level playing field and lead in an unbiased way that enables all employees to grow in their careers. Yet our collective outcomes do not reflect these good intentions. Women, particularly women of color, are significantly underrepresented in senior leadership compared to their proportions in the workforce; clearly, they are not progressing at rates equal to white men, who make up the largest proportion of leaders across industries. The 2019 Women in the Workplace study conducted by McKinsey and Lean In found that women lag men when it comes to first promotion to a managerial role. From this early imbalance, the leadership pipeline becomes cumulatively more gender-skewed over time.[4]

Individual managers have tremendous power over employees' career progression; not only do managers create the opportunities through which employees grow their skills and competencies (more on that in the following section), but they also assess performance and put forward candidates for promotion, in many cases unilaterally deciding if an employee advances to a higher level. The difference between a stagnant or sluggish career and one that flourishes apace can be a single supervisor, as one woman from our survey recounted: "An SVP at [one company] made it very difficult for my promotion to director, despite overwhelming high remarks by my own director-manager as well as my peers. When he finally approved it, he said, 'You have very strong capability and work experience, especially for a female engineer.' I wanted to ask him, do I not have strong capability compared to male engineers?" Another woman in our study noted how this phenomenon played out in her career: "The observable impact of noninclusive management was timing. My [male] peers appeared to have been given opportunity faster and promoted to executive levels sooner."

It can be difficult for women to break through a manager's reliance on swift, subjective judgments. A health care executive described watching one strong candidate be summarily rejected based on no clear rationale: "I had a very talented diversity candidate that a very senior person decided not to move forward with, when on paper they were the most qualified. I asked him to have a live conversation with this person because she was top talent. He ignored my recommendation and decided to just send an email telling her she did not get the job."

While we don't know the views and attitudes of this particular manager, it may not be accurate to assume that he was deliberately sidelining this candidate on the basis of her identity. In fact, it's highly likely that he believed he was being impartial and that his preferred candidate was simply a better choice on the merits, that his intuitive sense, honed by years of experience, was his best guide. Yet at the same time, it's also likely, given the fact that leadership in the health care industry is male-dominated (despite the strong representation of women in the health care workforce overall), that he ended up hiring another man like himself.[5] As a different woman in our study put it, "People that discriminate in the workplace are not always bad people. Most of the time they are unaware of what they are doing and have never seen a different way." This manager—and countless others—failed to step outside his comfort zone, to stop and question his instincts, and to reflect on whether he was giving adequate consideration to a candidate who didn't fit the standard mold.

It's well known that implicit biases (that is, the stereotypes we unconsciously associate with different groups) can skew our perception and decisions. While there has been scientific debate about the measurement and effect of these biases, a number of studies have shown that they influence how people interact with and treat others, including in the workplace.[6] If you work for a large company, or even a smaller one in certain industries such as tech, you've probably had some form of unconscious bias training. And even if not, you're probably familiar with the concept and understand that your perceptions may be influenced by subtle biases that are out of sync with your values. Is this awareness enough to help you stay objective and fair in your decisions?

While learning about unconscious bias provides helpful insight, that awareness is a first step, not the ultimate solution. In fact, researchers have found that bias trainings can actually *increase* discriminatory behaviors when they are delivered without any encouragement to overcome bias.[7] What's critical is a commitment to look for and address its influence on your perception and judgments. Whatever bias training you've received, whether through a formal program or just your own reading and learning, is a starting point. Knowing that unconscious bias exists doesn't automatically eliminate it, but you have the opportunity to dig into your processes and identify ways to minimize its impact. This can be as simple as investigating patterns that are gender-skewed. If you observe that male candidates have won out over women in three out of four recent searches, you might pull the résumés of each finalist and take a look at whatever evaluation materials are available, be they scoring sheets or simply your notes from debrief meetings. Look for differences in how men and women were described, whether they were asked different questions, and how their accomplishments and skills were weighted. These conversations, whether with colleagues or yourself, should be inquisitive, not accusatory, and should encourage dialogue about how candidates are being perceived and vetted.

Your investigations are likely to reveal that gender and other disparities show up in places where subjective judgments are more heavily relied on. Adopting evaluative methods that minimize the role of gut feel and provide an objective framework can help to reduce these gaps. One executive in our survey, working at a large publicly traded company in the United States lauded several of her past managers for implementing blind screening, in which "all names, genders, etc. were taken off of résumés prior to meeting candidates." And indeed, recent research has confirmed that anonymizing résumés reduces the chances that equally qualified women are overlooked in favor of male applicants.[8] By pairing best practices such as blind screening and standardized performance assessment with an ongoing commitment to looking at how your decisions affect outcomes for both white women and people of color, you can equalize opportunities and paths for everyone on your team.

Develop an objective lens for recruiting and rewarding employees by

- Deploying approaches that minimize subjective judgments that may be skewed by unconscious bias.

- Honing your ability to notice and explore patterns along lines of gender and other differences in hiring and promotion.

Inclusive Managers *Provide Developmental Opportunities and Feedback on an Equitable Basis*

In a 2019 report from the Center for Talent Innovation, 71 percent of more than three thousand executives said that the junior employees whose development they were guiding shared their gender and/or race.[9] This tendency to mentor and sponsor "mini-me" protégés leads to leadership pipelines that look overwhelmingly the same at every stage. It's crucial for managers to not only apply fair and consistent practices, as we discussed in the previous section, but also proactively provide guidance and support. Organizations can—and should— establish guidelines for staffing projects, providing feedback, and sponsoring training, but at the end of the day the one-to-one relation- ship between employee and manager shapes the extent to which these policies meaningfully influence employees' trajectories. Managers are able to offer the stretch assignments that raise visibility and expand skills, to provide insight into what employees need to do in order to improve, and to grant time and sometimes funding to spend on conferences and courses. In our survey of executive women, examples of how inclusive managers had facilitated respondents' success through these developmental supports were numerous. When asked to provide an example of inclusive management they had personally experienced, nearly 30 percent shared stories of bosses who had provided key development opportunities and advice.

One woman recounted how her manager "recommended that I apply for a new position that I had not even considered because I didn't believe I was qualified. Turns out I was great at it." Similarly, another described how her manager offered "job opportunities that he knew I could do even if they were a stretch for me at the time." And one recounted her experiences at a large retailer: "I joined the organization as a VP from outside of the company in the field of logistics. My manager was very supportive of me, ensured that I felt I had what I needed to be successful and gave me opportunities to showcase my accomplishments."

Many of these managers who provided critical development to the women in our survey were men. The profound impact of their mentorship is reflected in the success of women such as this executive, who today works for a large US insurance company:

I was offered a position in executive management ranks associated with an assignment I was reluctant to take, as it was not in my wheelhouse. Despite my lack of confidence and my declarations of incompetence, my boss persisted—helping me to define my career goals beyond doing an excellent job in my current role, helping me to understand what I brought to the table, and assuring me that I would be supported by him. This was in the late '90s in a virtually all-male–dominated industry. I would never have taken the job without that push, and there were men who were raising their hands for it.

This promotion was pivotal in her career, as similar moments are for so many. Managers' role in enabling and encouraging employees to take up such opportunities means that every day they are shaping the leadership pipeline in their companies and industries. In a longitudinal study for which we serve on the research team, about half of women who lacked supportive managers found that absence to be "very" or "extremely" detrimental to their careers. Conversely, among those who'd had supportive managers, the vast majority described the relationships as very or extremely beneficial to their careers.

Yet managers can only offer this kind of support if they strive to view employees through a lens that isn't distorted by assumptions about women's capability. If you're reading this book, you've already chosen to educate yourself about some of these misconceptions, such as the notion that women are less committed to their careers than men—a claim that has been debunked by social science. You can start putting that knowledge into practice today by, for instance, tracking how you distribute plum assignments among your reports. When an opportunity comes up that is sure to be a career boon but will entail taking on a particularly challenging project or working with an unpleasant client, do you decline to offer it to a qualified female employee, perhaps out of a desire not to burden her, as Ana Paula Pessoa's boss once did, or do you present the opportunity and let your employee weigh the decision? In our research with executive women, we heard many stories of managers simply failing to ask. One partner at a major auditing and consulting firm saw how it seriously hindered women's careers:

> I think one of the big factors in the leadership gender gap is the microdecisions that happen along someone's career path. The experiences that a professional gains over the course of their career will qualify them for potential promotions down the road, so it is critically important that those opportunities are made available across genders. When leadership decides which professional to assign to a strategic project, they may inject gender bias into their

thinking; for example, these strategic projects may require more hours, lots of travel, an overseas assignment, or a relocation. I have seen many instances where business leaders make assumptions that women can't do that or won't be willing to do that and count them out without even asking. Sometimes leaders even pat themselves on the back for "saving" a female from saying "no"—giving themselves credit for considering her, acknowledging she's a fantastic performer, but then not putting her in a position where she feels bad about declining the opportunity. It's almost like "I'm taking care of you by excluding you," and that mentality is a real issue. We should instead make sure she has a chance to decide for herself.

By contrast, another woman told us about a manager who did not see her parental status as a reason for limiting her opportunities and instead empowered her to lead: "My first male manager hired me when I was five months pregnant. He became my mentor in the banking industry. He pushed me to learn, make decisions, be creative and gave me opportunities to hold managerial positions at a very early age."

In 2018, our colleagues Robin J. Ely and Catherine H. Tinsley reviewed the research on three commonly held beliefs about what holds women back at work: that they lack negotiation skills or the desire to negotiate, that they are less confident than men, and that they are risk-averse.[10] After Ely and Tinsley reviewed multiple meta-analyses, each analyzing hundreds of studies, it became clear to them that these assumptions simply weren't borne out by the data. While some differences between men and women were detectable, they were also small to trivial in statistical terms. (By contrast, the relationship between sex and height is statistically large.) In other words, these differences were so slight as to be essentially meaningless in the real world.

If any of these beliefs about women ring true to you, we aren't suggesting that your observations are mistaken or that you're prejudiced. Rather, you may simply be relying, as most of us do, on incomplete information that tends to confirm the dominant narrative. Our recommendation is to take an inquisitive approach. Ely and Tinsley offer the story of a consulting firm with a gender gap in promotion, which was being attributed to a lack of confidence and drive among female hires. One regional leader was skeptical about that explanation, so she asked the researchers to help her investigate how supervisors were developing men and women on their teams. Together, they designed an experiment to understand whether managers' assumptions about gender differences were driving different treatment and what it might mean for women's performance. One group of supervisors was shown research on the lack of difference between men's and women's self-confidence, subtly encouraging them to question gendered assumptions, while a control group was not shown the research. The control group gave less actionable, relevant feedback to women employees, instead relying on vague praise and feel-good language, while the first group provided constructive comments to both men and women.[11] It became clear that default behavior toward women provided them with less useful feedback, which was likely the true underlying cause of the advancement gap. If the regional head had been content to rely on conventional wisdom, she wouldn't have discovered the real problem, much less been able to address it through taking steps to ensure that all employees received meaningful feedback.

For managers, getting curious instead of complacent is critical. Indeed, it's highly likely that individual supervisors at the consulting firm weren't aware of how differently they were managing men and women, but armed with insight, they could act to provide women with the same level of feedback that men received. Even if you don't manage other managers, you can investigate what you see on your own team; instead of assuming that a female employee is closing fewer deals because she's a weak negotiator, look into whether she has access to the same information and resources her male peers do or review whether her clients are systematically different in some way. Asking these questions is especially important for the women of color you manage, who have been shown to receive less support than both men and white women. Black women in particular tend to get less encouragement, less advocacy, and less guidance from their managers.[12]

Provide developmental opportunities and feedback
on an equitable basis by

- Tracking whom you mentor and advocate to ensure you aren't supporting only employees who share your race and/or gender.

- Challenging your assumptions about employees' preferences and aptitudes.

Inclusive Managers *Foster a Culture Where Everyone Matters*

Interpersonal exclusion—both subtle and blatant—was the most consistent theme that emerged in our survey of executive women. About 40 percent of all examples of noninclusive management recounted some form of being marginalized or left out of both work-related and social interactions, from the overt ("I've had numerous male managers who would golf only with men") to the more indirect ("My manager would never come to me to chat about issues or seek my opinion, but he did with the others—all men—on the team. He had all their cell numbers and texted them frequently. He did not once text me.")

Your interpersonal interactions and the social patterns on your team can undermine the work you've done to establish fairness in your formal management processes. When you form personal bonds only with employees who share your gender, those who are different from you have less access to the information, advice, and insights that you hold. Recent research at a large financial institution has found that socialization between male managers and male employees measurably boosts men's careers. Men who report to men are promoted more quickly than women (regardless of their managers' gender), and that advancement is associated with additional time that male managers and male employees spend together.[13] One woman in our own survey described how a manager prioritized spending time with same-gender colleagues: "[I had] a manager whose busy schedule often had him squeezing in one-on-one time with male colleagues after hours (over drinks, dinners, etc.), but female colleagues often had their meetings either cancelled or cut short to fit into the compressed workday."

It's natural to gravitate toward people who are similar to you, and we aren't suggesting that you don't form those relationships, but managing inclusively means getting to know the people you don't connect with as seamlessly. Not only does such a mindful approach help ensure you aren't inadvertently favoring some employees on the basis of gender (or race, or sexual orientation, or any other identity), but it also sets inclusion as the cultural norm for your team or department. Inclusive norms are critical to ensuring that employees who differ from the majority are valued and seen as full members of the group. One example from our survey illustrates how an inclusive culture enables employees to thrive even when they are in the numerical minority:

> At the beginning of my career, I was on a team of all men where we worked together on a matter that was essentially 24/7. I was included in every meeting, every dinner, every night out, client meetings, and asked to contribute substantively. On a particular issue, when I disagreed with another member of the team who was senior to me, my view was given serious consideration. I always felt like an important, contributing member of the team by all the men on the team. When a judge mistook me for a support person in open court, the leader of our team was quick to correct him.

By ensuring that she was a full participant in all aspects of the team's work and recognized as such, her manager signaled that women belonged, a message that not only enabled her success but also provided a counterpoint to any beliefs about women's lesser competence that teammates might have held, even unconsciously. This inclusive culture enacted and modeled an environment where women and men were on equal footing not just on paper but also in the day-to-day experience of the team.

Inclusive cultures take effort, and leading them can be uncomfortable at times. In the example we just noted, the manager had to point out the error of someone in authority in order to preserve the dignity of an employee—something that, while perhaps minor in this instance, could be fraught in many contexts. In the profile that follows this chapter, Wall Street executive Jack Rivkin makes a more confrontational move to call out bias exhibited toward his female employees. His willingness to swim against the tide of the dominant culture resulted in a high-performing department but wasn't always well received by others at the firm.[14]

Staying silent might seem easier in the moment, but the price is higher in the long run. One executive at a multinational telecommunications company experienced firsthand what it was like to have colleagues who failed to consider how their actions impacted others and what it meant that no one spoke up about it. The executive, a Black woman, told us about sitting in a meeting when the following happened:

> This guy who headed our most profitable business was complaining about how we were being treated in one market, and his way of explaining the unfairness was to say they treated us like the N-word, that commercially it was the equivalent of making us, quote, "sit at the back of the bus." Honestly, I think I just shut down in that meeting. The comment just kind of sat there. While it in no way defined or marred my overall excellent experience at the company, at the same time there was no assurance that he did not represent the corporation in speaking that way.

If others in the meeting, particularly white men and those with the most seniority, had stepped in and pointed out that equating a market disadvantage with racial oppression belittled the latter, it could have benefitted the entire team, especially if the conversation didn't end there. Our executive would have known that her identity as a Black woman was seen and valued and that the company wasn't cavalier about racial inequality. The speaker and others who may not have perceived the harmful nature of the comment would have been reminded that their perspective isn't universal. Without such an intervention, the executive was left feeling that her company allowed "some people in the work environment [to] get away with all kinds of things because they are performing, because they are bringing in a lot of money," at the expense of the team as a whole.

In these kinds of situations others, as with our executive, are often reluctant to speak up, to be the one to call out colleagues. And understandably so—in working environments where relationships are usually key to getting things done, no one wants to be branded as "difficult" or to confirm negative views about their gender or race. Managers can stand up for these employees and affirm their value not by avoiding uncomfortable moments but instead by embracing them as opportunities to grow. Those in management can model a constructive, candid approach that creates space for learning and deeper understanding and also makes it safe for employees to speak up when they feel marginalized or misunderstood. Managers can do this by being open about their own learning, acknowledging mistakes and missteps while reasserting a commitment to inclusive and equitable leadership.[15] Even when addressing a problem requires decisive action—such as terminating someone for sexual harassment—you can signal to employees that you aren't brushing the issue aside by holding a town hall–style conversation or check-ins to gauge how employees are feeling. As one talent management executive we interviewed put it, "The ultimate leader, in my view, is someone who strives to stay objective and seeks to better understand how they themselves interact and their impact on the people around them."

In contrast to the disheartening story above, another Black woman told us about a time when white male leaders at her law firm did stand up for her:

A client showed up in my office to talk about a complicated provision that a partner had written, and he said, "This doesn't make any sense. How am I supposed to understand this? This is not English. This is Swahili." I just kind of looked at him, and I didn't say anything. We discussed something else, and then he said it again. I responded, "You need to get out of my office right now." I went to the partner who had actually written the provision and told him. He kind of laughed, and then he looked at me and could tell I was not happy. He asked me to sit down and tell him exactly what had happened, after which he said, "Go back to your office, and we'll deal with this." He went and told the head of the practice group, who came to my office and asked me to tell him what happened. Later, he came back and told me he'd called the head of the client company and told him that was not the way his associates were supposed to be treated.

Foster an inclusive culture by

- Nurturing relationships with employees who are different from you.

- Affirming the value of and publicly recognizing the contributions of team members.

- Speaking up against biased or hurtful comments.

- Embracing difficult conversations.

Inclusive Managers *Effectively Leverage Diverse Perspectives*

Gender inclusion means more than making women feel welcome. If you're not soliciting and using their knowledge and expertise, you're not truly including them in the actual work of your team. In our survey of women executives, one consistent characteristic of noninclusive managers, both male and female, was an unwillingness or inability to listen to and take advantage of others' views and insights.

Superficial recognition that doesn't allow women to fully contribute won't placate employees who feel their voices are unheard. Indeed, lip service can be all the more frustrating, as expressed by one woman working in the health care industry: "I recently reported to someone I always thought was inclusive, but in hindsight he was not. He put women in top roles, but they did not get an equal voice. Many times, I was told what decisions were rather than being asked to make the decision or provide input." This experience is echoed by a legal professional: "The CEO had an inner circle where all decisions got made, and despite the fact that I reported to him, I was not part of that informal decision-making body. I was the only female on the executive team, and he made a point of including me in public events but not where information was shared and the decisions got made."

Not only does this sort of inclusion in name only demoralize employees, but it also deprives teams of the benefits of diversity. By seeking out and valuing perspectives grounded in employee's different experiences, you can deepen engagement and are also likely to gain insights that contribute to better work culture and performance. If you are leading a diverse team, you might be inclined to minimize differences in hopes of fostering unity and connection. But research has shown that trying to play down differences actually backfires: it creates a sense of isolation.[16] When team culture focuses on going along to get along, offering a contrary opinion becomes a risky prospect. While it makes sense to align priorities and foster a shared ethos among employees, it is crucial that managers welcome contributions and perspectives that challenge the status quo. One case in point happened at coworking space The Wing. In 2020 CEO Audrey Gelman had to address criticism that the company, despite a feminist mission, had inadequately addressed concerns among the women of color on its staff and failed to live up to its equity and inclusion rhetoric. Writing in *Fast Company*, she explained that by failing to listen to employees, Wing had missed important information about problems that worsened as they went unaddressed and ultimately damaged the company's reputation: "Rather than creating a healthy feedback loop and addressing with urgency the issues that members and employees identified, we prioritized business growth over cultural growth. There comes a time when your employees and customers know your business better than you do and when slowing down to listen becomes the smartest (and most strategic) thing you can do."[17]

The inclusive managers we heard about in our survey made employees feel heard and respected. They solicited input from across the organizational hierarchy and focused on what was best for the team rather than listening only to a few voices and maneuvering to enhance their own standing. "Midcareer, I had a boss in Hong Kong who was quite inclusive and progressive. He was . . . bringing in more diverse staff both locally and as expats and engaging many levels of the team," said one woman in our survey. One executive in consulting, who'd had dozens of managers over the course of more than thirty years, pithily summarized the key actions of her most inclusive managers: "Championed everyone on his team. [Was a] supporter, equally, of all on his team. Allowed each person to speak at meetings and solicited input from those that were quieter." We heard about managers who made sure to bring in the voices of women or other staff who were in the minority, "call[ing] for the opinions of women or underrepresented minorities if their voices were more quiet." Indeed, recent research has found that white men speak up the most and exert the most influence on group deliberation, even when white women or people of color in the group have more expertise.[18] Making a proactive effort to tap into the knowledge of others, as these managers did, can disrupt that pattern and help you leverage the power of the entire team.

One woman's first manager left a lasting impression by setting a tone of shared problem-solving: "[He] was extremely inclusive. Most meetings he had with our team of seven were together. Unless there was a reason for something personal to be discussed, everything was transparent." Inclusive managers know that ultimately, diversity enhances their own performance through added insight, as another executive we surveyed explained:

Early in my career I reported to women. As I won more senior roles, I started reporting to men, as they held the majority of the most senior roles. Only one of these men was particularly focused on inclusion. He had a very vast and active network from his background as a consultant. His philosophy on teams was that "the most difference creates the best long-term results." Because of his network, he was able to draw in a large variety of people with different backgrounds, cultures, and experiences.

Effectively leverage diverse perspectives by

- Recognizing the value of a range of perspectives.

- Ensuring the voices of those in the minority are fully heard.

Inclusive Managers *Champion Diversity, Equity, and Inclusion as Values and Aspirations*

The value of a diverse workforce and the importance of treating employees equitably and inclusively are rarely questioned today. Women who started working in the 1980s and 1990s, like many of those in our survey, witnessed a shift in how leaders spoke about gender and race and how they approached people management. One aerospace executive described this evolution:

> Early in my career, any reference to time off for family issues was *never* spoken of. It would result in public, negative statements about employees who spoke of it. It was also not unusual to hear inappropriate jokes that reflected bias in both race and gender. In later years—the 1990s and beyond—it was rare for leaders to speak publicly in a way that was not supportive of an inclusive workplace. In the early 2000s, our most senior leadership (CEO and below) made it clear that creating an inclusive environment was a required skill for executive leaders. It changed the course for many at work.

Naming inclusion as a value and a goal is not something that only top leaders must do, however. Despite much discussion, women today still aren't sure that their organizations truly prioritize equitable treatment. In a 2019 study, less than half of women—and just 35 percent of Black women—believed that promotion decisions at their companies were fair and objective.[19] In a 2018 study we conducted with a global sample of executive women, only 19 percent felt that their field or industry was doing enough to engage and retain women. What gives? It's news to no one that a frozen middle impedes change of all kinds, from implementing new technologies to improving organizational cultures, but the flipside is that frontline and middle managers can shape companies for the better. By being explicit about your commitment to inclusive management, you indicate to your employees that these values are a priority and unfreeze progress toward greater equity.

One way to make that commitment clear is by treating activities and projects related to diversity as legitimate and important. One woman in our inclusive management study pointed to a manager who supported participation in employee resource groups and funded dues in women's professional organizations. These actions don't simply provide opportunities for skill-building and networking for the individual employees who participate, but they also send a message that engaging in efforts to advance diversity and inclusion within the company or industry are worthwhile endeavors, not superfluous distractions from "real" work.

In addition, you can elevate inclusion to a business priority by setting concrete goals for yourself and your team. If you manage other managers, setting an expectation for your employees to implement inclusive practices widens your impact. Tracking performance is critical to making such expectations meaningful, and you can measure not just outcomes (such as attrition rates by gender) but also process. When it comes to the latter, you can look at what your employees are doing in real time: Are they attending bias trainings when asked? Do they apply evaluation rubrics consistently? Are they favoring same-gender colleagues when it comes to sharing information and insight?

Do they ostracize new hires who are different from the existing team? Are team members able to talk about difference, bias, and inequality in ways that are constructive and lead to learning? Getting specific about what employees need to do to work and lead inclusively will enable you to incorporate those goals into performance objectives and hold your team accountable.

Champion values of diversity, equity, and inclusion by

- Affirming the importance of and endorsing participation in diversity, equity, and inclusion activities and groups.

- Setting concrete goals for equitable and inclusive practices and holding your team accountable.

Cultivating these five attributes will help you make decisions, communicate, and collaborate in ways that enable your team to do more than just function. With conditions in place that make it possible for people to contribute to their fullest potential, stay engaged, and feel invested in shared goals, your team can thrive. Even so, you might find that some behaviors are more impactful than others in the context of your organization, or you may identify additional actions you can take to manage inclusively. Feedback from your team might spur you to rethink how you address disparities or set norms. You could find yourself wrestling with a new kind of challenge that isn't fully addressed in these pages. What defines effective management has changed over time and will continue to change, as will what we understand about inclusive management. Our development of the principles in this chapter was partly inspired by one large tech company's efforts to identify and measure the characteristics of effective management. After implementing a program that trained and evaluated managers on key attributes, the company saw measurable improvements in managerial performance and effectiveness.[20] Yet even these attributes, as useful as they were and are, have evolved over time. In 2018, ten years after the launch of the project, the list was revised and expanded. As the company had changed and grown more complex, so too had what it took to be a great manager within it. The very nature of managing, particularly in the complicated world we live in, means that this chapter cannot be an exhaustive and final guide. Research will illuminate new factors that perpetuate inequality and need to be addressed. Employee expectations will evolve. The social context will become different. And your own capabilities, insights, and aspirations will grow and shift.

What is here to stay is the understanding that inclusion is integral to good management. In fact, one of the changes the aforementioned company made was to its third managerial attribute, which in 2008 read "Expresses interest/concern for team members' success and personal well-being" but in 2018 was updated to "Creates an inclusive team environment, showing concern for success and well-being." Recognizing that simply 'paying attention' to team members doesn't necessarily create an environment where they can all succeed and are valued equally, the company knew that it was time to explicitly prioritize inclusion as a managerial competency. And the updated list of behaviors proved to be even more highly correlated with team turnover, satisfaction, and performance than the original version.[21] Managing inclusively makes a difference—to your own effectiveness, to the people you lead, and to your organization as a whole.

BRINGING INCLUSIVE MANAGEMENT TO WALL STREET

Jack Rivkin

The late Jack Rivkin is famous in finance circles for turning around a disorganized and underperforming investment research department, along the way creating practices that became standard across the field.[22] Upon his death in 2016, he was widely remembered for taking the now-shuttered firm Shearson from fifteenth to first place in *Institutional Investor*'s definitive ranking of industry analysts and for mentoring some of Wall Street's brightest stars. What fewer know is how the Shearson research department became an island of gender inclusion and fair treatment for women in a sea that was not just male-dominated but characterized by outright sexism.

In the late 1980s, when Rivkin was hired to head up Shearson's global equity research department, Wall Street was well known for a hypermasculine culture, and women were a distinct minority throughout the finance industry. The proportion of female equity analysts—researchers who study industries and companies and make recommendations about the stocks that investors should trade—was roughly 15 percent across the field.[23] When Rivkin joined Shearson in 1987, women made up 20 percent of its analysts.

Many banks didn't see a problem with this status quo. Teena Lerner, an analyst tracking the biotechnology industry, explained: "During the late 1980s, top firms developed the unsavory reputation of being particularly difficult places for women to work. People from some firms would brag that every woman there had quit." Judy Sanders, a human resources executive at Shearson, concurred that "most of Wall Street had a powerful culture that allowed only a particular type of person to succeed."[24]

Rivkin's management approach ran directly counter to this culture. Rather than participate in or ignore the ways that women were marginalized, Rivkin was vocal about women's value and about inclusive management as effective management. In Chapter 5, we mentioned an investment firm that dramatically increased the proportion of women hired after diversifying its interview panels to include more women. The firm was Rivkin's, and those gender-diverse interview panels were designed to show candidates that in his department, there was no single model for success. "Our recruiting process was set up to evaluate talent and to send a signal that no matter what strengths or weaknesses you have, we know how to make you successful," he explained in an interview.[25] Implementing these inclusive processes propelled Shearson's research department to the head of the pack when it came to recruiting and hiring women analysts. Five years after Rivkin took the helm, Shearson's proportion of female analysts jumped to 30 percent, double the industry average.

Whereas most research departments focused on trying to hire away high performers from other firms, in effect tacitly endorsing traditional gender-biased definitions of success, Rivkin's strategy was weighted toward potential. He was attuned to the value of recruiting early-career women and enabling their success before they experienced the biases and stymied growth that spurred women to exit the field at higher rates than men. Women analysts hired at Shearson tended to be younger than average for the industry and consequently attained ranked status earlier in their careers. The average age of a ranked female analyst at Shearson was thirty-one, compared to an industry average of thirty-five.

One of Rivkin's first hires, Josie Esquivel, quickly became one of Shearon's highest-performing analysts; just eighteen months after joining, she was a runner-up on *Institutional Investor*'s annual list, the definitive ranking of equity researchers by their clients. In an interview, Esquivel described being able to flourish under Rivkin's leadership in large part because he didn't expect her—or anyone—to fit a narrow mold: "We have always been given the freedom to be ourselves and create our own style. As long as I was producing, my style didn't matter." (Esquivel in fact became well known for her distinctive style, writing lively reports with humorous titles and sporting fashion-forward attire—both of which set her apart from the more buttoned-up norm.) Overall, Rivkin fostered a culture where gender diversity was normalized, according to a contemporary of Eqsuivel's: "[Shearson] had a unique ability to make women welcome in the department and make us feel in the mainstream socially. I never felt I had to pretend to be a male to fit in." Cultivating a culture that was welcoming and fair was a guiding principle. Famously, Rivkin hewed to a no-jerk policy, which meant that while performance was critical, it didn't trump collegiality. Bad behavior was not to be excused, no matter how brilliant the jerk; Rivkin knew that turning a blind eye was poisonous for the culture at large. "No matter how good an analyst may be," he explained, "given the structure we are trying to create here, I am not going to bring a jerk into the department."[26]

As the no-jerk policy suggests, not only was Rivkin focused on removing barriers to female talent, but he also preferred to keep out those who didn't share his belief that women and men were equally capable. "Some male analysts opted out because they were uncomfortable being interviewed by so many female analysts, who were actually evaluating them and could possibly have become their team leaders," he explained. "That was fine with us."[27] Nor was Rivkin uncomfortable challenging colleagues who exhibited bias. One female analyst who worked for Rivkin recounted a meeting she attended with another female analyst, several senior male sales executives, and Rivkin. During the meeting, she recalled, one of the sales executives "turned to us and asked 'So what do the girls think?'

Jack turned to us and said we didn't have to answer that question."[28] In prioritizing the dignity of his women employees over camaraderie with other senior leaders, Rivkin sent a clear message about his values and about the value of the women on his team.

In tandem with preventing a toxic culture, Rivkin fostered an environment where women were rewarded based on performance, not assumptions about their commitment to work. He had long supported the careers of women with children, including promoting an analyst with young sons to the position of research director at the firm Paine Webber in the early 1980s. At Shearson, flexible hours were normalized and not equated with lower performance. Rivkin leaned on objective evaluation metrics and provided actionable feedback (something that, as we discuss elsewhere in this book, women are less likely than men to receive). As a result, women saw a clear path to success; the firm remained a competitive environment but one in which opportunities for high achievement weren't restricted by gender. As Lerner described, "You felt that management was on your side, trying to improve you. They were giving you these measurements and telling you how you stacked up for your own benefit."[29] Rather than haphazard development accruing to those whom senior colleagues decided to take under their wings, analysts had equal access to education, information, and advice. With longtime deputy Fred Fraenkel, Rivkin developed a program, designed around leveraging individual strengths, to accelerate analysts' ability to understand and predict trends. As Esquivel explained, "Jack and Fred believed you could develop . . . in a number of different ways; there was no 'right' way to do it."[30]

In response to these innovations in hiring, training, and performance management, the best female analysts on Wall Street flocked to join Rivkin's department. Because of the male-dominated nature of the field, women were already attuned to factors beyond compensation and prestige when assessing new opportunities. Women who were willing to consider switching firms had questions beyond "what's my salary, what's my bonus," as Fraenkel remembered in an interview. "Women were much more focused on 'Am I going to step into quicksand where they hate women, there's a glass ceiling, where they don't make accommodations for the things I need?'"[31] Under Fraenkel and Rivkin's leadership, Shearson stood out for credibly telling women they wouldn't get stuck in quicksand. Instead, they could expect to receive support to realize their full potential. And the numbers confirmed that Shearson was exceptionally effective at developing its analysts: Just under 12 percent of the firm's analysts achieved ranked status, compared to under 8 percent across the field. Shearson analysts also achieved ranking more quickly than those at other firms—dramatically so in the case of women, who made the cut with just 3.73 years of experience at the firm, compared to an average length of 6.26 years at other research departments. More than 60 percent of the women analysts in Rivkin's department held ranked status, compared to an average below 30 percent at competing firms and just 2 percent across the industry. By 1991 nearly a quarter of all ranked female analysts worked for the firm, compared to less than 4 percent in 1987. No other major investment bank employed as many of the industry's top-performing female analysts. As it rose steadily in the *Institutional Investor* rankings, the Shearson research department appeared poised to begin a long run as an industry leader on the basis of its inclusive approach to hiring, training, and assessment.

However, Rivkin's unconventional people-focused management style—which also included instituting casual Fridays and team-building off-site retreats—did not win him favors with his superiors. While fiercely devoted to his own department, Rivkin had little patience for the intricacies of firm politics, especially when dealing with senior colleagues whom he felt didn't understand the complexities of equity research. In 1992 he abruptly left the firm, shocking many of the analysts who had become stars under his tutelage.[32] Over the next handful of years, the department's high performers, including Esquivel, followed, with turnover rates among ranked analysts going from single-digit percentages to above 20 percent.

In 1994 alone, 57 percent of ranked women analysts left Shearson for competing firms. Fred Fraenkel also departed, frustrated at his inability to maintain the culture and team he and Rivkin had built in the face of a new cost-cutting regime and attempts by firm leadership to force the research department to adopt a conventional approach to hiring and managing talent. With these departures, the department soon tumbled in the rankings. And it was no longer a leader when it came to gender diversity. By 1995, the firm was lagging instead of leading the industry in its gender composition; under 15 percent of its analysts were women, and it counted no women among its ranked analysts.[33]

This precipitous decline underscores the critical role of managers in advancing and sustaining equity and inclusion. Rivkin had instituted numerous practices that helped level the playing field, but his departure and new restrictions from firm leadership left no one to champion and maintain them. Without a manager to steward it, the distinctive culture that Rivkin had cultivated was subsumed by broader firm and industry norms, and the advantage it once had when it came to recruiting and retaining talented women evaporated. No longer an island of inclusion or excellence, Rivkin's former department held less appeal as a prospective employer—or a current one. As Esquivel recalled, in the months prior to her own departure, "Every other day, analysts were leaving the firm. If you were not leaving, then you were looking around."[34] The swiftness of both the firm's rise and its decline underscores how managers and systems work together. Leadership at the highest level is needed to implement and steward the latter, which is why Rivkin's innovations never made it past his own department and why they weren't sustainable once his superiors withdrew their tacit support. Without permission, much less endorsement, from those at the top, the local systems Rivkin and Fraenkel had implemented couldn't outlast their tenure. Ultimately, leadership at all levels is critical to carrying out even the most equitable and inclusive systems on a day-to-day basis.

CONCLUSION

A BREAKTHROUGH MOMENT

Tumble outta bed and I stumble to the kitchen,
pour myself a cup of ambition.

—Dolly Parton, "9 to 5"

In 1980, long before the coauthors of this book entered the workforce, *9 to 5* became the second-highest-grossing film of the year (exceeded in ticket sales only by *Star Wars: The Empire Strikes Back*).[1] At a time when workplace harassment, differential treatment, and demeaning language toward women were widely accepted, the film offered a satisfying fantasy of justice as three women, played by stars Jane Fonda, Dolly Parton, and Lily Tomlin, exact revenge on their outrageously sexist boss. While the average workplace of today is a vast improvement over that of the film—in which women are physically harassed and openly passed over for promotion in favor of less capable men, and hardly anyone bats an eye at denigrating jokes and remarks—the lyrics of the film's title track, which became a *Billboard* hit and earned Parton a Grammy, continue to ring true. The song tells of aspirations that shrink and crumble under the pressure of an unequal reality, paths to advancement blocked, contributions that go uncredited and unrewarded, and a profound sense of frustration with such unfair conditions. Forty years later, these themes recur in the stories of women quoted in this book across the spectrum of industries, geographies, and career stages.

But we didn't write this book to assert that the status quo is intractable. On the contrary, we decided to gather our own and others' research about gender inequality at work because we believe that the current moment is one of immense opportunity. One of the executives we interviewed described feeling "like we're at the base camp at Mount Everest" when it comes to gender equity. "We still have a long way to go, but it's base camp. We've made the seventeen-thousand-foot journey to reach the mountain." She's right on both counts. Collectively, we've surmounted and dismantled major hurdles to women's careers; behind us lies a trail of broken barriers. At the same time, the mountain before us has come into sharp relief. Deeply embedded obstacles to women's advancement are consistently revealed through scholarly investigation, journalistic exploration, and real workplace experiences. In the first half of this book, we endeavored to explain how these obstacles evolve across women's careers. Strategies deployed early on become less effective as women move up, as we detailed in Chapter 2. At each stage, from entry level all the way to the boardroom, developing a toolkit for navigating an unequal workplace is a core competency—and an additional mental load—for women. We believe it's crucial to understand the nature of these barriers and the factors that cause them to linger, which is why we've taken care to explain the sources of gendered disadvantage and tell the stories of women navigating through it. Without understanding the nature of today's gender gaps, they can't be closed—indeed, attempts to do so may even undermine best intentions. Yet arriving at the mountain means that we can begin to craft a path upward and onward; the climb may yet be arduous, but it's surmountable.

One reason we're hopeful is that workplace gender inequality has become harder to dismiss. Social media, along with the increasing reliance of traditional media on social platforms, has meant that women's lived experiences of bias and discrimination are part of the global conversation in unprecedented ways. When we first began putting together our ideas for this book #MeToo hadn't ignited, and sexual harassment was not a high-priority topic for the companies we researched. But the movement forced businesses to take seriously their responsibility for organizational cultures that were allowing harassment to flourish in the shadows. In the most recent round of data collection for an ongoing study we help lead, three-quarters of men said that post #MeToo, they had developed greater empathy for the challenges faced by women at work. Other examples of changing expectations are seen in new legislation. A few years ago it was considered vanishingly unlikely that mandates for gender diversity on corporate boards would appear in the United States. But then, California passed a law requiring that companies comply with a minimum level of representation for women. Washington State enacted a similar measure two years later. Likewise, it was virtually unheard of for companies to disclose gender pay gaps—until regulatory requirements in the United Kingdom spurred multinational firms such as Citigroup to share data even beyond the minimum required.

We also see cause for optimism as more and more attention is paid to the experiences of women of color, particularly Black women, who face both different and additional barriers compared to their white peers. Throughout this book, we have attempted to highlight some key research on the intersection of race and gender and call out phenomena whereby women of color are especially marginalized, though we have undoubtedly left some important facets unaddressed. For instance, we noted in Chapter 3 that until very recently, the conversation about board diversity has been focused almost entirely on gender. (Michele Hooper, in the profile following that chapter, also makes this observation and rightly chastens boards and governance organizations for it.) A failure to acknowledge and address how corporate governance is dominated by whites is all too clear in the abysmally low proportion of board seats held by women of color. We are hopeful that attention is now shifting. Recent industry reports have devoted more space to parsing the data on board racial diversity, and California leg-islators have proposed a law, modeled on the gender mandate, that seeks to outlaw all-white boards in the state.[2] In a similar vein, more conversations about race-based pay gaps are occurring. The UK gov-ernment, which already mandates disclosure of gender pay dispari-ties, is weighing a rule that would require companies to disclose data on differences in compensation by race and ethnicity.[3] And the coro-navirus pandemic has shone a spotlight on existing and increasing dis-advantages faced by Latinas and Black women in particular, including higher rates of unemployment and lower pay.[4] To ignore the perni-cious effects of racism and racial bias is to overlook all we need to do to advance the representation of *all* women into leadership, a stance that we see more organizations and gender-equity advocates adopting.

Moments of breakthrough are times of transition, and thus they are also moments of precarity. Will business and society redouble efforts to address the inequalities that shape lives and careers, or will aspira-tions for more just and inclusive workplaces crumble under the weight of doubt and pushback? Skepticism and backlash toward organizational and cultural changes are quite real. A 2020 executive order prohibited federal agencies from engaging in staff training discussing the con-cept of white privilege or drawing on the field of critical race theory, referring to such programs as "propaganda effort[s]."[5] The "Google memo" of 2017, in which an employee asserted that women have less aptitude for and interest in technical jobs than men, was hailed by like-minded media commentators.[6] Yet rather than reasons to despair, we see these events and many others like them as calls to action. There are no magic bullets, but our aim is to arm readers with the knowl-edge and tools to support a collective ambition to make change.

We have spent many pages explicating the often subtle nature of gender inequality today to help readers better understand the condi-tions that perpetuate it. Half measures that fail to get at the roots of inequality all too often produce limited results. A poignant case in point is unfolding before our eyes. When we began writing this book, the world hadn't heard of the novel coronavirus. As we conclude, it is contorting the world economy, straining health care systems, and transforming how work gets done. In this new reality, parents have found themselves without childcare, thrust into being both full-time employees and full-time caregivers with little support. Just as quickly as these new conditions snapped into place came the awareness that women were bearing a disproportionate burden. As early as March 2020, a poll found that women were more likely than men to report that their lives had been disrupted by the virus. Later in the year, studies of the pandemic's effect on families found that mothers had reduced their work hours four to five times more than fathers and were taking on more of the child care and housework burdens.[7] Despite all the gains we've made for women at work, a governing paradigm in which men's careers are given priority remains in place. Yet many of the men we spoke to in Chapter 4 are charting a different course, demonstrating in their choices as partners and managers what it looks like to enact and enable more egalitarian norms. A pandemic-era example was seen in a viral tweet from the education minister of Sierra Leone, who shared a photo of himself carrying his young child while participating in a video call and inviting others to "share with the world how you worked from home as a leader."[8]

Everyone has a stake in advancing gender equality. Men stand to gain from loosening the stereotypical expectations that force an artificial and untenable divide between work and love—the men who are fighting to be both caregivers and professionals are doing so not only to share the load but also to share equally in the joy and fulfillment of family. Organizations, too, win out when they stop adhering to outmoded assumptions about gender and work. Biased beliefs (conscious and unconscious) and their associated behaviors result in women being systematically undervalued by employers. In the absence of a commitment to advancing gender equity, managers and companies needlessly limit their ability to leverage talent—widely acknowledged to be the most important resource in a knowledge-based economy, where people's decision-making and problem-solving generate value. Creating a workplace that enables women to thrive isn't a favor that companies bestow on female employees. Removing sources of systematic disadvantage means unleashing and reaping the full benefit of their talent. We aren't talking about a simplistic business case where adding women means adding profits. (See Chapter 3 for a discussion of the research on diversity and performance.) Rather, we're urging you to open your eyes to the shortsightedness of making gender equity a low-priority goal—nice to have but extraneous to your most important work. Nothing could be further from the truth. When you overcome the biases and change the structures that lead to women being undervalued and stymied, you put yourself out ahead of peers who allow gender-based barriers to stand.

In our profile of Jack Rivkin, we pointed out that Rivkin saw the value in making his department a place where women analysts could thrive and gained a clear advantage against competing firms after putting those conditions in place. His team's swift rise in the industry rankings provides one compelling case of how a gender-equitable environment can unleash women to succeed—to become, in the parlance of investment research, "stars." Dismantling the structures that marginalize women can also improve the overall culture of an organization. A comprehensive study of multinational companies in South Korea conducted in the mid-2000s found that they were hiring and promoting more women into managerial roles than peer firms based locally, pushing back against cultural perceptions that women didn't belong in such jobs, especially if it gave them authority over male employees. The researchers discovered that the presence of these female managers disrupted hidebound norms that precluded transparency, inquiry, and debate, and these cultural changes led to increased company productivity.

The researchers conducted in-depth qualitative fieldwork to understand exactly how the presence of women managers was invigorating the firms that hired and promoted them. They found that men had been more immersed in command-and-control cultures at home, at school, and in military service (which was compulsory only for men).

As a result, women employees were more adept at fostering the collaborative, reflective management styles suited to the moment.[9] What's notable about this explanation is the way in which women's greater facility at what companies needed stemmed from skills they gained navigating an unequal world. Women hadn't been exposed to the same training and development as men, because gender roles dictated that women be more focused on home and family than on work and leadership. Yet despite these roadblocks, women who did pursue managerial careers took the talents they developed in this context and applied them to great success.

In fact, discrimination has often propelled women to develop, out of necessity, skills that make them exceptionally suited to leadership. Take the glass cliff phenomenon wherein companies tend to appoint women to lead in troubled times.[10] Broadly speaking, this pattern suggests that women are likely to be quite familiar with managing through crisis, having watched plum assignments go to favored male peers while they, by contrast, were often relied on to put out fires. Similarly, we know that women get excluded from the socializing and relationship building so critical to success in many fields. As a result, they are more resourceful about building their networks; they look outside their organizations and rely less heavily on their immediate coworkers. This strategy, borne of exclusion, can mean that women's performance is less tied to their current workplace than men's: Women can switch jobs and bring with them a robust proverbial Rolodex, ready to hit the ground running.[11] Another example: in Chapter 2 we found that cultivating resilience was critical to the success of women who had surmounted obstacles and attained leadership. Some of our colleagues conducted an in-depth study of African American women who had reached the C-suite or managing partner level and likewise found that resilience was key to their climb.[12] The persistence of gender inequality at work spurs women, especially women of color, to develop extra measures of flexibility and toughness.

Readiness, resourcefulness, resilience: On a still-uneven playing field, it's no wonder that these terms characterize the women who make it to the top. Yet even as we laud these traits, we should remember that many women still on the climb are finding themselves stalled or derailed even as they strive to cultivate all the right skills and capabilities. A 2019 study that collected data from 329 companies with more than thirteen million employees collectively found that between entry and director levels, white women's share of the leadership pipeline has already shrunk by 13 percent and women of color's by a shocking 50 percent.[13] Companies are losing talented women, and it's a vicious cycle. Women leave companies when they don't see a path to advancement, and a lack of women in positions of power can leave female employees feeling alienated and less trusting of each other and of female managers.[14]

Decades ago, the three lead characters of *9 to 5* banded together instead, challenging a system that excluded and diminished them. The longtime manager who saw her promotion prospects blocked knew that she was fighting the same battle as the secretary deflecting lewd comments and a new colleague entering the workforce postdivorce. Rather than focus narrowly on how to overcome individual hurdles, all three women saw a broader, more foundational set of problems and set about to rectify them (albeit in comedic fashion). We know that numerous gender-based disparities are outside the scope of this volume and acknowledge that our focus on professional women leaves out scores of other women workers who contend with more dire and more entrenched disadvantages. However, we hope that in making the case for systemic change, we have made clear that the commitment of everyone—of all genders and at all levels—is needed in the movement toward greater equality. We are heartened by emerging forms of solidarity in the fight against workplace discrimination, such as the work of Time's Up, a legal defense fund founded by a star-studded list of entertainment professionals that works on behalf of women across the economic spectrum. Gender equity profoundly enhances all our lives and all our workplaces, and now is the time to keep fighting for it. We should no longer be satisfied with seeing individual women break through barriers—it's time for glass-shattering organizations to clear away the sharp edges and shards that continue to keep women from achieving their full potential. It's time for ceilings to come down so that all of us—men, women, business, and society—can turn toward a sky full of greater possibility.

FROM INNOVATOR TO ADVOCATE

Ilene H. Lang

"A teacher said that I couldn't be a leader because I was a girl," Ilene Lang recalls. "I became a feminist at the age of eleven when I heard that." Lang's commitment to gender equality, which she terms her lifelong avocation, would ultimately bring her to Catalyst, a nonprofit focused on advancing women in the workplace. Along the way her own career journey mapped the evolution in women's professional opportunities, bringing her from an era of normalized discrimination to one where gender is far less determinative yet still hinders women's advancement.

Lang entered Radcliffe College in the fall of 1961, a member of one of the last classes to experience the separate and unequal system dividing Radcliffe from Harvard College, to which only men were admitted. At the time Lang matriculated, Radcliffe graduates were still being awarded a separate degree, despite being taught the same curriculum by the same faculty. That practice had been eliminated by the time Lang graduated in 1965, but women were not on equal footing. "There was a four-to-one ratio of men to women. We were second-class citizens. We couldn't go to Lamont Library, which was restricted to Harvard undergraduates. At our fiftieth reunion, we were still complaining about it—it was very formative," she explains. (Women were allowed access to Lamont in 1967, and joint admissions began in 1975. By 1977, "sex-blind admissions" eliminated the four-to-one standard.[15])

Lang grew up in Chicago and was valedictorian of her high school class. The title of her valedictory speech, "Observe the

Opportunity," reflected her desire to chart her own path—an approach that would later inform her decision to enter the new field of computer technology. But before pursuing a career in an emerging and rapidly growing industry, Lang experienced the social upheaval that was expanding women's opportunities. As she looked for a postgraduation job, technology was appealing—not only because the proximity of schools such as Harvard and MIT meant new companies were cropping up but also because the young industry seemed like it might be open to women. "A Radcliffe friend and I joked that we ought to look at tech companies, because it was an industry so desperate for talent they'd even hire a woman," she explains. Indeed, there were open doors; Lang joined a technology consulting firm, and her friend went to work at IBM.

Lang's new employer was largely made up of MIT engineers who had developed a massive data center. Lang was hired to write proposals and documentation, and the job was fortuitous not only because it set Lang on the path to a tech career. "The president's chief of staff had gone to the Harvard-Radcliffe Program in Business Administration. She became a mentor to me," Lang recalls, and she encouraged Lang to consider pursuing an MBA at Harvard, something Lang kept in mind as she spent several years working in technology and steeping herself in the emerging research on computing. In 1970 when the stock market crashed, her growing company hit a wall, and she decided it was time. Lang enrolled at Harvard Business School (HBS) in 1971, one of fewer than forty women in a class of more than eight hundred students. While women were still very much in the minority at HBS, societal gender norms were changing rapidly. "The 1960s were an awakening," Lang explains, "and the 1970s brought significant changes. The year I graduated with my MBA, there were two foundational Supreme Court cases in the span of just a couple of months. One was *Roe v. Wade*, and the other was the AT&T class-action suit, where the company was found to be discriminating against women." (AT&T paid $38 million in back pay and raises to settle an

Equal Employment Opportunity Commission case claiming gender and racial discrimination by the company.)[16] "Women raced into the business world, convinced that they would succeed," she reflects. Indeed, much media coverage at the time held that it was just a matter of time until women would achieve parity with men.

Against this backdrop, Lang was leveraging her early experience in software, her new degree, and her natural bent for adventure to launch her career. "I have entrepreneurial genes—my grandparents on both sides were entrepreneurs and built successful family businesses. I was comfortable with a certain amount of risk taking," she notes. By the early 1980s, venture capital money was flooding the tech industry, and exciting developments in computing were happening, it seemed, every day. "My next-door neighbor bought an amazing new computer from a company called Symbolics," remembers Lang, who soon parlayed her enthusiasm into a job with Symbolics. "They needed someone to do communications and documentation—which fit my experience. I was in the right place at the right time." Lang was one of very few women at the company and the only mother in a leadership role. "I had two young children with a third on the way, so the company set me up with home computing, allowing me to work flexibly. I was a role model for women and men alike, a responsibility I took very seriously. Years later, former colleagues would reach out to tell me that they were better able to navigate working while parenting because of the example I set. 'Pay it forward!' I advised. That's how change happens."

As vice president of software, Lang helped to take Symbolics public and ended her tenure as vice president of marketing. In the early 1990s, she joined Lotus as vice president of international product development. She led a global team, with offices in Dublin, Tokyo, Singapore, and Cambridge, Massachusetts. Partnering with IBM and the China Academy of Sciences, she established a global quality assurance lab in Beijing that enabled the company to bring products to the global market more swiftly: "We used technology, of course, but the key was developing communication, formal proto-cols, and trust to enable people to work together in parallel. In those days we didn't call it 'diversity and inclusion,' but that's what it was. The cultural transformation at Lotus was profound." Lang was promoted to senior vice president of the desktop business group, responsible for 50 percent of Lotus's worldwide business. When IBM bought Lotus, Lang was recruited by Digital Equipment Corpora-tion, where she founded AltaVista, an early search engine that quickly outstripped the capabilities and popularity of its competitors. Digital Equipment Corporation took steps toward an initial public offering for AltaVista but later withdrew the filing, at which point Lang left, moving on to adviser, director, and CEO roles at four more internet companies.

Though Lang built a high-profile career as a tech executive, when the dot-com bubble burst in 2000, her entrepreneurial genes were itching for a change. "I had led three dot-coms in five years. I was ready for something else. I served on several corporate boards, I was advising early-stage companies, investing in women-led technology start-ups, and working with some of the venture capitalists in the Boston area, but I was looking for what was next. I wanted a change." Lang served on several nonprofit boards and was intrigued by the possibility of leaving the private sector, but none of the nonprofits she supported ignited in her the kind of passion she knew was needed for leading a mission-driven organization—until she heard about Catalyst's search for a new president. Catalyst—part think tank, part consulting firm—had been advising companies about how to enable women's careers since 1962, when founder Felice Schwartz championed the idea that mothers had a place in corporate America. By the time Lang got a call about the job, Catalyst's work had expanded to address barriers to women's advancement into executive leadership and onto corporate boards as well as combating widespread gender biases such as the notion that women lack ambition. Lang was immediately excited about the prospect. "I realized this was a career capstone, that my avocation would become my job. I was so passionate about advancing women and equality for women; it was the job for me." After breaking through barriers as a female leader, it was now time for Lang to devote herself to tearing them down altogether.

Lang's time at Catalyst may have been a capstone, but her career was far from over when she took the helm in 2003. There was no shortage of leadership challenges. New York City was still recovering from the 9/11 terrorist attacks, and the forty-year-old organization needed to accelerate its embrace of technology as well as tailor its efforts to the increasing complexity of the modern workplace. The meaning of gender equality was itself shifting, with greater understanding of how race and ethnicity, sexual orientation, and other dimensions of identity shaped women's experiences. As Lang explains:

> The perspective I have today was sharpened by my experience at Catalyst, by understanding the frameworks of stereotypes and implicit bias, about structural and systemic barriers. I marvel that trillions of dollars are spent to make women feel inadequate so they can spend trillions more being "fixed." What we need to do is fix workplace policies, practices, and cultures! I recognized patterns in my own career experiences—for example, the importance of sponsors as well as mentors. Mentors advise, sponsors put skin in the game. Every opportunity that came my way, from Symbolics, to Lotus, to AltaVista, to Catalyst, resulted from sponsors, women and men who knew me and put their reputational capital on the line for me.

Under Lang's leadership, Catalyst expanded its work on women of color and LGBTQ issues, conducted more research and programming outside the United States, and launched an initiative to engage men in advancing gender equity. Lang also steered Catalyst through some inauspicious times, most notably the 2008 financial crisis. "Two weeks into our new fiscal year, with a board-approved growth plan,

Lehman Brothers melted down," she remembers. "Many of our staff and board wanted us to hunker down and cut back." Instead, Lang and her team asked the board to resist the urge to scale back. "Our chairman said, 'You have cash in the bank for a rainy day, and it's pouring outside. Our companies are cutting back, and we need to depend on Catalyst being there for us.' So, we didn't pull back. We did not freeze salaries; we gave raises and promotions. We didn't hire; rather, we invested in current staff. It was counterintuitive, but it brought the team together and sharpened our focus on our values and the future." It was a smart strategy. Catalyst emerged from the crisis in a stronger position, and two years later, on the eve of its fiftieth anniversary, the board approved and funded Catalyst's first major gift campaign, raising millions of dollars to expand the company's global influence and its impact on the conversation about workplace equity.

Lang retired as president and CEO of Catalyst in 2014 and remains an honorary director. She is also an adviser to Trewstar, an executive search firm that places women on corporate boards, and is an investor in and adviser to the Women's Venture Capital Fund, which invests in gender-diverse leadership teams. Lang is particularly excited about how collective understanding of gender continues to evolve. "By questioning the nature of gender, we're questioning the foundation of gender stereotypes. Today we are learning that gender and race are social constructs, and this helps us define problems and opportunities differently." Yet even as Lang considers how much has changed in her lifetime, she recognizes that we are still grappling with fundamental inequalities. Progress is not inevitable, she points out. "It's harder to be an optimist these days," in light of backlash against advances in gender and racial justice. Nevertheless, Lang continues to see equality as a shared mission that we can all embrace. "Leaders speak out, set goals, act, take responsibility, and are accountable. Being a leader means being a change agent in times of challenge. We still have a lot of work ahead of us."

GENDER BALANCE SHEET

A Harvard Business School Case Study

In the introduction to this book, we referenced our involvement in the ongoing work to advance gender equity at our own institution, Harvard Business School (HBS). It's not lost on us that HBS figures, in many respects, as a bastion of male leadership.[1] Scores of the men, most of them white, who dominate the top ranks of business and other sectors are graduates of the school. The school has yet to be led by a female dean. Women students have not reached 50 percent of any MBA class. Only about a quarter of faculty members are women, and the school has tenured only two Black women in its history.[2] We would be remiss to write about the barriers that working women face without turning a clear eye to our own employer, which has enormous influence on business. What is the state of gender equity at the school today? How far have we come, and what work still remains unfinished?

Women began earning MBAs at HBS in the early 1960s. Obtaining a professional degree was one tool women were using to break into leadership at that time. Such credentialing provided a boost for what *Ms.* cofounder Letty Cottin Pogrebin called "the longest, most arduous journey" from "the cold steel typing table" of secretarial work to "the warm walnut desk" of the executive.[3] Yet obtaining an MBA at HBS could be its own grueling journey. Speaking at a 2014 alumnae event, Dean Nitin Nohria apologized for the mistreatment women had experienced at the school, acknowledging to a crowd of six hundred women that many had been "disrespected, left out, and unloved by the school." "The school owed you better," Nohria said, "and I promise it will be better."[4] To be sure, as the following pages will illustrate, HBS is a better place for women than it was fifty, twenty, or even ten years ago. Yet as Nohria's statement implies, we have room to improve, and the history and present state of gender at the school deserve a close look.

In some respects, the story of women at HBS presents a case study in organizational change—its possibilities, its limitations, and its uneven, partial nature. It's not the story of a leader who did away with inequities in one fell swoop. Nor is it a story of women's demands for better treatment being consistently met. It doesn't provide a neat, linear narrative of continuous improvement—there are breakthrough moments followed by periods of inertia, along with cycles of momentum and backlash. Across the last decade, we've seen significant progress but know that we must sustain it in the years to come. One example: In the early 2010s, women students became represented among Baker Scholars, the highest academic honor at the school, at a proportion commensurate with their representation in the MBA class. After years of a gender gap and efforts by women students to investigate its causes and spark conversation about it, this development was a sign that the school had become a place where women could reach their full potential. To be sure, as this epilogue will detail, the culture of the school has changed massively since women were first admitted. But in recent years the proportion of women among Baker Scholars dipped below representative levels.[5] Our ongoing focus and commitment will be critical to preventing gender gaps in achievement from reemerging.

The pages that follow will attempt to identify where we've made real progress on gender equity as well as expose where we've continued to fall short. Today, HBS educates students in the context of widespread awareness about multiple forms of inequality. Leaders and companies are expected to actively contribute to building a better world, and the continued predominance of white men in positions of power is being challenged with renewed force.[6] Women were first admitted to HBS in 1963, but the first Black woman, who became a co-founder of the African American Student Union, did not enter for another four years. Women of color have by and large been less visible in the discourse about gender at the school, and much of the history of progress toward gender equity has failed to account for the ways in which their experiences differ from those of white women. It is our hope that examining our past and current efforts to address gender inequality will enable the school to acknowledge its shortcomings and, as a result, redouble its commitment to becoming a place that enables everyone to thrive. At the same time, by unpacking what *has* worked, we aim to illuminate some of the key components of institutional change and remind readers that transformation is always possible.

Admitted—But Not Accepted

HBS faculty first began teaching women in the 1930s, moonlighting at Radcliffe College's certificate program in personnel administration. In 1959 HBS began admitting graduates of that program into the second year of the MBA, although they were still barred from applying to the full two-year program.[7] The late US Supreme Court justice Ruth Bader Ginsburg, who entered Harvard Law School in 1956, was among the last cohort of women to be formally excluded from applying directly to HBS. As she recounted in a 2015 *New York Times* interview, her decision to pursue a legal career was in part shaped by the fact that "the business school wasn't taking women. So that left law."[8] In 1962, the HBS faculty voted to directly admit women; eight women matriculated the following year. That first cohort was made up of women who, like the vast majority of their male peers, were white. The first

Black woman to directly enter the MBA, Lillian Lincoln Lambert, was admitted in 1967.

By the time it came up for a formal vote, the question of admitting women was uncontroversial, suggesting that the school was lagging, rather than leading, societal views about the place of women. As one faculty member who was at the 1962 meeting recalled, "There had been a lot of discussion about it, there was no question it was going to be enacted and . . . that meeting . . . was really kind of a light-hearted meeting. It was a foregone conclusion, and it was about time." Yet despite the ease with which the school went coed, women were treated differently from their male peers. Early applicants were considered in a separate pool, and women students initially lived on the Radcliffe College campus, ferried to and from HBS by taxi at the school's expense. Nor could they eat in the campus dining hall with the rest of their classmates.[9] Women students were well aware that they were anomalous, even deviant, and were accustomed to being asked to justify their presence on campus. One 1967 alumna developed a clever retort: "At first, I would give my earnest response about how I wanted to be a consultant," she recalled. "And after three or four times, I started saying, 'I'm here because I want to be the CFO of General Motors, and if you're nice to me I might get you a job.'" She was not alone in turning to humor as a way of acknowledging and even embracing the challenges of being a female MBA student. In 1969, the student newspaper *The Harbus* published "Female B-Schoolers Get Screw-tinized," in which the (female) author noted wryly that "one advantage of being a woman at Harvard Business School is that you are a scarce and therefore noticeable commodity (and I use that term advisedly)."[10]

Although female students found a hostile reception from a number of male classmates—and at least one professor barred women from enrolling in his popular course—attending HBS was nevertheless a pathway to opportunities that were generally unavailable to women. Upon graduating, Barbara Franklin, whose profile appears earlier in this book, was pleased to receive several job offers, noting that "we women were more concerned about [finding jobs], certainly more than the men were." One aspiring leader decided to pursue an MBA after realizing that the traditional career ladder was one she would have difficulty even stepping onto, much less climbing. Working at a large technology company and seeing that virtually all of its senior executives had come up through sales management, she asked her manager if she could go into sales. "He said the company had not had a woman in sales since World War II, and 'it will take an event of comparable significance before we'd ever consider it again,'" she recalled in an interview. It was at that point that she decided to apply to HBS, hoping that a Harvard degree would help future employers see beyond her sex.

In the early years after women's admittance, little else about the school seemed to change. The few dozen women who graduated in the 1960s sat in classrooms surrounded by men on a campus not designed to accommodate them. Jay Light, who earned an MBA and a doctorate at HBS before joining the faculty and later becoming dean of the school, described the environment that greeted his female peers at the time:

> I came in to HBS in 1966, and I believe there were seven women in the class of '67. It was a difficult, lonely, frustrating experience for them. I mean, you can imagine; these women were true pioneers. They didn't come here because it was a comfortable thing to do. They didn't come here because anyone expected them to come here, and in fact people didn't expect them to come here—neither their parents nor the faculty here nor anyone else expected them to do it. They did it because they really wanted to. And none of the place was set up in terms of physical infrastructure, in terms of social interactions, in terms of everything—nothing was set up to be hospitable to them.

By the decade's end, however, a shift was slowly beginning. As the national dialogue about women's roles in society ramped up, so too did the campus conversation. In 1969 dormitories for women opened, and a female student was named a Baker Scholar for the first time.[11] As women became more fully a part of the school, they began expecting more from it.

The number of female students was growing—fifty enrolled for the 1969–1970 academic year—yet the school's approach to their integration was more ad hoc and haphazard than deliberate and considered. Many women "did not feel that their viewpoints were pertinent or seriously considered," as several alumnae remembered in interviews. A 1976 alumna who spent two years working for a large multinational firm before coming to HBS recalled, "My experience in a factory in Texas still did not fully prepare me for HBS. The school was not very welcoming to women students. There was one ladies' room in Aldrich [the main classroom building]. They didn't know what to do with us; professors didn't know what to call us. It was a period of social upheaval, and people were trying to find their way."

Some male students did express derision and hostility toward their female classmates and indeed were disparaging of any students who did not fit the traditional white male mold. There were just fifty-eight Black students, of more than six hundred students, in the class of 1971.[12] One 1971 alumna recalled:

> At the beginning of the first year, there was a feeling on the part of some of the [white] men enrolled that the school had bent its standards to let underqualified African Americans and women in and that therefore, because of us, ten white guys per section didn't get in. It seemed that the white males resented the Blacks more than they resented the women in terms of chair space. But we were all sort of tokens, perceived that way.

And a 1972 alumna we interviewed was even less sanguine about how some of her classmates reacted to her presence:

> Male classmates would occasionally approach me with visible anger in the hallways and say, "What are you doing here? What right do you have to be here?" They would actually come up to

my face and say this. I would tell them, "I intend to use my MBA. I want to do exactly what you want to do with it." But that didn't stop it. They would say things like "Oh, aren't you just here to find a husband?"—not realizing I was already married—and "My best friend applied and didn't get in. Now you've taken his place."

Meanwhile, the faculty posture toward female students was driven more by individual instructors' dispositions than a clear institutional stance. Men remained the vast majority of faculty in the 1970s; 6 of 180 professors were women, and none of them were tenured. (From 1908 to the early 1960s, just 2 women held faculty appointments at HBS, Henrietta Larson and Elizabeth Abbott Burnham.[13]) While some professors actively encouraged more women to apply to HBS, others were visibly uncomfortable having women in their classrooms. One alumna described faculty attitudes as ranging from indifferent to marginalizing: "There were a few professors that didn't care very much about us women being there; they just cared that you were able to answer the questions and do the work. But there were others who never called on a woman unless it was a discussion of a woman's product—for example, something that he felt was domestic in nature."

And some students contended with overt bigotry in the classroom. Recounted one 1971 alumna, "We had professors who, in the middle of a class, would look at the women and the African Americans and say, 'Is this too difficult for you?'" Another remembered that "some [professors] were very discriminatory, would not call on the women and [would] dismiss you," and yet another said, "One of the professors made it very clear that he believed women did not belong in the classroom. Another actively discouraged women from taking his second-year elective course."

Starting a Movement

Women students became more and more dissatisfied with this status quo and began to speak out against it. A *Harbus* opinion piece by a first-year student named Ilene Lang, whose profile appears earlier in this book, called out the "incredulity," "condescension," and "derision" that women faced—from "jokes about women's work, women's liberation, and women's physical, mental, and emotional frailties" to "case writers' habit of referring to women workers as girls."[14] In early 1971, a group of women met to discuss establishing a women's student group. The club, then called Harvard Business Women, held its first official meeting in April of that year, and today it remains one of the largest and most active student organizations at the school. Two founding leaders, Marnie Tattersall and Betty Eveillard, described the new group to the *Harbus* as a "clearinghouse" for women students' needs and interests, with the aim of fostering community among women students and tackling what they diplomatically termed "sources of obstruction" to women's "optimal educational experience."[15] Early on, members stressed that the organization was pragmatic in nature, "not a women's lib group or even a very radical women's group." They were keenly aware that, as the article put it, "many of the men students turn up their nose at the thought of a 'women's group.'"[16]

Despite strategically downplaying the club's connection to the feminist movement, its leaders recognized that supporting women students' success would nevertheless mean confronting the ways in which they remained marginalized. Though the HBS administration was not opposed to the formation of the group, which soon became known as the Women's Student Association (WSA), HBS was still far from prioritizing women's needs. Even something as fundamental as providing facilities for women in Aldrich Hall, where virtually all classes were held, remained a sticking point more than a decade after women were admitted. Leslie Levy, the 1975–1976 WSA president, recalled how this issue was more significant than it might seem on the surface: "If women wanted to go to the bathroom, they had to go to the basement. Finally, we got the administration to designate one formerly men's bathroom on every other floor. There was a lot of joking, because they didn't take out the urinals." Susan Posner, 1977–1978 president, likewise explained that the bathrooms were seen as a microcosm of the larger problem: "We mentioned the fact that it wasn't quite sending out the right message to women as being appreciated and wanted."

Indeed, more than a decade after HBS became coed, women students questioned how truly welcome they were not only in light of campus infrastructure but also given how few women were in positions of authority at the school. "I can specifically remember two female professors," one alumna recalled. "But other than that, we did not see any other women in any kind of leadership positions, nor in our cases." (Case studies made up the majority of the school's curriculum, as they still do today.) The fledgling WSA provided a mechanism for women to voice such concerns and press the school to adopt a more gender-inclusive culture. One of the WSA's first goals toward that end was to recruit female applicants to the school; Eveillard, Tattersall, and their classmates accounted for less than 5 percent of the MBA class of 1972.

The WSA approached the school administration with proposals for attracting women applicants but didn't receive much support, so the club mounted its own initiatives to make HBS more visible to young women. Beverly Brandt, also a member of the class of 1972, helped organize these efforts:

> We wanted to increase the number of qualified women who would consider HBS as a graduate school choice. We had no money for advertising, of course, but we approached some of the top women in the world, the tops in their field, and invited them to speak on campus. We spread the word to all local colleges with female students, encouraging them to attend, see that we were there, and learn that they were welcome to apply.

Bringing high-profile female leaders to campus also gave the women already there a sense of their own potential at a time when the vast majority of positions to which MBAs might aspire were held by men.

"One of the things I think so many of us struggled with was not really having female role models," said Tattersall in an interview. The WSA hosted a talk by Gloria Steinem in 1971, and Muriel Siebert, the first woman to sit on the New York Stock Exchange, spoke in 1972 at Women in Management Day.[17] The following year the WSA hosted its first Career Day, featuring alumnae leaders from multiple industries.

The WSA also turned attention to the portrayal—or lack thereof—of women in the curriculum. In 1972, the club presented to school researchers "Guidelines for Avoiding Discrimination against Women in Written Materials."[18] This effort was ongoing in 1975, when the WSA asked companies as well as alumni to send in case ideas featuring women. The club also began collecting examples of sexist and discriminatory language in cases.[19] By 1980, the WSA had launched its formal Case Editing Committee focused on "the equal treatment of the sexes in HBS cases."[20] That year John McArthur was named dean of the school, and the administration began to more actively support the WSA. Ginger Graham, 1985–1986 WSA president, explained how a partnership began to blossom:

> There were almost no women case protagonists, and often the women who did appear in cases were portrayed as secretaries, wives, or assistants. There might be a woman mentioned at the start of a case—"As Jim was packing to leave for his trip, his wife was folding his shirts, watching him ponder his big trip," something like that. The WSA worked with the administration to initiate a project to modernize some of the language and begin to address the lack of women protagonists. The school had to be committed to this effort, as each of the changes in case material had to be approved, authors had to be contacted, revisions suggested and approved and materials reissued; it was not a trivial commitment for the school itself. The process engaged all the students, and encouraged them to be editors of the case material in a way that led to more representative and appropriate language around

gender and other biases. Separate initiatives were launched to identify women in business who could be protagonists, and new case material was created. We had the commitment of Dean McArthur and Professor Regina Herzlinger, the WSA faculty sponsor, and support from the school for the resources to implement the changes. I think it resulted in higher-quality case materials, and it continued the march to improve the context in which women students read about other women leaders, discuss women in leadership positions, and see themselves as future leaders.

As the curriculum slowly began to evolve, so too did the gender composition of the faculty. Professor Herzlinger, whose profile appears after this epilogue, became the first woman to earn tenure at Harvard Business School in 1980, although this milestone did not signal an immediate shift to a more gender-diverse era for the school's faculty. Even as the number of female professors gradually increased, gender inequities were a source of contention. A female professor of marketing brought suit against HBS, alleging that gender discrimination had contributed to her being denied tenure in 1983.[21] The case polarized the campus, as a student at the time recalled: "Lines were drawn. You were either for or against; there was no middle ground."

As the school neared the twenty-year anniversary of women's admittance change was afoot, but the campus remained dominated by white, heterosexual, US-born men. Acknowledging this fact was not a part of campus culture, and students who didn't fit the mold often felt the need to minimize their differences from the norm. A 1982 alumna recalled, "There were five gay and lesbian students in our section, including me, and none of us were out because it was either not comfortable or not safe to be out. I heard lots of antiwomen rhetoric and homophobic comments. That was a very negative experience." Another alumna noted that the default sense of who HBS students were remained male: "My spouse was invited to the garden club. . . . They just sent out the mass mailing to all the spouses. He wasn't offended, but it was awkward. We still had urinals in the women's restrooms almost twenty years after women had been admitted. So, it was pretty clear that Harvard hadn't quite embraced women at that time."

Confronting a Culture

Despite some progress, it was clear that simply opening the doors of HBS to women as well as other marginalized and underrepresented people wasn't enough to truly diversify the school. A more concerted effort was needed if the student body was to evolve past its homogenous roots. In the late 1960s the African American Student Union had begun working with administrators to recruit more Black students, and the WSA followed suit. By 1982, the WSA and the admissions office had jointly developed a system through which alumnae could recommend female applicants.[22] Collaboration on recruiting women ramped up as the decade went on, as 1988–1989 WSA president Carol Schwartz explained: "The school was trying to figure out ways to reach out and identify women from nontraditional backgrounds and encourage them to come to HBS. During my term as president, there were a number of meetings where this was discussed." In 1988, the Committee to Increase the Number of Women at HBS was formed to investigate why only a quarter of the applicant pool was female, especially considering that women made up 40 to 50 percent of applicants to most law schools at the time. "I think [the administration was] conscious of the numbers," 1989–1990 WSA president Julia Sass Rubin said. "They were genuinely trying, but they were fighting some broader societal trends. And we helped them think this stuff through. We gave them a way to focus on the issue." The WSA also expanded its own independent programming for prospective women, actively recruiting women by hosting Admitted Student Days, mailing WSA brochures with personal notes, and running phone-a-thons for members to call admitted women and encourage them to enroll.[23]

Meanwhile, the WSA maintained its advocacy for the women already on campus. Although it was now far less common to have their presence openly questioned by fellow students, women were not always receiving the full benefit of the MBA curriculum. In 1985 the WSA, drawing on interviews and surveys as well as admissions data, reported that first-year women felt "not very comfortable in class" and were less satisfied than their male peers with how often they were able to participate in case discussions. These findings were particularly worrisome given that a student's class participation accounted for half of his or her grade. And indeed, the WSA's research revealed that women tended to outscore men on blind-graded exams yet were underrepresented in honors, making it clear that participation scores were holding down women's marks.[24] Karen Dawes, 1980–1981 WSA president, explained how the dearth of women made it challenging to speak in class: "You were in a room with eighty people, and maybe ten were women. The first day you walk in, and you realize that there are not many other people who look like you. From my discussions with women, and in my experience, it's a little tougher to jump in and be part of the discussion."

In response, women faculty, staff, and students created programs to discuss these challenges and remind women students that they indeed belonged at the school. Professor Lynda Applegate, who joined the faculty in 1986, recalled an effort to bring women together, affirm their place in the classroom, and galvanize them to continue pushing the school toward greater inclusion:

> HBS students take all their first-year courses together in "sections" of several dozen students. When I first began teaching at the school, one of the first things I noticed was that the women students were very focused on how to fit in within these groups; there were only a few women in each section. I worked with other female faculty and staff to launch something we called the "Women Students' Welcome," where all of the women on the faculty and MBA staff, along with second-year women students, welcomed the incoming women. We held it in the campus auditorium at the start of the academic year, and we opened the session

by asking the students to look at the accomplished women all around them in the room. We then asked them to compare how this experience felt with what they experienced in the classroom. It led to a fantastic discussion, and we always closed by encouraging them to join the WSA and to continue to work together to increase the power of women at HBS.

Sometimes, women's experience of marginalization went beyond simply being in the numerical minority. As Robin Hacke, 1983–1984 WSA president, described:

> I did not plan to get involved [with the WSA]. But something happened in my section: Midway through the year, one of the guys thought it would be really entertaining to take all of the students' seat cards and put all the women on one side of the room on a particular day. Talking about it now, with the distance of all these years, it seems ridiculous that anybody would care where they sat. But it was one of those hot buttons that really hit me. The idea that all the women would be shunted off to the side got me thinking about the WSA as an organization of interest to me. And we were in the years where it was common, on people's birthdays, to have belly dancers and strippers come into class. That kind of sealed the deal for me. I just thought, this is not a very congenial environment for women. At the time I think there were nineteen women in my section out of ninety-one people. So that prompted me to get involved.

The kinds of incidents that galvanized Hacke continued well into the next decade, coming to a head in the spring of 1998 when six male students were disciplined for sexual harassment, including passing explicit notes to female classmates and class visitors. The incidents received considerable coverage in the press; first publicly revealed by *Inc.* magazine, they were also reported on by the Associated Press, the *Boston Globe*, the *New York Times*, and the *Wall Street Journal*. The media coverage came at the end of a long period of struggle within the school, beginning in late 1996 when students who had experienced harassment met with administrators. No formal action was taken in response to these initial meetings, although in the spring of 1997 several faculty and administrators—including the chair of the MBA program and the director of student standards—wrote to students about harassment, pressing them to "think about these issues" and "help in identifying inappropriate behaviors."[25] The WSA was unsatisfied with the muted response: "It felt like we were being placated," one member recalled.

The club didn't accept the school's initial reluctance to do more than provide a general admonishment. Although administrators first claimed that there was little they could do to address specific incidents unless a student initiated a formal complaint, victims feared that coming forward with such complaints would harm their future career opportunities and professional networks, as the student newspaper noted at the time.[26] To spur more action from the school, WSA members began tracking communications between students and administrators, investigating relevant laws and regulations, and soliciting support from individual faculty members whom they thought would be sympathetic. As one alumna explained, "In some ways we were project managers, trying to collect [information], to see whom we could find that would be an influence. [It was] persistence. Collecting the notes, collecting the stories, refusing to just let it disappear."

Soliciting support from faculty proved crucial. "We booked appointments, and we tried to figure out who could be an ally and who might be concerned about these issues. And we tried to be strategic about it, to think about who had influence, who might be open to it, and finally we found enough [faculty] that could be helpful," recalled another alumna. Ultimately, around the time the scandal became public, another memo to students acknowledged the pattern of incidents, and six students were formally sanctioned.[27] The process had been flawed and halting but ultimately compelled the HBS community to acknowledge and address the harassment. "[Without the WSA], it would have just languished," one alumna argued. The incident also prompted the school to articulate and disseminate its set of

"Community Values," which continues to be displayed in classrooms and other locations on campus today.

Embracing Change?

By the early twenty-first century campus dynamics had evolved considerably, not least because of the reckoning occasioned by the harassment scandal. And HBS had begun to look very different. Classrooms once crowded with white men in ties and with crewcuts were now filled with a more diverse set of students; by 2005, women made up 35 percent of the MBA class, and over 30 percent of students came from outside the United States.[28] Even so, a sense of true belonging could still be elusive for female students. A 2006 alumna found the school inclusive and respectful about some kinds of cultural difference but still somewhat retrograde when it came to gender dynamics: "I think, because it's such a global school, that people are used to others being different. But there's still a sense that women aren't supposed to be in certain roles or that you can treat women a certain way. Tone is huge." Nitin Nohria, who taught a required organizational behavior course in the early 2000s, observed such attitudes whenever his students discussed case studies that featured female leaders:

> When there were women protagonists in a case, people had questions about how they managed work/family balance. Men had families too, but we didn't seem to ask those questions about men. So, if the women in the classroom experienced the conversations around women protagonists as always having these gendered dimensions, then it probably made it harder to imagine further opportunities that felt equal relative to the men.

As gender disparities moved ever higher on the agenda of school leadership, the WSA pressed for more dialogue. In 2009, the club once again analyzed data on grades and found that female students were still underrepresented in the ranks of honors recipients as well as overrepresented among students who failed their first year.[29] Mary Ellen Hammond, 2008–2009 WSA president, was startled to see the disparity:

> First-year honors got released, and I just looked at the list. I remember putting the numbers together and sending it to my copresident, Anne Himpens, with a note saying "Nearly 40 percent of the class, and well below 10 percent of those receiving honors?" And Anne did some Google searching, and she came up with a list from a few years earlier; she worked the numbers, which showed a similar result. My response was, I think we've got something we should talk about.

The following year, a team of women students worked with a faculty adviser, Professor Kathleen McGinn, to examine the underlying causes of the gaps. Their findings pointed to a range of likely factors, including unconscious biases among instructors and a shortage of female role models in the form of both faculty and case protagonists. Subtle biases about female leaders also pervaded the classroom. Nohria had observed a pattern in his own classes, wherein "for all of our women case protagonists, somehow the discussion almost inevitably raised questions such as 'Did these women succeed because they were lucky? Or did they succeed because they were competent?' We didn't seem to ask the same questions about the men."

Speaking up in class was still fraught, with women often feeling more constrained in voicing their perspectives. As a *Harbus* article on the results of the student study noted, "many women admit to self-editing in the classroom to manage their out-of-classroom image."[30] As the school neared its sixth decade as a coed institution, many wondered—in the pages of the *Harbus*, in club meetings, and in conversations with one another—whether an MBA held as much value for women as men. "If HBS points to the fact that some number of CEOs in *Fortune* 500 companies are HBS alums and is willing to take credit for that, then the school should also factor in the proportion of women—or lack thereof—[in leadership] and take some responsibility for that," said a 2011 alumna. "I do think the learning environment is a factor."

Nohria became dean of the school in 2010 and believed he had a clear mandate to address gender differences in academic achievement. "While admissions and enrollment statistics revealed [that] we were accepting and enrolling male and female students with similar scores, experiences, achievements, and aptitudes," he explained, "we were not seeing parity in terms of performance once they were on campus." The WSA's advocacy and investigation had brought the issue to the fore, making it hard for both students and faculty to ignore. Women's underrepresentation in honors began to be acknowledged and discussed in official faculty meetings as well as informally around the campus. In 2013 the school commemorated the fiftieth anniversary of women's admission, further spotlighting lingering gender disparities. For Nohria, the year offered an occasion to underscore the centrality of gender equity to his role as dean. At the official anniversary celebration in the spring of 2013, he declared to a crowd of more than eight hundred alumni that "if feminism means to be deeply committed to equality of men and women, then I am a feminist."[31]

Writing Different Stories

A number of programs to address gender gaps were implemented in the early 2010s. There were assessments of calling patterns to look at whether women had equal opportunities to speak in class, and classroom "scribes" who monitored student contributions provided hard data that faculty could rely on when evaluating participation, which made up a third to half of a student's course grade. Workshops on effective participation were offered to all students, in line with the idea that women might undercontribute relative to their knowledge and expertise. (Indeed, research confirms that formal encouragements for women to contribute their ideas, especially in stereotypically masculine areas such as finance, can help ensure that female students with relevant expertise speak up.)[32] Plus, a new required course that didn't rely on the traditional case method but instead employed experiential, small group–based learning techniques was adopted.

The school also made efforts to cultivate new norms outside the classroom, such as switching from self-selected study groups to assigned clusters that put students together with a diverse range of classmates. There was resistance and backlash—some students considered the changes, according to a 2013 *New York Times* article, "intrusive social engineering." Yet even so, student satisfaction ratings went up, and a satisfaction gap between men and women closed.[33]

The individual impact of each of these various interventions is hard to fully tease out, but they were part and parcel of changing culture. Grade gaps in many required courses and in honors recipients had closed just prior to the implementation of many interventions, suggesting that heightened dialogue had sparked a broad commitment to tackling the problem. The tools and innovations that the school embraced likely then strengthened and legitimized this shared desire to close the gaps and helped institutionalize our initial burst of progress. The formal measures also reflect a prioritization of the issue that is essential to fostering change. Time will tell if HBS has dedicated adequate resources and attention to gender equity over the long-term, but these initial formalized efforts reinforced a sense of urgency and import that had bubbled up.

Some disparities have lingered. Narrowed gaps in satisfaction may have been driven by white women's experiences, thus obscuring ways in which women of color, who are in the numerical minority, weren't reaping the benefits of some of these changes. Nonetheless, women students are no longer seen as anomalous, and their male classmates are certainly not questioning their very presence on campus. In 2016, LaToya Marc and Libby Leffler became the first all-female ticket to be elected copresidents of the student body. And in 2019, eight out of ten section presidents were women, the highest-ever proportion.[34] (Each

MBA class consists of ten sections of about ninety students who take their first year of courses together and elect classmates to serve as community leaders.)

Along with many colleagues, we ourselves have tried to tackle what we believe continues to be a root cause of lingering gender inequity: an overrepresentation of white male leaders in the curriculum. At HBS, cases make up the overwhelming majority of assigned readings and form the basis for most class sessions, particularly in the first year of the MBA when all students take a standard set of courses. In 2015, we did a thorough analysis of progress toward diversity in cases over the preceding six years. There had been an increase in cases published with female protagonists over that time period, bringing the total proportion close to 25 percent. We also looked at what was happening across required and elective courses as well as in HBS's executive education programs. The required curriculum had the greatest representation of female protagonists, and current data show that this proportion has increased over time, although such cases remain in the minority at 23 percent (vs. 67 percent with a male protagonist and 11 percent without an identifiable protagonist).[35] While we don't have current comparative data for the elective curriculum or executive education, new offerings in both programs feature courses with a focus on women leaders—the elective "How Star Women Succeed" discussed below and the Women on Boards executive education program, which thus far has educated more than four hundred women and seen increased demand year over year. (For more about Women on Boards, see Chapter 3.)

Because the case method is the core of students' academic experience, a lack of female protagonists can mean that leadership itself seems to skew male, as one recent alumna told us: "In our leadership class, out of maybe twenty-five protagonists, maybe three were women. We read about many great leaders, but it was hard to personally see myself in their shoes." One faculty member we interviewed agreed that our images of leadership remain too limited. "I think we all—students, faculty, everybody—need to be exposed to a range of types of people that are in leadership positions," she noted. "Partly it's role modeling—to have students in the class say, 'Oh I could see myself doing that.'" Indeed, a long line of social science research has found that female students' self-perception and performance are influenced by the presence or absence of women role models. For instance, studies looking at the effects of reading about or seeing portraits of successful women found that these activities boosted female students' belief in their own competence and their public speaking ability.[36]

Male leaders dominate business education, even beyond the curriculum at our own institution. An analysis of data from the Case Centre, a global clearinghouse, found that just 11 percent of bestselling and award-winning cases published between 2009 and 2015 included a female protagonist.[37] Another study, of cases published by Ivey, the second-largest (after HBS) case publisher in the world, found that only 19 percent of cases published in a one-year period featured female protagonists. Even when they appear, women leaders can be marginalized. The same study found that female protagonists were minimized relative to other characters in their cases and that female-protagonist cases included fewer direct quotes from the protagonists, compared to those cases featuring male leaders.[38] Moreover, students may bring biases, often unconscious, into their reading. We spoke to a dozen faculty members about gender in the classroom, and we analyzed student evaluations for one required MBA course. In that course, cases with female protagonists received lower ratings from male (though not from female) students, holding other factors, such as the faculty member teaching the case, constant. We don't have enough data to understand what drives these lower ratings, but they may reflect subtle biases about gender and leadership. Anecdotally, we heard that cases about highly accomplished women sometimes elicit skepticism. One instructor who taught a case about a Black female executive explained: "The problem with having it be a case about great success is that students still dismiss the female protagonist, because then 'it's all PR.'" Such a comment can be a learning opportunity—if the instructor chooses to make it one. One faculty member told us how he tried to turn such assumptions into questions that encourage students to reflect on why they've doubted a female leader. "When it comes up in class that Fred is brilliant but Jane is lucky, that's a real teaching opportunity," he explained. "I can point out, hey, in the last class we did with Fred as a protagonist, he was great, brilliant, blah blah blah. Why do you think that Jane or Ingrid or Christine is lucky?"

We thought that one way to counter the persistent sense that women leaders are anomalous would be to flip the script, so to speak, and offer a course in which they were the rule rather than the exception. The course we developed, "How Star Women Succeed," is aimed partly at equipping students with the skills necessary to navigate workplace challenges but also seeks to inform them about how they can enable women on their own future teams to succeed. Through exploring the leadership experiences of women in a range of fields, including finance, law, telecommunications, and consulting, the course offers a different experience to students who are accustomed to a male-dominated curriculum and, in many cases, a male-dominated workplace prior to business school. As one 2013 alumna who took the course explained:

> I enrolled because there is a dearth of female protagonists in the cases we study in the required and elective curricula at HBS. I was intrigued to take a class where the majority of the case protagonists were female and to learn what, if anything, is different about women's leadership style and how women navigate some of the complexities and challenges that may be specific to gender. That was compelling to me, especially as I looked at graduating in the near future and reentering the workforce with fewer women at management levels. I know as I continue to move forward, that will increasingly be the case. It was for me a way to gather war stories, examples, and role models that I could draw on as I progressed in my own career.

In interviews we conducted with other former students of the course, we found that the impact of studying the trajectories of female leaders—and often hearing from them directly as class speakers—improved their ability to navigate career decisions and obstacles. As one interviewee explained, "There were a lot of things that other women had done that made me aware of things that I could change about my own actions or behavior." And similarly, another said, "I think it better equipped me just in the anecdotes and stories and lessons learned—if I encounter similar situations, I can recall some of the lessons and the cases and decide what to do about my situation or avoid certain situations altogether." Beyond these practical tactics, we also heard that the course expanded students' aspirations, as one interviewee described: "The course inspired me to think really, really big and to think much more strategically and spend a lot of time on active career planning." Another alumna echoed, "It's helped me challenge myself to think, am I doing what I really want to be doing? Why am in the job I'm in? What am I gaining? What's the long-term goal?"

Just as importantly, the course also gave students tools with which to advocate for gender inclusion, as recounted by several former students. While most students who took the course were women, men also enrolled. One male student found himself becoming more aware of the gender biases all around him:

> There are things I learned from [the course] that I use all the time in the workplace. I find myself calling out behaviors. And it spurred a whole bunch of conversations with the [2016] election. One of the other men who took the class and I would text, effectively daily, with the hashtag #HSWS [How Start Women Succeed], with regard to anything that Hillary did, because there was this double standard. I was very attuned to that.

Another alumnus pushed for changes to his firm's hiring approach after he returned to his finance career postgraduation:

> It makes it much easier to speak up once you feel like you have some subject-matter knowledge. Just recently our team was reviewing a list of potential first-round interviews, and I and a

colleague went to our HR team and said, "There's one female on a list of fifty interviews. You've got to be kidding me; what are we doing?" They unfortunately gave us blank stares and blamed the "pipeline," so the two of us took it upon ourselves to fix the problem short-term and push for a more recurring solution in the future.

The male students who enrolled in a course on advancing women's leadership were, admittedly, a small and self-selected group. But they aren't the only men on campus who joined the conversation about gender equity. Not all male students were supportive of the growing focus on gender in the early 2010s. Alexandra Daum, copresident of the WSA in 2013–2014, recalled that some felt that "women were getting too much attention and that is wasn't actually helpful for them or the school." Yet at the same time, she and the other WSA leaders were hearing from men who wanted to contribute but didn't know how or even if they should. For decades, gender at the school had been purely a "women's issue"; combating gender inequality had been a part of campus life but one that men had little engagement with. That began to change on the heels of the fiftieth anniversary of women's admission, as more and more men decided to join in.

A New Chapter, an Uncertain Unending

In response to both criticism and enthusiasm from their male classmates, the WSA launched a new program called Manbassasdors in 2013. Alumna Tara Hagan helped found the group as the WSA's vice president of male involvement. She wanted men on campus to know "[they] are invited into the conversation." As she explained in an interview, "Some men haven't talked much about gender equality, and it's hard to go from 'I've never talked about it' to 'I can talk about it eloquently and say all the right things.' You're still trying to figure it out. Manbassadors delivers the conversation but also tries to lower the bar for jumping in." Two hundred men (over 30 percent of male MBA students) joined the inaugural Manbassadors cohort. Hagan saw a key aim of the program as "chang[ing] how women feel in the classroom, knowing that there are men advocating for gender issues. Part of it is to create a social movement, changing the dynamic." Likewise, Daum felt that Manbassadors could create a culture change: "Just by signing up they're adding fuel to the fire, saying I care about this, I'm on board." The program also meant men had a way, as 2014 alumnus and Manbassador cofounder David Wolfish put it, "to engage with the WSA in a clear, open way" and see that issues affecting women matter to everyone. Wolfish's classmate Santiago Ocejo described the program as fostering a more sophisticated discussion: "I don't see the Manbassadors as 'supporting' women in a simplistic way but as a venue for men to get involved in these issues. Men should see this as an important part of their training and education."

The Manbassador program became a permanent arm of the WSA and over time an increasingly visible group—especially when the national dialogue about workplace gender discrimination grew louder in the late 2010s. As Matt Piltch, an active member of Manbassadors from 2017 to 2019 and a member of the WSA board for the 2018–2019 year, pointed out, "#MeToo made the world, including HBS, a lot more aware of the systemic nature of these issues." Piltch's classmate Kyle Emory led the Manbassadors in a campaign to expand participation: "We made a really big push to involve and engage the community. And we changed the Manbassadors pledge to be more focused on action, not just talking about gender equity," explained Emory. The number of male students affiliating themselves with the group more than doubled, to 480 (nearly 90 percent of the men in the class of 2019). Now, it was no longer only women students who challenged school administrators to address issues of sexism. Piltch recalled that "we didn't receive any comment [about #MeToo] from the administration until December of 2017, and I was surprised and frankly found that to be problematic. So, I started working within the Manbassador cohort on a memo about what HBS could do to address diversity and inclusion broadly, but specifically issues around sexual violence and gender inequity." Piltch also worked with WSA copresidents Erica Santoni and Alexis Wolfer on a series of proposals for further curricular changes, including a call for greater diversity of case protagonists, coaching for faculty, and integration of implicit bias and other kinds of diversity trainings into the student experience. By insisting that attention to gender as well other axes of inequality should be part of management education, allied male and female students hoped to impact not only the school but also business at large.

MBA students are on campus for just two years, but their influence on companies, industries, and various communities might last for decades. As Emory explained, changing the world also means changing students' mindsets: "We're trying to grow, and it's an uncomfortable space to be operating in. How do we improve as men, as allies, in taking these incremental steps?" Despite the profound changes in business and society since the 1960s, many of today's student leaders see a long way to go, and the numbers bear out their view. Women are still outnumbered by male classmates, making up 43 percent of the HBS class of 2021. Women's lower representation at HBS and in MBA programs more generally is out of sync with broader trends in education. In 2018 women earned 38 percent of MBAs, and a 2017 study found that the proportion of women applying to MBA programs has remained virtually unchanged since 2012.[39] Yet by 2016, women made up a slight majority of medical students in the United States, and in 2017 female law students surpassed the 50 percent mark at US law schools.[40]

Moreover, despite the changed nature of the MBA experience today as compared to fifty, thirty, or even twenty years ago, women graduates' career prospects still lag men's. Even among this elite population, the value proposition of an MBA has yet to equalize. A longitudinal alumni study we're involved with has found that women graduates are significantly less likely than men to be in supervisory roles, have profit-and-loss responsibility, and be in top management positions. They are also less satisfied with how their careers play out: Women report lower satisfaction then men on multiple fronts, including opportunities for advancement, professional accomplishments, and opportunities for meaningful work.[41] Related research comparing Black with white alumni has found some of the same disparities, with more white alumni in supervisory and leadership positions and the largest differences existing between Black women and white men. Black alumni also reported lower career satisfaction than their white counterparts.[42]

These findings accord with other research, including a global study of four thousand MBAs from multiple institutions whose authors found that women experienced slower career advancement and evinced less career satisfaction than their male counterparts and that male grads were twice as likely to be CEOs or senior executives.[43] Likewise, a study of University of Chicago MBAs from the classes of 1990 through 2006 found that women's postgraduation starting salaries were on average $15,000 less than the salaries of their male counterparts, and this pay disparity only widened over the years.[44] A recent survey by the *Financial Times* of graduates from the paper's ranked business schools found that three years postgraduation, men were making more than their female peers in every sector including those that employ more women, such as health care and education.[45]

This book has focused on the change still needed in organizations and industries to shift these trends, but it's clear to us that educational institutions such as our own have a role to play in mitigating workplace inequalities. The stated mission of HBS is to educate leaders who make a difference in the world. Business leadership lacks diversity of all kinds, thereby constraining, we would argue, the potential for its positive impact on the world. Our Black women graduates are systematically less likely than their peers—Black and white men as well as white women—to see someone who looks like them in senior management and are most likely to say that their race and gender created career obstacles.[46] The world is certainly not reaping the full benefit of their talents. Moreover, HBS doesn't always deliver a truly equal educational experience, even today. In the summer of 2020, rising second-year student Chichi Anyoku spoke at a school-wide discussion on race and racism held in the wake of the murders of Black citizens across the United States by police and vigilantes. Anyoku recounted racist incidents she both witnessed and was victimized by in and outside the classroom.[47] It was a sobering reminder that, as an institution, we haven't dismantled the barriers, both cultural and structural, that diminish the experience of being a student at HBS.

Yet the school has been profoundly transformed by the women, including women of color, who have made their way here. The seeds of this book were planted nearly a decade ago, when HBS decided to take a look at the school's history on the occasion of the fiftieth anniversary of women's admittance. As we, along with numerous colleagues, researched the experiences of women on campus across the years, it became clear that the school, for all its continued limitations, is as welcoming to women as it is today in large measure because women insisted that it truly include them. Even when women were a tiny fraction of the MBA class, they claimed their place in the classroom and asked a powerful institution to make room for their needs and ambitions. In this epilogue we've seen how the WSA played a pivotal role in illuminating what was missing at HBS. Women students brought female leaders to campus when almost no women faculty stood at the front of the classroom, and they called out biases in the course materials they were supposed to learn from. They also asked questions: Why were so few women applying to HBS two decades after the school opened its doors to them? Why couldn't students report sexual harassment anonymously? Why were there so few women leaders featured in the curriculum? Why didn't women achieve academic honors at the same rate as male classmates?

Putting such issues on the table opened up space for the school to address them and to make real progress on the underlying problems the questions revealed. Not unlike the employee resource groups at many companies, the WSA has been a venue for students who share an important identity to give voice and visibility to challenges they face. All too often, such groups are not leveraged effectively. Instead of being seen as a resource for diagnosing inequities and charting a path toward organizational change, they become a way to ventilate concerns about inequality in hopes that air time alone will satisfy concerned employees. Or they help to attract candidates who see the group as a sign of commitment to diversity and equity yet are not actually empowered to take action or influence decisions. This lip-service approach is a missed opportunity of immense proportions. At HBS, the WSA and other student clubs advocating for underrepresented communities have helped administrators understand what drives disparities, piloted programs to address them, and made many inequities discussable. In response, school leaders have leaned in at key moments, using their power to make institutional change. As this epilogue makes clear, the journey toward true equity and inclusion is a marathon, not a sprint. HBS is still in the race, and we hope that our story inspires other educators, as well as the organizations that employ our graduates, to keep running too.

A PIONEER'S PATH

Professor Regina E. Herzlinger

Growing up in a tight-knit Orthodox Jewish community in 1950s Brooklyn, Regina Herzlinger was determined to have a career. "I was always a great reader and very curious—I read an entire children's encyclopedia by the age of five—but I was also interested in being financially secure," she explains. "My family were Holocaust victims who had lost everything—family and resources—and I wanted to become financially secure in a way that couldn't be taken away from me, and to be a professional." To further this goal, she took the unusual step of leaving the community to enter MIT, studying economics, in the early 1960s. After graduating, she had to forge a path that actualized her capabilities and ambitions at a time when virtually no role models for working women existed. Although her choices were limited, Herzlinger did find a foothold in management:

Finance, my first choice of occupation, is still today an industry with a notable shortage of women, and this was also true in the mid-1960s. I would have wanted to go work for an investment bank, but I had zero chance of being employed. So, I went to work for a consulting firm, and I had a staff of forty by the time I was twenty-six years old. I was very successful, but I wanted to have children, and as a consultant I was constantly on a plane and rarely saw my husband. [Herzlinger had married an MIT classmate in 1966.] So, I thought, well, what do I like to do? I really liked the research and interaction of consulting. And I thought about how I could replicate that experience without being on a plane all my life.

Harvard Business School (HBS) seemed like an ideal place to fulfill her goals, and Herzlinger applied. "It was the only place I applied, not only to get a doctorate but also to join the faculty," she recalls. "That was a 'denial' kind of activity—there were no women on the faculty; there were hardly any women students. But because I am who I am, I see my path and I'm not going to be easily deterred."

Herzlinger's determination proved fruitful: She was admitted to HBS's doctoral program, studying financial control, where she became interested in nonprofit management. Her doctoral thesis on measuring productivity at a local medical center piqued her interest in the health care sector, and she built a research and teaching agenda on these interests, despite there being virtually no precedent at the school for the kind of scholarship she pursued. "When I was tenured, people said, she's okay but she has these strange interests. She is interested in nonprofits and health care, and those are verticals that do not fit at HBS. As usual, I paid no attention." In the early 1980s, Herzlinger became the first woman to advance to tenure at HBS and is today a renowned scholar of the health care industry—a topic no longer seen as strange by her colleagues and indeed studied by many others.[48] By 2020, she had published more than fifty field-based teaching cases, numerous *New York Times* and *Wall Street Journal* editorials as well as six books. She was also at work on a new book and teaching materials about health care innovation.

Yet, for a time it was uncertain that Herzlinger would even be able to have an academic career at HBS. Although asked to join the faculty as an assistant professor upon completing her doctorate in 1971, she was initially told by the dean that as a woman, she would not be permitted to teach MBA students. Realizing that this arrangement would seriously hinder her career, she decided to leave. "This is a teaching school," she recalls thinking. "So [without teaching] I'm not going to have a career here. I didn't leave angry; I just thought, this is not the right time for me to be here." She went to work for the governor of Massachusetts, but before long she received an invitation to return—this time with the full status of teaching faculty: "The dean called me and said, we've changed our minds. You can come back, and you can teach. And I came back. That was what I wanted." Herzlinger would later become one of the first two faculty members voted 'best instructor' by students.

Herzlinger was not inhibited by her unusual status as a woman teaching at an institution with few female students, let alone faculty. While she was certainly a pioneer, she was driven less by the desire to attain a precedent-defying position than by an interest in using HBS as a platform to address what she saw as urgent questions:

Women of my age were generally the first to do what they did professionally, but rather than being "the first," I was more motivated by the Hebrew phrase *tikkun olam*. It means you want to fix the world. But I was aware of and tried to be helpful to my female colleagues. For example, amid widespread debate about the "glass ceiling" in the 1990s, MBA applications from women declined. I was worried that women were needlessly depriving themselves of a wonderful career, and I wrote a *Wall Street Journal* editorial that argued that the problem of a shortage of women CEOs was caused as much by a shortage of viable candidates at the time as by sexism. I predicted there would be more than twenty women CEOs of public firms in the twenty-first century as the pipeline of women with such interests and skills grew. I believe that this was helpful in reversing a worrisome downward trend among women in our applicant pool.

Over the years, Herzlinger continued to explore new professional territories even after breaking through one set of barriers. In the 1980s she launched a medical device company with her husband, a PhD physicist, which, as she explains, "wasn't that much different from coming to HBS when I did. We were just going to do it, and we did it." At the same time, the Herzlingers were also raising two children and found themselves navigating work and family as that topic became increasingly prominent in the discourse about women's careers. They pursued an egalitarian partnership that allowed both spouses to pursue professional goals—an approach perhaps still ahead of its time. As she describes:

> It wasn't true in my own marriage, but in most marriages, women still have primary responsibility for the children, and the family's social life, and everything else. So, you have to have a career that enables you to balance those things. When my students come and ask for my advice, the number of men who ask about work-family balance—I could count them on one hand over fifty years, whereas for women it's a very important issue.

Through her roles as a teacher, researcher, and entrepreneur, Herzlinger has impacted many thousands of students and scholars, as well as health care practitioners and their patients. In addition, she has been a groundbreaking presence in numerous boardrooms and has also helped shape policy debates. She has served on the boards of more than a dozen publicly traded companies, typically as chair or member of the audit or pension committee, given her doctoral training in accounting, and often as the first woman at the table. With characteristic frankness, Herzlinger draws on her own observations to note the drawbacks to boardroom homogeneity:

> I think boards need diversity of all sorts, but what they really need are people who understand the business. And what you frequently see on boards are people who are CEOs, who come from the same kind of roles as the top management of the company they oversee. And that similarity between directors and management could ultimately be a negative; when their fellow CEO gets into trouble, directors are very sympathetic, perhaps unduly so. That's when boards are really important, when the

company gets into trouble—and you've got the wrong kind of board if everyone on it is a CEO who does not really understand the business.

Today, Herzlinger continues to be a leading voice for innovation and consumer focus in health care. Like a number of her HBS colleagues, she has spent considerable energy translating the insights of research into guidance for policy makers. She authored 2008 presidential candidate John McCain's health care plan and has addressed the US House of Representatives on the health care sector. A 2018 *Wall Street Journal* editorial coauthored with Joel Klein, former Bill Clinton–era assistant US attorney general, helped make the case for expanding the use of health reimbursement arrangements, a rule the federal government adopted the following year. Herzlinger's work on expanding consumer choice in health insurance was also cited in a *Wall Street Journal* editorial jointly authored by the US secretaries of health and human services, labor, and treasury, after the publication of which she chaired a Washington, DC, panel on health care innovation.[49]

Herzlinger's influence on the health care sector has also extended from her long-running MBA course, "Innovating in Health Care." It was the first health care course to be offered at HBS and has evolved with the changing nature of the industry. (Student business plans written for the course have to date launched at least six billion-dollar firms.) In 2014, Herzlinger launched "Innovating in Health Care" as a massive open online course, making the course available to thousands of learners beyond HBS. Today, she continues to break the mold in her academic field, developing a nontraditional textbook on health care innovation. As she explains, "I'm very excited about it, because the subject doesn't get taught. Innovation gets taught, and health care gets taught, and how to do medical research gets taught. What people don't teach is how you actually innovate in this environment, and that's what my course focuses on. It's not a standard course." To spur more teaching on health care innovation, Herzlinger founded the Global Educators Network for Health

Innovation Education (thegeniegroup.org), a nonprofit aimed at helping schools and instructors develop curricula; since the group's founding, it has helped more than twenty schools around the world to create programs or courses on health care innovation.

Regina Herzlinger's path has itself been innovative. Over a career spanning six decades, she has often been the first to explore important questions and lay claim to seats typically occupied by men. Her pioneering work and pioneering presence have presaged dramatic changes to women's roles in business and society. Looking back, Herzlinger notes that she always believed in an inexorable and positive trend toward more diversity, including greater representation of women, in management and leadership, and is glad that she has survived long enough to see meaningful progress.

NOTES

Introduction

1. Likhitha Butchireddygari, "Historic Rise of College-Educated Women in Labor Force Changes Workplace," *Wall Street Journal*, August 20, 2019, https://www.wsj.com/articles/historic -rise-of-college-educated-women-in-labor-force-changes-workplace-11566303223; Jonnelle Marte, "Women Gained in Income and Jobs in 2018, U.S. Census Data Shows," Reuters, September 10, 2019, https://www.reuters.com/article/us-usa-economy-census-women/women-gained-in -income-and-jobs-in-2018-us-census-data-shows-idUSKCN1VV2IQ.

2. "Quick Take: Women in the Workforce–Global," Catalyst, January 30, 2020, https://www .catalyst.org/research/women-in-the-workforce-global/.

3. Michelle Stohlmeyer Russell, Matt Krentz, Katie Abouzahr, and Meghan Doyle, "Women Dominate Health Care—Just Not in the Executive Suite," Boston Consulting Group, January 7, 2019, https://www.bcg.com/en-us/publications/2019/women-dominate-health-care-not-in -executive-suite.aspx.

4. Emma Hinchcliffe, "A New Low for the Global 500: No Women of Color Run Businesses on This Year's List," *Fortune*, August 10, 2020, https://fortune.com/2020/08/10/a-new-low-for-the -global-500-no-women-of-color-run-businesses-on-this-years-list/.

5. Paula England, Andres Levine, and Emma Mishel, "Progress toward Gender Equality in the United States Has Slowed or Stalled," *Proceedings of the National Academy of Sciences* 117, no. 13 (2020): 6990–6997.

6. "Degrees Conferred by Race and Sex," National Center for Education Statistics, 2019, https://nces.ed.gov/fastfacts/display.asp?id=72.

Chapter One

1. "Voice of the Female Millennial," in *The Female Millennial: A New Era of Talent*," Pricewater houseCoopers, 2015, https://www.pwc.com/jg/en/publications/the-female-millennial_a-new-era-of -talent.pdf.

2. Robin J. Ely, Pamela Stone, Laurie Shannon, and Colleen Ammerman, *Life & Leadership after HBS*, Harvard Business School, 2015, https://www.hbs.edu/gender/faculty-research/life -and-leadership-after-hbs/Pages/default.aspx.

3. "Facts over Time—Women in the Labor Force," US Department of Labor, https://www .dol.gov/wb/stats/NEWSTATS/facts/women_lf.htm#CivilianLFSex.

4. David S. Pedullaa and Sarah Thébaud, "Can We Finish the Revolution? Gender, Work-Family Ideals, and Institutional Constraint," *American Sociological Review* 80, no. 1 (2015): 116–139.

5. Name has been changed.

6. Shelley J. Correll, "SWS 2016 Feminist Lecture: Reducing Gender Biases in Modern Workplaces: A Small Wins Approach to Organizational Change," *Gender & Society* 31 (2017): 725–750; Monica Biernat, M. J. Tocci, and Joan C. Williams, "The Language of Performance Evaluations: Gender-Based Shifts in Content and Consistency of Judgment," *Social Psychological and Personality Science* 3, no. 2 (2012): 186–192; Eden B. King, Whitney Botsford, Michelle R. Hebl, et al., "Benevolent Sexism at Work: Gender Differences in the Distribution of Challenging Developmental Experiences," *Journal of Management* 38, no. 6 (2012): 1835–1866.

7. Madeline E. Heilman and Michelle C. Haynes, "No Credit Where Credit Is Due: Attributional Rationalization of Women's Success in Male-Female Teams," *Journal of Applied Psychology* 90, no. 5 (2005): 905–916.

8. Madeline E. Heilman and Julie J. Chen, "Same Behavior, Different Consequences: Reactions to Men's and Women's Altruistic Citizenship Behavior," *Journal of Applied Psychology* 90, no. 3 (2005): 431–441.

9. Robin J. Ely, Pamela Stone, and Colleen Ammerman, "Rethink What You 'Know' about High-Achieving Women," *Harvard Business Review*, December 14, 2014, 100–109.

10. "Voice of the Female Millennial."

11. Rachel Thomas, Marianne Cooper, Ellen Konar, et al., *Women in the Workplace 2017*, https://womenintheworkplace.com/2017.

12. Alice H. Eagly and Linda L. Carli, *Through the Labyrinth: The Truth about How Women Become Leaders* (Boston: Harvard Business Press, 2007).

13. "List: Women CEOs of the S&P 500," Catalyst, October 2, 2019, https://www.catalyst.org/research/women-ceos-of-the-sp-500/.

14. Klaus Schwab, Richard Samans, Saadia Zahidi, Till Alexander Leopold, and Vesselina Ratcheva, *The Global Gender Gap Report 2017*, World Economic Forum, 2017, http://www3.weforum.org/docs/WEF_GGGR_2017.pdf.

15. Paul A. Gompers, Vladimir Mukharlyamov, Emily Weisburst, and Yuhai Xuan, "Gender Effects in Venture Capital," SSRN, June 4, 2014, https://papers.ssrn.com/sol3/papers.cfm?abstract_id=2445497.

16. Boris Groysberg, *Chasing Stars: The Myth of Talent and the Portability of Performance* (Princeton, NJ: Princeton University Press, 2010).

17. Kathleen L. McGinn and Katherine L. Milkman, "Looking Up and Looking Out: Career Mobility Effects of Demographic Similarity among Professionals," *Organization Science* 24, no. 4 (2013): 1041–1060.

18. Rachel Thomas, Marianne Cooper, Ellen Konar, et al., *Women in the Workplace 2019*, https://wiw-report.s3.amazonaws.com/Women_in_the_Workplace_2019.pdf.

19. "Voice of the Female Millennial."

20. Thomas et al., *Women in the Workplace 2017*.

21. Robin J. Ely, Pamela Stone, Laurie Shannon, and Colleen Ammerman, *Life & Leadership after HBS*, Harvard Business School, 2015, https://www.hbs.edu/gender/faculty-research/life-and-leadership-after-hbs/Pages/default.aspx.

22. Ely, Stone, and Ammerman, "Rethink What You 'Know.'"

23. Lakshmi Ramarajan, Kathleen McGinn, and Deborah Kolb, *An Outside-Inside Evolution in Gender and Professional Work*, Working paper, Harvard Business School, November 2012, https://www.hbs.edu/faculty/Pages/item.aspx?num=43734.

24. Ely, Stone, and Ammerman, "Rethink What You 'Know.'"

25. Thomas et al., *Women in the Workplace 2017*.

26. Robin J. Ely and Irene Padavic, "What's Really Holding Women Back?," *Harvard Business Review*, March–April 2020, 58–67; Irene Padavic, Robin J. Ely, and Erin M. Reid, "Explaining the Persistence of Gender Inequality: The Work-Family Narrative as a Social Defense against the 24/7 Work Culture," *Administrative Science Quarterly* 65, no. 1 (2019): 61–111.0

27. Gretchen Livingston and Kim Parker, "8 Facts about American Dads," Pew Research Center, June 12, 2019, https://www.pewresearch.org/fact-tank/2019/06/12/fathers-day-facts/; Clare Lyonette and Rosemary Crompton, "Sharing the Load? Partners' Relative Earnings and the Division of Domestic Labour," *Work, Employment and Society* 29, no. 1 (2015): 23–40; Suzanne M. Bianchi, Liana C. Sayer, Melissa A. Milkie, and John P. Robinson, "Housework: Who Did, Does or

Will Do It, and How Much Does It Matter?," *Social Forces* 91, no. 1 (2012): 55–63; Liana C. Sayer, Suzanne M. Bianchi, and John P. Robinson, "Are Parents Investing Less in Children? Trends in Mothers' and Fathers' Time with Children," *American Journal of Sociology* 110, no. 1 (2004): 1–43.

28. Ely, Stone, and Ammerman, "Rethink What You 'Know.'"

29. Caitlyn Collins, Liana Christin Landivar, Leah Ruppanner, and William J. Scarborough, "COVID-19 and the Gender Gap in Work Hours," *Gender, Work & Organization*, 2020, doi:10.1111/gwao.12506.

30. Erin Reid, "Why Some Men Pretend to Work 80-Hour Weeks," *Harvard Business Review*, April 28, 2015, https://hbr.org/2015/04/why-some-men-pretend-to-work-80-hour-weeks.

31. Sreedhari D. Desai, Dolly Chugh, and Arthur P. Brief, "The Implications of Marriage Structure for Men's Workplace Attitudes, Beliefs, and Behaviors toward Women," *Administrative Science Quarterly* 59, no. 2 (2014): 330–365.

32. "Voice of the Female Millennial."

33. Joan C. Williams, Mary Blair-Loy, and Jennifer L. Berdahl, "Cultural Schemas, Social Class, and the Flexibility Stigma," *Journal of Social Issues* 69, no. 2 (2013): 209–234.

34. Pamela Stone, *Opting Out? Why Women Really Quit Careers and Head Home* (Berkeley: University of California Press, 2007).

35. Williams, Blair-Loy, and Berdahl, "Cultural Schemas, Social Class, and the Flexibility Stigma."

36. Shelley J. Correll, Stephen Benard, and In Paik, "Getting a Job: Is There a Motherhood Penalty?," *American Journal of Sociology* 112, no. 5 (2007): 1297–1339.

37. Melissa J. Hodges and Michelle J. Budig, "Who Gets the Daddy Bonus? Organizational Hegemonic Masculinity and the Impact of Fatherhood on Earnings," *Gender and Society* 24, no. 6 (2010): 717–745.

38. Fran Worden Henry, *Toughing It out at Harvard: The Making of a Woman MBA* (New York: McGraw-Hill Book, 1983).

39. Matt Hazenbush, *Application Trends Survey Report 2019*, Graduate Management Admission Council, 2019, https://www.gmac.com/-/media/files/gmac/research/admissions-and-application-trends/application-trends-survey-report-2019.pdf.

40. Forté Foundation, fortefoundation.org, accessed 2019.

41. Rusty B. McIntyre, Rene M. Paulson, and Charles G. Lord, "Alleviating Women's Mathematics Stereotype Threat through Salience of Group Achievements," *Journal of Experimental Social Psychology* 39, no. 1 (2003): 83–90; Ioana M. Latu, Marianne Schmid Mast, Joris Lammers, and Dario Bombari, "Successful Female Leaders Empower Women's Behavior in Leadership Tasks," *Journal of Experimental Social Psychology* 49, no. 3 (2013): 444–448.

42. Leonardo Bursztyn, Thomas Fujiwara, and Amanda Pallais, "'Acting Wife': Marriage Market Incentives and Labor Market Investments," *American Economic Review* 107, no. 11 (2017): 3288–3319.

43. Amy J. C. Cuddy, Peter Glick, and Anna Beninger, "The Dynamics of Warmth and Competence Judgments, and Their Outcomes in Organizations," *Research in Organizational Behavior* 31 (2011): 73–98.

44. Alice H. Eagly and Steven J. Karau, "Role Congruity Theory of Prejudice toward Female Leaders," *Psychological Review* 109, no. 3 (2002): 573–598.

45. Caroline T. Zhang, "Barbara Hackman Franklin HBS '64, Former Secretary of Commerce," *Harvard Crimson*, May 29, 2014, https://www.thecrimson.com/article/2014/5/29/barbara-hackman-franklin-hbs/.

46. Lee Stout, *A Matter of Simple Justice* (University Park: Pennsylvania State University Libraries, 2012).

Chapter Two

1. Bureau of Labor Statistics, "Women in the Labor Force: A Databook," *BLS Reports*, https://www.bls.gov/opub/reports/womens-databook/2018/home.htm; "Pyramid: Women in S&P 500 Companies," Catalyst, January 15, 2020, https://www.catalyst.org/research/women-in-sp-500-companies/.

2. Emma Hinchcliffe, "The Number of Female CEOs in the Fortune 500 Hits an All-Time Record," *Fortune*, May 18, 2020, https://fortune.com/2020/05/18/women-ceos-fortune-500-2020/.

3. "Historical List of Women CEOs of the Fortune: 1972–2020," Catalyst, May 28, 2020, https://www.catalyst.org/research/historical-list-of-women-ceos-of-the-fortune-lists-1972-2020/.

4. Claire Cain Miller, Kevin Quealy, and Margot Sanger-Katz, "The Top Jobs Where Women Are Outnumbered by Men Named John," *New York Times*, April 24, 2018, https://www.nytimes.com/interactive/2018/04/24/upshot/women-and-men-named-john.html.

5. Dominic-Madori Davis, "One of the Only 4 Black Fortune 500 CEOs Just Stepped Down—Here Are the 3 That Remain, *Business Insider,* July 21, 2020, https://www.businessinsider.com/there-are-four-black-fortune-500-ceos-here-they-are-2020-2.

6. Dion Rebouin, "Only 1 Fortune 500 Company Is Headed by a Woman of Color," Axios, January 14, 2019, https://www.axios.com/fortune-500-no-women-of-color-ceos-3d42619c-967b-47d2-b94c-659527b22ee3.html.

7. Ellen McGirt, "PwC Releases Its First-Ever Diversity Report," *Fortune*, August 27, 2020, https://fortune.com/2020/08/27/pwc-diversity-report-first-ever/.

8. Madeline E. Heilman, "Gender Stereotypes and Workplace Bias," *Research in Organizational Behavior* 32 (2012): 113–135; Anne M. Koenig, Alice H. Eagly, Abigail A. Mitchell, and Tiina Ristikari, "Are Leader Stereotypes Masculine? A Meta-analysis of Three Research Paradigms," *Psychological Bulletin* 137, no. 4 (2011): 616–642.

9. Heather Murphy, "Picture a Leader. Is She a Woman?," *New York Times*, March 16, 2018, https://www.nytimes.com/2018/03/16/health/women-leadership-workplace.html.

10. Cira Cuberes and Boris Groysberg, "Success Strategies of Star Women in Consulting" (unpublished manuscript, Harvard Business School, 2012).

11. Jane Stevenson, "Presentation on 'Women CEOs Speak' Report" (Harvard Business School, November 29, 2017).

12. Jamie Tarabay, "Julie Bishop Quits Australian Politics, Adding to Exodus of Conservative Women," *New York Times*, February 21, 2019, https://www.nytimes.com/2019/02/21/world/australia/julie-bishop-liberals.html.

13. Kara Swisher, "Hitting the Glass Ceiling, Suddenly, at Pinterest," *New York Times*, August 14, 2020, https://www.nytimes.com/2020/08/14/opinion/pinterest-discrimination-women.html.

14. Cuberes and Groysberg, "Success Strategies of Star Women in Consulting."

15. Lily Jampol and Vivian Zayas, "Gendered White Lies: Women Are Given Inflated Performance Feedback Compared with Men," *Personality and Social Psychology Bulletin*, doi:10.1177/0146167220916622; Shelley J. Correll and Caroline Simard, "Research: Vague Feedback Is Holding Women Back, *Harvard Business Review*, April 29, 2016, https://hbr.org/2016/04/research-vague-feedback-is-holding-women-back; Eden B. King, Whitney Botsford, Michelle R. Hebl, et al., "Benevolent Sexism at Work: Gender Differences in the Distribution of Challenging Developmental Experiences," *Journal of Management* 38, no. 6 (2012): 1835–1866; Theresa K. Vescio, Sarah J. Gervais, Mark Snyder, and Ann Hoover, "Power and the Creation of Patronizing Environments: The Stereotype-Based Behaviors of the Powerful and Their Effects on Female Performance in Masculine Domains," *Journal of Personality and Social Psychology* 88, no. 4 (2005): 658–672.

16. Katherine B. Coffman, Christine L. Exley, and Muriel Niederle, "When Gender Discrimination Is Not about Gender," Working Paper, Harvard Business School, 2017.

17. Rachel Thomas, Marianne Cooper, Ellen Konar, et al., *Women in the Workplace 2018*, https://womenintheworkplace.com/2018.

18. Courtney L. McCluney and Verónica Caridad Rabelo, "Conditions of Visibility: An Intersectional Examination of Black Women's Belongingness and Distinctiveness at Work," *Journal of Vocational Behavior* 113 (2019): 143–152; Allison Cook and Christy Glass, "Above the Glass Ceiling: When Are Women and Racial/Ethnic Minorities Promoted to CEO?," *Strategic Management Journal* 35, no. 7 (2019): 1080–1089.

19. Victoria L. Brescoll and Eric Luis Uhlmann, "Can an Angry Woman Get Ahead? Status Conferral, Gender, and Expression of Emotion in the Workplace," *Psychological Science* 19, no. 3 (2008): 268–275.

20. Ashleigh Shelby Rosette and Robert W. Livingston, "Failure Is Not an Option for Black Women: Effects of Organizational Performance on Leaders with Single versus Dual-Subordinate Identities," *Journal of Experimental Social Psychology* 48, no. 5 (2012): 1162–1167.

21. Stephanie Forshee, "Women CEOs Negotiate Higher Severance Pay," *Agenda*, 2020, https://www.agendaweek.com/c/2674993/325193; Felice B. Klein, Pierre Chaigneau, and Cynthia E. Devers, "CEO Gender-Based Termination Concerns: Evidence from Initial Severance Agreements," *Journal of Management*, November 21, 2019, doi:0149206319887421.

22. Joan C. Williams, Mary Blair-Loy, and Jennifer L. Berdahl, "Cultural Schemas, Social Class, and the Flexibility Stigma," *Journal of Social Issues* 69, no. 2 (2013): 209–234; Pamela Stone, *Opting Out? Why Women Really Quit Careers and Head Home* (Berkeley: University of California Press, 2007).

23. Irene Padavic, Robin J. Ely, and Erin M. Reid, "Explaining the Persistence of Gender Inequality: The Work–Family Narrative as a Social Defense against the 24/7 Work Culture," *Administrative Science Quarterly* 65, no. 1 (2020): 61–111.

24. Laura Morgan Roberts, Anthony J. Mayo, Robin J. Ely, and David A. Thomas, "Beating the Odds," *Harvard Business Review*, April 2018, 126–131.

Chapter Three

1. Olga Emelianova and Christina Milhomem, *Women on Boards: 2019 Progress Report*, MSCI, December 2019, https://www.msci.com/documents/10199/29f5bf79-cf87-71a5-ac26-b435d3b6fc08.

2. James Thorne, "Moves to Lift Board Diversity Highlight Inaction among Private Companies," Pitchbook, February 28, 2020, https://pitchbook.com/news/articles/moves-to-lift-board-diversity-highlight-inaction-among-private-companies.

3. Deloitte and the Alliance for Board Diversity, *Missing Pieces Report: The 2018 Board Diversity Census of Women and Minorities on Fortune 500 Boards*, https://www2.deloitte.com/us/en/pages/center-for-board-effectiveness/articles/missing-pieces-fortune-500-board-diversity-study-2018.html.

4. Daniel Thomas, "Company Boards Pressed to Improve Ethnic Minority Representation," *Financial Times*, July 1, 2020, https://www.ft.com/content/022b3540-39ca-4f47-b409-5a15cca6d2aa.

5. Emma Hinchliffe, "GM's Board Will Have More Women Than Men. It's Not the Only One," *Fortune*, May 20, 2019, http://fortune.com/2019/05/20/women-boards-fortune-500-2019/.

6. Anja Kirsch, "The Gender Composition of Corporate Boards: A Review and Research Agenda," *Leadership Quarterly* 29, no. 2 (20118): 346–364.

7. PricewaterhouseCoopers, *The Collegiality Conundrum: Finding Balance in the Boardroom: PwC's 2019 Annual Corporate Directors Survey*, https://www.pwc.com/us/en/services/governance-insights-center/assets/pwc-2019-annual-corporate-directors-survey-full-report-v2.pdf.pdf

8. PricewaterhouseCoopers, *Turning Crisis into Opportunity: PwC's 2020 Annual Corporate Directors Survey*, https://www.pwc.com/us/en/services/governance-insights-center/assets/pwc-2020-annual-corporate-directors-survey.pdf.

9. Amanda Gerut, "Appointments of Black Board Members Skyrocket," *Agenda,* November 6, 2020, https://www.agendaweek.com/c/2951303/368723/appointments_black_board_members_skyrocket.

10. PricewaterhouseCoopers, *The Collegiality Conundrum*.

11. Isabelle Solal and Kaisa Snellman, "Why Investors React Negatively to Companies That Put Women on Their Boards," *Harvard Business Review*, November 25, 2019, https://hbr.org/2019/11/why-investors-react-negatively-to-companies-that-put-women-on-their-boards.

12. Marianne Bertrand, Sandra E. Black, Sissel Jensen, and Adriana Lleras-Muney, "Breaking the Glass Ceiling? The Effect of Board Quotas on Female Labor Market Outcomes in Norway," National Bureau of Economic Research, June 2014 (revised June 2017), https://www.nber.org/papers/w20256.pdf.

13. Lauren Rivera, Ann Shepherd, and Gené Teare, "Research: Gender Diversity on Start-Up Boards Is Worse Than You Think," *Harvard Business Review*, December 11, 2019, https://hbr.org/2019/12/research-gender-diversity-on-start-up-boards-is-worse-than-you-think.

14. Department for Business, Energy, and industrial Strategy and Andrew Griffiths, "Revealed: The Worst Explanations for Not Appointing Women to FTSE Company Boards" [Press release], GOV.UK, May 13, 2018, https://www.gov.uk/government/news/revealed-the-worst -explanations-for-not-appointing-women-to-ftse-company-boards.

15. Matteo Tonello, "Corporate Board Practices in the Russell 3000 and S&P 500: 2019 Edition," The Conference Board, https://www.conference-board.org/topics/board-practices -compensation/Corporate-Board-Practices-2019.

16. Patrick Durkin, "Gender Diversity Claims Undermined as Eight Women Dominate Top Boards, *Australian Financial Review*, February 3, 2019, https://www.afr.com/leadership/gender -diversity-claims-undermined-as-eight-women-dominate-top-boards-20190201-h1aqay.

17. Edward H. Chang, Katherine L. Milkman, Dolly Chugh, and Modupe Akinola, "Diversity Thresholds: How Social Norms, Visibility, and Scrutiny Relate to Group Composition," *Academy of Management Journal* 62, no. 1 (2019): 144–171.

18. Marion Hutchinson, Janet Mack, and Kevin Plastow, "Who Selects the 'Right' Directors? An Examination of the Association between Board Selection, Gender Diversity and Outcomes, *Accounting & Finance* 55, no. 4 (2015): 1071–1103; Szymon Kaczmarek, Satomi Kimino, and Annie Pye, "Antecedents of Board Composition: The Role of Nomination Committees," *Corporate Governance: An International Review* 20, no. 5 (2012): 474–489.

19. Rosabeth Moss Kanter, "Warren Buffett Has the Right Answer to Crony Capitalism: Women," CNN, March 6, 2020, https://www.cnn.com/2020/03/04/perspectives/warren-buffett -annual-letter-corporate-governance/.

20. Ethan Wolff-Mannn, "Buffett Rejects Diversity Measure for Berkshire, but Throws Support behind Its Goal," *Yahoo! Finance*, May 2, 2020, https://finance.yahoo.com/news/buffett -rejects-diversity-measure-but-throws-support-behind-its-goal-001730183.html.

21. Anja Kirsch, "The Gender Composition of Corporate Boards: A Review and Research Agenda," *Leadership Quarterly* 29, no. 2 (2018): 346–364; Renée B.Adams, "Women on Boards: The Superheroes of Tomorrow?," *Leadership Quarterly* 27, no. 3 (2016): 371–386; Alice H. Eagly, "When Passionate Advocates Meet Research on Diversity, Does the Honest Broker Stand a Chance?," *Journal of Social Issues* 72, no. 1 (2016): 199–222; David A. Carter, Frank D'Souza, Betty J. Simkins, and W. Gary Simpson, "The Gender and Ethnic Diversity of US Boards and Board Committees and Firm Financial Performance," *Corporate Governance: An International Review* 18, no. 5 (2010): 396–414; Deborah Rhode and Amanda K. Packel, "Diversity on Corporate Boards: How Much Difference Does Difference Make?," *Delaware Journal of Corporate Law* 39, no. 2 (2010): 377–426.

22. Kimberly D. Krawiec, John M. Conley, and Lissa L. Broome, "A Difficult Conversation: Corporate Directors on Race and Gender, *Pace International Law Review* 26, no. 1 (2014): 13–22.

23. Anita Williams Woolley, Christopher F. Chabris, Alex Pentland, Nada Hashmi, and Thomas W. Malone, "Evidence for a Collective Intelligence Factor in the Performance of Human Groups," *Science* 330, no. 6004 (2010): 686–688; Clint A. Bowers, James A. Pharmer, and Eduardo Salas, "When Member Homogeneity Is Needed in Work Teams: A Meta-Analysis, *Small Group Research* 31, no. 3 (2000): 305–327.

24. Cristian L. Dezsö and David Gaddis Ross, "Does Female Representation in Top Management Improve Firm Performance? A Panel Data Investigation," *Strategic Management Journal* 33, no. 9 (2012): 1072–1089.

25. Ye Dai, Gukdo Byun, and Fangsheng Ding, "The Direct and Indirect Impact of Gender Diversity in New Venture Teams on Innovation Performance," *Entrepreneurship Theory and Practice* 43, no. 3 (2019): 505–528; Sarah E. Gaither, Evan P. Apfelbaum, Hannah J. Birnbaum, Laura G. Babbitt, and Samuel R. Sommers, "Mere Membership in Racially Diverse Groups Reduces Conformity," *Social Psychological and Personality Science* 9, no. 4 (2018): 402–410; Katherine W. Phillips, "How Diversity Makes Us Smarter," *Scientific American*, October 1, 2014, https://www.scientificamerican.com /article/how-diversity-makes-us-smarter; Katherine W. Phillips, Michelle Duguid, Melissa Thomas-Hunt, and Jayaram Uparna, "Diversity as Knowledge Exchange: The Roles of Information Processing, Expertise, and Status," in *The Oxford Handbook of Diversity and Work*, ed. Quinetta M. Roberson (Oxford: Oxford University Press, 2013), 157–178; Daan van Knippenberg and Michaéla C. Schippers, "Work Group Diversity," *Annual Review of Psychology* 58, no. 1 (2007): 515–541.

26. Robin J. Ely, Irene Padavic, and David A. Thomas, "Racial Diversity, Racial Asymmetries, and Team Learning Environment: Effects on Performance," *Organization Studies* 33, no. 3 (2012): 341–362; Robin J. Ely and David A. Thomas, "Cultural Diversity at Work: The Effects of Diversity Perspectives on Work Group Processes and Outcomes," *Administrative Science Quarterly* 46, no. 2 (2001): 229–273.

27. "La vie en rose," *The Economist*, May 6, 2010, https://www.economist.com/business/2010 /05/06/la-vie-en-rose.

28. Tonello, "Corporate Board Practices in the Russell 3000 and S&P 500."

29. Ross Kerber, "Women's Share of US Corporate Board Seats Rises, but Not Top Roles: Study," Reuters, February 3, 2020, https://www.reuters.com/article/us-usadirectors-women /womens-share-of-us-corporate-board-seats-rises-but-not-top-roles-study-idUSKBN1ZX1K3.

30. Laura Casares Field, Matthew E. Souther, and Adam S. Yore, "At the Table but Can't Break through the Glass Ceiling: Board Leadership Positions Elude Diverse Directors," *Journal of Financial Economics* (forthcoming, last revised October 2, 2019), 2nd Annual Financial Institutions, Regulation and Corporate Governance Conference, http://dx.doi.org/10.2139/ssrn.2810543.

31. Ibid.

32. Boris Groysberg and Deborah Bell, "Dysfunction in the Boardroom," *Harvard Business Review,* June 2013, 88–95.

33. Andy Logan and Brendan Gill, "For Love," *New Yorker*, April 16, 1954.

34. Stefanie K. Johnson, David R. Hekman, and Elsa T. Chan, "If There's Only One Woman in Your Candidate Pool, There's Statistically No Chance She'll Be Hired," *Harvard Business Review*, April 26, 2016, https://hbr.org/2016/04/if-theres-only-one-woman-in-your-candidate-pool -theres-statistically-no-chance-shell-be-hired; Larissa Myaskovsky, Emily Unikel, and Mary Amanda Dew, "Effects of Gender Diversity on Performance and Interpersonal Behavior in Small Work Groups," *Sex Roles* 52, nos. 9–10 (2005): 645–657.

35. Alison M. Konrad, Vicki Kramer, and Sumru Erkut, "Critical Mass: The Impact of Three or More Women on Corporate Boards," *Organizational Dynamics* 37, no. 2 (2008): 145–164.

36. Paul Shukovsky, "Washington State Mandates Gender Diversity on Corporate Boards," Bloomberg Law, March 5, 2020, https://news.bloomberglaw.com/business-and-practice /washington-state-mandates-gender-diversity-on-corporate-boards.

37. Jennifer Rankin, "EU Revives Plans for Mandatory Quotas of Women on Company Boards, *The Guardian*, March 5, 2020, https://www.theguardian.com/world/2020/mar/05/eu -revives-plans-for-mandatory-quotas-of-women-on-company-boards.

38. Ruth Mateos de Cabo, Siri Terjesen, Lorenzo Escot, and Ricardo Gimeno, "Do 'Soft Law' Board Gender Quotas Work? Evidence from a Natural Experiment," *European Management Journal* 37, no. 5 (2019): 611–624; Siri Terjesen, Ruth V. Aguilera, and Ruth Lorenz, "Legislating a Woman's Seat on the Board: Institutional Factors Driving Gender Quotas for Boards of Directors," *Journal of Business Ethics* 128, no. 2 (2015): 233–251.

39. John Beshears, Iris Bohnet, and Jenny Sanford, "Increasing Gender Diversity in the Boardroom: The United Kingdom in 2011 (A)," Harvard Business School Case 918-006, October 2017 (revised July 2019).

40. D. Thomas, "Top UK Groups Reach Board Gender Target, but Smaller Companies Trail," *Financial Times*, February 8, 2020, https://www.ft.com/content/47d7cba0-49b2-11ea-aeb3 -955839e06441.

41. Corilyn Shropshire, "Illinois Bill Requiring Minorities on Corporate Boards 'Gutted'; Lawmakers Pass Version Calling for Disclosure, Report Card," *Chicago Tribune,* June 4, 2019, https://www.chicagotribune.com/business/ct-biz-corporate-diversity-bill-passed-gutted-20190603 -story.html.

42. Victor E. Sojo, Robert E. Wood, Sally A.Wood, and Melissa A.Wheeler, "Reporting Requirements, Targets, and Quotas for Women in Leadership," *Leadership Quarterly* 27, no. 3 (2016): 519–536.

43. Marta Geletkanycz, Cynthia E. Clark, and Patricia Gabaldon, "Research: When Boards Broaden Their Definition of Diversity, Women and People of Color Lose Out," *Harvard Business Review*, October 3, 2018, https://hbr.org/2018/10/research-when-boards-broaden-their -definition-of-diversity-women-and-people-of-color-lose-out; Aaron A. Dhir, "Diversity in the

Boardroom: A Content Analysis of Corporate Proxy Disclosures," *Pace International Law Review* 26, no. 1 (2014): 6–12; Christiane Schwieren, "The Gender Wage Gap—Due to Differences in Efficiency Wage Effects or Discrimination?," Maastricht University, Maastricht Research School of Economics of Technology and Organization (METEOR), January 1, 2003.

44. Sir John Parker and the Parker Review Committee, *Ethnic Diversity Enriching Business Leadership: An Update Report from the Parker Review*, February 5, 2020, https://assets.ey.com/content /dam/ey-sites/ey-com/en_uk/news/2020/02/ey-parker-review-2020-report-final.pdf.

45. PricewaterhouseCoopers, *The Evolving Boardroom: Signs of Change*, 2018, https://www.pwc .com/us/en/governance-insights-center/annual-corporate-directors-survey/assets/pwc-annual -corporate-directors-survey-2018.pdf.

46. Hugh Son, "Goldman Won't Take Companies Public without 'At Least One Diverse Board Candidate,' Says CEO," CNBC, January 23, 2020, https://www.cnbc.com/2020/01/23/goldman -wont-take-companies-public-that-dont-have-at-least-one-diverse-board-candidate-ceo-says.html.

47. Michelle Chapman and Stan Choe, "Nasdaq Seeks Mandatory Board Diversity for Listed Companies," Associated Press, December 1, 2020, https://apnews.com/article/business-board -of-directors-38bceb1f1579518b5b1d97df5b029569.

48. M. J. Anderson, "Investors Back Proposal Targeting C-Suite Diversity," Agenda, 2019, http://www.agendaweek.com/.

49. Jason Del Rey, "Amazon Employees Are Outraged by Their Company's Opposition to a Plan to Add More Diversity to Its Board," Vox, May 8, 2018, https://www.vox.com/2018/5/8 /17328466/amazon-jeff-bezos-board-diversity-proposal-shareholder-vote; Jason Del Rey, "Amazon Will Adopt a 'Rooney Rule' to Increase Board Diversity after Its Initial Opposition Sparked Employee Outrage," Vox, May 14, 2018, https://www.vox.com/2018/5/14/17353626/amazon -rooney-rule-board-diversity-reversal-shareholder-proposal.

50. Heidrick & Struggles, *Board Monitor: US 2019*, May 28, 2019, https://heidrick.com /Knowledge-Center/Publication/Board_Monitor_US_2019.

51. Amanda Gerut, "From One Woman to Three—Networks Expand as Women Join Boards," Agenda, 2020, https://www.agendaweek.com/c/2863703/355523/from_woman_three _networks_expand_women_join_boards.

52. Anne Steele, "California Rolls Out Diversity Quotas for Corporate Boards," *Wall Street Journal*, October 1, 2020, https://www.wsj.com/articles/california-rolls-out-diversity-quotas-for -corporate-boards-11601507471.

53. Boris Groysberg, Richard P. Chapman, and Yo-Jud Cheng, *2016 Global Board of Directors Survey*, Spencer Stuart, 2016, https://www.spencerstuart.com/-/media/pdf%20files /research%20and%20insight%20pdfs/wcd-board-survey-2016_041416.pdf.

54. Groysberg and Bell, "Dysfunction in the Boardroom."

55. Heidrick & Struggles, *Board Monitor*.

56. "Women on Boards: A Course Becomes a Movement," HBS Alumni Stories, June 6, 2017, https://www.alumni.hbs.edu/stories/Pages/story-bulletin.aspx?num=6265.

57. "The Data on Women Leaders," Pew Research Center, 2018, https://www .pewsocialtrends.org/fact-sheet/the-data-on-women-leaders/.

58. "Susan Schiffer Stautberg '67 Remarks," Wheaton College, May 20, 2017, https:// wheatoncollege.edu/commencement/past-commencements/commencement-2017-archive /honorary-degrees-2017/susan-schiffer-stautberg-67-remarks/.

Chapter Four

1. Taffy Brodesser-Akner, "The Company That Sells Love to America Had a Dark Secret," *New York Times*, April 23, 2019, https://www.nytimes.com/2019/04/23/magazine/kay-jewelry -sexual-harassment.html; Jenny Singer, "Here Are All the Famous Men Who Have Tried to Come Back from #MeToo," *Forward*, April 25, 2019, https://forward.com/schmooze/420038/here-are -all-the-famous-men-who-have-tried-to-come-back-from-metoo/.

2. Jena McGregor, "How #MeToo Is Reshaping Employment Contracts for Executives," *The Washington Post*, October 31, 2018, https://www.washingtonpost.com/business/2018/10/31/how -metoo-is-reshaping-employment-contracts-executives/?utm_term=.5f9a6d3da7f1; Aliya Ram,

"Tech Investors Include #MeToo Clauses in Start-up Deals," *Financial Times*, March 18, 2019, https://www.ft.com/content/5d4ef400-4732-11e9-b168-96a37d002cd3.

3. Katrin Bennhold, "Another Side of #MeToo: Male Managers Fearful of Mentoring Women," *New York Times*, January 27, 2019, https://www.nytimes.com/2019/01/27/world/europe/metoo-backlash-gender-equality-davos-men.html; Victoria Brescoll, *Has #MeToo Unintentionally Increased Male Managers' Fear of Mentoring & Interacting with Female Colleagues?*, presented at the Harvard Business School Gender & Work Symposium, Boston, MA, 2019, https://www.hbs.edu/about/video.aspx?v=1_0cnfry9u; Sheryl Sandberg and Marc Pritchard, "The Number of Men Who Are Uncomfortable Mentoring Women Is Growing," *Fortune*, May 18, 2019, https://fortune.com/2019/05/17/sheryl-sandberg-lean-in-me-too/.

4. Elizabeth R. Johnson, Laurie Shannon, Robin J. Ely, Peter Glick, and Colleen Ammerman, *Sexual Harassment Experiences & Beliefs*, presented at the Harvard Business School Gender & Work Symposium, Boston, MA, 2019, https://www.hbs.edu/about/video.aspx?v=1_w8fm8m1b.

5. Roberta Rincon, "The Importance of Men as Allies: A Review of the Literature," *Society of Women Engineers Magazine*, April 11, 2019.

6. L. Morrow, S. Allis, J. F. Stacks, and B. B. Dolan, "Why Not a Woman?," *Time* 123, no. 23 (1984): 20.

7. Pam Belluck, "N.I.H. Head Calls for End to All-Male Panels of Scientists," *New York Times*, June 12, 2019, https://www.nytimes.com/2019/06/12/health/collins-male-science-panels.html.

8. David R. Hekman, Stefanie K. Johnson, Maw-Der Foo, and Wei Yang, "Does Diversity-Valuing Behavior Result in Diminished Performance Ratings for Nonwhite and Female Leaders?," *Academy of Management Journal* 60, no. 2 (April 2017): 771–797; Sarah J. Gervais and Amy L. Hillard, "Confronting Sexism as Persuasion: Effects of a Confrontation's Recipient, Source, Message, and Context," *Journal of Social Issues* 70, no. 4 (2014): 653–667; Benjamin J. Drury and Cheryl R. Kaiser, "Allies against Sexism: The Role of Men in Confronting Sexism," *Journal of Social Issues* 70, no. 4 (2014): 637–652; Alexander M. Czopp and Margo J. Monteith, "Confronting Prejudice (Literally): Reactions to Confrontations of Racial and Gender Bias," *Personality and Social Psychology Bulletin* 29, no. 4 (2003): 532–544.

9. David M. Mayer, "How Men Get Penalized for Straying from Masculine Norms," *Harvard Business Review*, October 8, 2018, https://hbr.org/2018/10/how-men-get-penalized-for-straying-from-masculine-norms.

10. Michael S. Kimmel, "What Do Men Want?," *Harvard Business Review*, December 1993, 50–63.

11. Claire Cain Miller, "Millennial Men Aren't the Dads They Thought They'd Be," *New York Times*, July 15, 2019, https://www.nytimes.com/2015/07/31/upshot/millennial-men-find-work-and-family-hard-to-balance.html.

12. Jeff Green, "Dads Say They Deserve Parental Leave, but Only in Theory," Bloomberg, April 18, 2018, https://www.bloomberg.com/news/articles/2018-04-18/dads-say-they-deserve-parental-leave-even-if-they-don-t-take-it.

13. Emily Peck, "Big Bank Settles Claims That It Discriminated against Men," *Huffington Post*, May 30, 2019, https://www.huffpost.com/entry/jpmorgan-chase-parental-leave-discrimination_n_5ceee71ce4b0888f89d06ab8?ncid=engmodushpmg00000004&guccounter=1.

14. Noam Scheiber, "Couple's Suit over Parental Leave Is New Challenge to Big Law Firm," *New York Times*, August 14, 2019, https://www.nytimes.com/2019/08/14/business/economy/jones-day-lawsuit.html.

15. Noam Scheiber, "Attitudes Shift on Paid Leave: Dads Sue, Too," *New York Times*, September 15, 2015, https://www.nytimes.com/2015/09/16/business/attitudes-shift-on-paid-leave-dads-sue-too.html.

16. Isabella Jibilian and Kate Taylor, "SoulCycle's Ex-CEO Said 'Paternity Leave Is for Pussies,' a New Lawsuit Filed by an Exec Who Was Fired 32 Days after Giving Birth Alleges," *Business Insider*, August 12, 2020, https://www.businessinsider.com/soulcycle-fired-pregnancy-discrimination-exec-lawsuit-2020-8.

17. Michelle Obama, *Becoming* (New York: Crown, 2018).

18. Max Abelson and Rebecca Greenfield, "Wall Street Dads Find Parental Leave Easier to Get Than to Take," Bloomberg, June 13, 2019, https://www.bloomberg.com/news/articles/2019-06-13/wall-street-dads-find-parental-leave-easier-to-get-than-to-take.

19. "Parental Leave Survey," Deloitte, 2016, https://www2.deloitte.com/content/dam/Deloitte/us/Documents/about-deloitte/us-about-deloitte-paternal-leave-survey.pdf.

20. Sarah Thébaud and David S. Pedulla, "Masculinity and the Stalled Revolution: How Gender Ideologies and Norms Shape Young Men's Responses to Work–Family Policies," *Gender & Society* 30, no. 4 (2016): 590–617.

21. Michelle Peluso, Carolyn Heller Baird, and Lynn Kesterson-Townes, *Women, Leadership, and the Priority Paradox*, IBM, 2019, https://www.ibm.com/thought-leadership/institute-business-value/report/womeninleadership.

22. Rachel Thomas, Marianne Cooper, Ellen Konar, et al., *Women in the Workplace 2017*, https://womenintheworkplace.com/2017.

23. Hannah Fingerhut, "In Both Parties, Men and Women Differ over Whether Women Still Face Obstacles to Progress," FACTANK: News in the Numbers, August 16, 2016, https://www.pewresearch.org/fact-tank/2016/08/16/in-both-parties-men-and-women-differ-over-whether-women-still-face-obstacles-to-progress/.

24. Jillesa Gebhardt, "On Equal Pay Day 2019, Lack of Awareness Persists," Survey Monkey, https://www.surveymonkey.com/curiosity/equal-pay-day-2019/#.

25. Ellen Wulfhorst, "Men Still Don't Grasp the Depth of Gender Inequality at Work," *Huffington Post*, August 13, 2020, https://www.huffpost.com/entry/gender-inequality-work-politics_l_5f353430c5b6fc009a62674a.

26. William J. Scarborough, Danny L. Lambouths, and Allyson L. Holbrook, "Support of Workplace Diversity Policies: The Role of Race, Gender, and Beliefs about Inequality," *Social Science Research* 79 (2019): 194–210.

27. Diana C. Mutz, "Status Threat, Not Economic Hardship, Explains the 2016 Presidential Vote," *Proceedings of the National Academy of Sciences* 115, no. 19 (2019): E4330–E4339; Robert Schrank, "Two Women, Three Men on a Raft," *Harvard Business Review,* May–June 1994, 68–76.

28. Juliana Menasce Horowitz and Ruth Igielnik, "A Century after Women Gained the Right to Vote, Majority of Americans See Work to Do on Gender Equality," Pew Research Center, July 7, 2020, https://www.pewsocialtrends.org/2020/07/07/a-century-after-women-gained-the-right-to-vote-majority-of-americans-see-work-to-do-on-gender-equality/.

29. "The WSA and Manbassadors Team Up to Survey Student Views on Gender Inequity," *The Harbus*, March 2, 2019, http://www.harbus.org/2019/the-wsa-and-manbassadors-team-up-to-survey-student-views-on-gender-inequity/.

30. Robin J. Ely, Pamela Stone, Laurie Shannon, and Colleen Ammerman, *Life & Leadership after HBS*, Harvard Business School, May 2015, https://www.hbs.edu/gender/faculty-research/life-and-leadership-after-hbs/Pages/default.aspx.

31. Elad N. Sherf, Subrahmaniam Tangirala, and Katy Connealy Weber, "It Is Not My Place! Psychological Standing and Men's Voice and Participation in Gender-Parity Initiatives," *Organization Science* 28, no. 2 (2017): 193–210.

32. Adam M. Grant, "Why So Many Men Don't Stand Up for Their Female Colleagues," *The Atlantic*, April 29, 2014, https://www.theatlantic.com/business/archive/2014/04/why-men-dont-stand-up-for-women-to-lead/361231/.

33. W. Brad Johnson and David G. Smith, "How Men Can Become Better Allies to Women," *Harvard Business Review*, October 12, 2018, https://hbr.org/2018/10/how-men-can-become-better-allies-to-women.

34. Jeanine Prime and Corinne A. Moss-Racusin, *Engaging Men in Gender Initiatives: What Change Agents Need to Know*, Catalyst, 2009, https://www.catalyst.org/research/engaging-men-in-gender-initiatives-what-change-agents-need-to-know/.

35. Boris Groysberg and Katherine Connolly, "Great Leaders Who Make the Mix Work," *Harvard Business Review*, September 2013, 68–76.

36. Paul A. Gompers, Vladimir Mukharlyamov, Emily Weisburst, and Yuhai Xuan, "Gender Effects in Venture Capital," SSRN, June 4, 2014, https://papers.ssrn.com/sol3/papers.cfm?abstract_id=2445497; Paul Gompers and Silpa Kovvali, "The Other Diversity Dividend," *Harvard Business Review*, July–August 2018, 72.

37. Bennhold, "Another Side of #MeToo"; Gillian Tan and Katia Porzecanski, "Wall Street Rule for the #MeToo Era: Avoid Women at All Cost," Bloomberg, December 3, 2018, https://

www.bloomberg.com/news/articles/2018-12-03/a-wall-street-rule-for-the-metoo-era-avoid-women
-at-all-cost.

38. Promundo-US, *So, You Want to Be a Male Ally for Gender Equality (and You Should): Results from a National Survey and a Few Things You Should Know*, 2019, https://promundoglobal.org
/resources/male-allyship/.

39. Chio Verastegui, Freek Jorna, Jenny Boddington, and Sue Morphet, "Better Together: Increasing Male Engagement in Gender Equality Efforts in Australia," Bain, March 19, 2019, https://www.bain.com/insights/better-together-increasing-male-engagement-in-gender-equality
-efforts-in-australia/.

40. Emily Shaffer, Negin Sattari, and Alixandra Pollack, *Interrupting Sexism at Work: How Men Respond in a Climate of Silence*, Catalyst, 2020, https://www.catalyst.org/research/interrupting
-sexism-silence/.

41. Mary King, Malin Ortenblad, and Jamie J. Ladge, "What Will It Take to Make Finance More Gender-Balanced?," *Harvard Business Review*, December 10, 2018, https://hbr.org/2018/12/what-will
-it-take-to-make-finance-more-gender-balanced; Katie Abouzahr, Jennifer Garcia-Alonso, Matt Krentz, Michael Tan, and Frances Brooks Taplet, "How Millennial Men Can Help Break the Glass Ceiling," Boston Consulting Group, November 01, 2017, https://www.bcg.com/en-us/publications
/2017/people-organization-behavior-culture-how-millennial-men-can-help-break-glass-ceiling.aspx.

42. Robin J. Ely, Pamela Stone, Laurie Shannon, and Colleen Ammerman, *Life & Leadership after HBS*, Harvard Business School, 2015, https://www.hbs.edu/gender/faculty-research/life
-and-leadership-after-hbs/Pages/default.aspx.

43. Valentin Bolotnyy and Natalia Emanuel, "Why Do Women Earn Less Than Men? Evidence from Bus and Train Operators," Working paper, Harvard University, July 5, 2019, https://scholar.harvard.edu/bolotnyy/publications/why-do-women-earn-less-men-evidence-bus
-and-train-operators-job-market-paper.

44. Anne-Marie Slaughter, *Unfinished Business: Women Men Work Family* (New York: Random House, 2015); Lisa Belkin, "Huggies Pulls Ads after Insulting Dads," *Huffington Post*, March 12, 2012, https://www.huffpost.com/entry/huggies-pulls-diaper-ads_b_1339074?guccounter=1.

45. Gretchen Livingston and Kim Parker, "8 Facts about American Dads," Pew Research Center, June 23, 2019, https://www.pewresearch.org/fact-tank/2019/06/12/fathers-day-facts/.

46. Scheiber, "Couple's Suit over Parental Leave Is New Challenge to Big Law Firm."

47. Brad Harrington, Fred Van Deusen, Jennifer Sabatini Fraone, and Samantha Eddy, *The New Dad: Take Your Leave Perspectives on Paternity Leave from Fathers, Leading Organizations, and Global Policies*, The New Dad, 2014, https://www.fatherhood.gov/sites/default/files/resource_files/e000003047.pdf.

48. Jennifer Petriglieri, *Couples That Work: How Dual-Career Couples Thrive in Love and Work* (Boston: Harvard Business Review Press, 2019).

49. Alexis Ohanian, "Alexis Ohanian: Paternity Leave Was Crucial after the Birth of My Child, and Every Father Deserves It," *New York Times*, August 12, 2019, https://parenting.nytimes
.com/work-money/alexis-ohanian-paternity-leave.

50. Yoon Min-sik, "Korean Fathers Can Get Longest Paid Leave in OECD," *Korea Herald*, December 2, 2015, http://www.koreaherald.com/view.php?ud=20151202001017.

51. Ben Waber, "Why I Require New Fathers Who Work for Me to Take Paternity Leave," Quartz, May 22, 2018, https://qz.com/work/1284912/paid-parental-leave-why-i-require-new
-fathers-who-work-for-me-to-take-it/.

52. John West, "Japan Is a Poor Performer on Gender Equality. Can the 'Womenomics' Initiative Help?," Brink, August 1, 2019, https://www.brinknews.com/japan-is-a-poor-performer-on
-gender-equality-can-the-womenomics-initiative-help/; Brook Larmer, "Why Does Japan Make It So Hard for Working Women to Succeed?," *New York Times*, October 17, 2018, https://www.nytimes
.com/2018/10/17/magazine/why-does-japan-make-it-so-hard-for-working-women-to-succeed.html.

53. Mokoto Rich, "Japan's Working Mothers: Record Responsibilities, Little Help from Dads," *New York Times*, February 2, 2019, https://www.nytimes.com/2019/02/02/world/asia/japan
-working-mothers.html.

54. Mokoto Rich, "A Japanese Politician Is Taking Paternity Leave. It's a Big Deal," *New York Times*, January 15, 2020, https://www.nytimes.com/2020/01/15/world/asia/japan-koizumi-paternity
-leave.html.

55. This profile draws on Siri Chilazi, Aneeta Rattan, and Oriane Georgeac, "Ros Atkins and the 50:50 Project at the BBC," London Business School Case Study 20-010, March 2020.

56. *The 50:50 Project, Impact Report 2019*, http://downloads.bbc.co.uk/aboutthebbc/reports/reports/5050-may-2019.pdf.

57. *50:50: The Equality Project, Impact Report 2020*, http://downloads.bbc.co.uk/aboutthebbc/reports/reports/5050-april-2020.pdf.

58. Ibid.

Chapter Five

1. Boris Groysberg and Katherine Connolly, "JPMorgan Chase: Tapping an Overlooked Talent Pool," Harvard Business School Case 415-066, May 2015 (revised May 2018), https://www.hbs.edu/faculty/pages/item.aspx?num=48876.

2. J. Yo-Jud Cheng and Boris Groysberg, "Innovation Should Be a Top Priority for Boards. So Why Isn't It?," *Harvard Business Review*, September 21, 2018, https://hbr.org/2018/09/innovation-should-be-a-top-priority-for-boards-so-why-isnt-it.

3. Tina Lee and Julie Sweet, *Advancing Women as Leaders in the Private Sector*, 2018, https://advancingwomeninbusiness.com/wp-content/uploads/2018/10/Advancing-women-as-leaders-in-the-private-sector_report.pdf.

4. Sheryl Estrada, "Leaders Say Gender Equity Is Important, but Less Than 50% Have Multi-year Strategy, HR Dive, March 9, 2020, https://www.hrdive.com/news/leaders-say-gender-equity-is-important-but-less-than-50-have-multi-year-s-1/573741/.

5. Herminia Ibarra, Robin J. Ely, and Deborah M. Kolb, "Women Rising: The Unseen Barriers," *Harvard Business Review*, September 2013, 60–67.

6. Miller McPherson, Lynn Smith-Lovin, and James M. Cook, "Birds of a Feather: Homophily in Social Networks," *Annual Review of Sociology* 27, no. 1 (2001): 415–444.

7. Paul A. Gompers, Kevin Huang, and Sophie Calder-Wang, *Homophily in Entrepreneurial Team Formation*, Harvard Business School Working Papers, May 16, 2017, https://ssrn.com/abstract=2973329.

8. Matt L. Huffman and Lisa Torres, "It's Not Only 'Who You Know' That Matters: Gender, Personal Contacts, and Job Lead Quality, *Gender & Society* 16, no. 6 (2002): 793–813.9

9. LinkedIn Talent Solutions, "LinkedIn's Former Head of Global Solutions on Hiring Diverse Teams," YouTube, January 30, 2019, https://www.youtube.com/watch?v=mUpogdpzaqM&feature=youtu.be.

10. Danielle Gaucher, Justin Friesen, and Aaron C. Kay, "Evidence That Gendered Wording in Job Advertisements Exists and Sustains Gender Inequality," *Journal of Personality and Social Psychology* 101, no. 1 (2001): 109–128.

11. Marise Ph. Born and Toon W. Taris, "The Impact of the Wording of Employment Advertisements on Students' Inclination to Apply for a Job," *Journal of Social Psychology* 150, no. 5 (2010): 485–502.

12. Kieran Snyder, "Language in Your Job Post Predicts the Gender of Your Hire," Textio, June 21, 2016, https://textio.ai/gendered-language-in-your-job-post-predicts-the-gender-of-the-person-youll-hire-cd150452407d.

13. Katherine B. Coffman, Manuela Collis, and Leena Kulkarni, *When to Apply?*, Harvard Business School Working Paper, February 2019, https://www.hbs.edu/faculty/Pages/item.aspx?num=57230.

14. Lisa Abraham and Alison Stein, *Words Matter: Experimental Evidence from Job Applications*, Working paper, August 9, 2020, https://drive.google.com/file/d/1YKifRzy_kWuIIdB3MLS4VHht3okJa8pa/view.

15. Roberto M. Fernandez and Isabel Fernandez-Mateo, "Networks, Race, and Hiring," *American Sociological Review* 71, no. 1 (2006): 42–71; Roberto M. Fernandez and M. Lourdes Sosa, "Gendering the Job: Networks and Recruitment at a Call Center," *American Journal of Sociology* 111, no. 3 (2005): 859–904; Brian Rubineau and Roberto M. Fernandez, "Missing Links: Referrer Behavior and Job Segregation," *Management Science* 59, no. 11 (2013): 2470–2489.

16. Corinne A. Moss-Racusin, John F. Dovidio, Victoria L. Brescoll, Mark J. Graham, and Jo Handelsman, "Science Faculty's Subtle Gender Biases Favor Male Students," *Proceedings of the National Academy of Sciences* 109, no. 41 (2012): 16474–16479; András Tilcsik, "Pride and Prejudice: Employment Discrimination against Openly Gay Men in the United States," *American Journal of Sociology* 117, no. 2 (2011): 586–626; Marianne Bertrand and Sendhil Mullainathan, "Are Emily and Greg More Employable Than Lakisha and Jamal? A Field Experiment on Labor Market Discrimination," *American Economic Review* 94, no. 4 (2004): 991–1013; Claudia Goldin and Cecilia Rouse, "Orchestrating Impartiality: The Impact of 'Blind' Auditions on Female Musicians," *American Economic Review* 90, no. 4 (2000): 715–741.

17. Boris Groysberg and Katherine Connolly, "BlackRock: Diversity as a Driver for Success," Harvard Business School Case 415-047, February 2015, https://www.hbs.edu/faculty/pages /item.aspx?num=48640.

18. Isabelle Régner, Catherine Thinus-Blanc, Agnès Netter, Toni Schmader, and Pascal Huguet, "Committees with Implicit Biases Promote Fewer Women When They Do Not Believe Gender Bias Exists," *Nature Human Behaviour* 3 (2019): 1171–1179.

19. Eric Luis Uhlmann and Geoffrey L. Cohen, "Constructed Criteria: Redefining Merit to Justify Discrimination," *Psychological Science* 16, no. 6 (2005): 474–480.

20. Heather Sarsons, "Recognition for Group Work: Gender Differences in Academia," *American Economic Review* 107, no. 5 (2017): 141–145.

21. Katherine B. Coffman, Christine L. Exley, and Muriel Niederle, "The Role of Beliefs in Driving Gender Discrimination," Harvard Business School Working Paper No. 18-054, December 2017 (revised January 2020), https://www.hbs.edu/faculty/Pages/item.aspx?num=53686.

22. Shelley J. Correll, Stephen Benard, and In Paik, "Getting a Job: Is There a Motherhood Penalty?," *American Journal of Sociology* 112, no. 5 (2007): 1297–1339.

23. Lauren A. Rivera and András Tilcsik, "Class Advantage, Commitment Penalty: The Gendered Effect of Social Class Signals in an Elite Labor Market," *American Sociological Review* 81, no. 6 (2016): 1097–1131.

24. Boris Groysberg, *Chasing Stars: The Myth of Talent and the Portability of Performance* (Princeton, NJ: Princeton University Press, 2010); Ashish Nanda, Boris Groysberg, and Lauren Prusiner, "Lehman Brothers (A): Rise of the Equity Research Department," Harvard Business School Case 906-034, January 2006 (revised June 2008), https://www.hbs.edu/faculty/pages/item.aspx?num =32959.

25. Jordan Siegel, Mimi Xi, and Christopher Poliquin, "Talent Edge Initiative," *Harvard Business Review*, October 21, 2010, https://store.hbr.org/product/baxter-s-asia-pacific-talent-edge -initiative/711408?sku=711408-PDF-ENG.

26. Iris Bohnet, Alexandra van Geen, and Max Bazerman, "When Performance Trumps Gender Bias: Joint vs. Separate Evaluation," *Management Science* 62, no. 5 (2015): 1225–1234.

27. Frank L. Schmidt and John E. Hunter, "The Validity and Utility of Selection Methods in Personnel Psychology: Practical and Theoretical Implications of 85 Years of Research Findings," *Psychological Bulletin* 124, no. 2 (1998): 262–274.

28. Stephanie K. Johnson and Jessica F. Kirk, "Dual-Anonymization Yields Promising Results for Reducing Gender Bias: A Naturalistic Field Experiment of Applications for Hubble Space Telescope Time," *Publications of the Astronomical Society of the Pacific* 132, no. 1009 (2020), https://iopscience.iop.org /article/10.1088/1538-3873/ab6ce0/pdf; Goldin and Rouse, "Orchestrating Impartiality."

29. Jeanna Smialek, "How the Fed Is Trying to Fix Its White Male Problem," *New York Times*, October 2, 2019, https://www.nytimes.com/2019/10/02/business/economy/federal-reserve-diversity -hiring.html.

30. Anne Sraders, "Goldman Sachs Removed This One Word from Some Recruiting Materials—and Saw Female Hires Soar," *Fortune*, December 10, 2019, https://fortune.com/2019/12 /10/goldman-sachs-removed-this-one-word-from-some-recruiting-materials-and-saw-female-hires -soar/.

31. Groysberg, *Chasing Stars*.

32. Louise Marie Roth, *Selling Women Short: Gender and Money on Wall Street* (Princeton, NJ: Princeton University Press, 2006).

33. Boris Groysberg and Deborah Bell, "Dysfunction in the Boardroom," *Harvard Business Review*, June 3, 88–95.

34. Herminia Ibarra, "Homophily and Differential Returns: Sex Differences in Network Structure and Access in an Advertising Firm," *Administrative Science Quarterly* 37, no. 3 (1992): 422–447.

35. Alexandra Kalev, "Cracking the Glass Cages? Restructuring and Ascriptive Inequality at Work," *American Journal of Sociology* 114, no. 6 (2009): 1591–1643.

36. David A. Thomas, "Truth about Mentoring Minorities: Race Matters," *Harvard Business Review* April 1, 2001, 98–107; David A. Thomas and John A. Gabarro, *Breaking Through: The Making of Minority Executives in Corporate America* (Boston: Harvard Business School Press, 1999).

37. Irene E. De Pater, Annelies E. M. Van Vianen, and Myriam N. Bechtoldt, "Gender Differences in Job Challenge: A Matter of Task Allocation," *Gender, Work & Organization* 17, no. 4 (2010): 433–453.

38. Christine L. Nittrouer, Michelle R. Hebl, Leslie Ashburn-Nardo, Rachel C. E. Trump-Steele, David M. Lane, and Virginia Valian, "Gender Disparities in Colloquium Speakers at Top Universities," *Proceedings of the National Academy of Sciences* 115, no. 1 (2018): 104–108.

39. Eden B. King, Whitney Botsford, Michelle R. Hebl, Stephanie Kazama, Jeremy F. Dawson, and Andrew Perkins, "Benevolent Sexism at Work: Gender Differences in the Distribution of Challenging Developmental Experiences," *Journal of Management* 38, no. 6 (2012): 1835–1866.

40. Curtis K. Chan and Michel Anteby, "Task Segregation as a Mechanism for Within-Job Inequality: Women and Men of the Transportation Security Administration," *Administrative Science Quarterly* 61, no. 2 (2016): 184–216.

41. Linda Babcock, Maria P. Recalde, Lise Vesterlund, and Laurie Weingart, "Gender Differences in Accepting and Receiving Requests for Tasks with Low Promotability," *American Economic Review* 107, no. 3 (2017): 714–747.

42. Madeline E. Heilman and Julie J. Chen, "Same Behavior, Different Consequences: Reactions to Men's and Women's Altruistic Citizenship Behavior," *Journal of Applied Psychology* 90, no. 3 (2005): 431–441.

43. Ibarra, Ely, and Kolb, "Women Rising."

44. Herminia Ibarra, Nancy M. Carter, and Christine Silva, "Why Men Still Get More Promotions Than Women," *Harvard Business Review*, September 2010, 80–126.

45. Rachel Thomas, Marianne Cooper, Ellen Konar, et al., *Women in the Workplace 2017*, https://womenintheworkplace.com/2017.

46. Francine D. Blau, Janet M. Currie, Rachel T. A. Croson, and Donna K. Ginther, "Can Mentoring Help Female Assistant Professors? Interim Results from a Randomized Trial," *American Economic Review* 100, no. 2 (2010): 348–352.

47. Jennifer L. Berdahl, Marianne Cooper, Peter Glick, Robert W. Livingston, and Joan C. Williams, "Work as a Masculinity Contest," *Journal of Social Issues* 74, no. 3 (2018): 422–448.

48. Amy J. C. Cuddy, Peter Glick, and Anna Beninger, "The Dynamics of Warmth and Competence Judgments, and Their Outcomes in Organizations," *Research in Organizational Behavior* 31 (2011): 73–98; Alice H. Eagly and Steven J. Karau, "Role Congruity Theory of Prejudice toward Female Leaders," *Psychological Review* 109, no. 3 (2002): 573–598.

49. Victoria L. Brescoll and Eric Luis Uhlmann, "Can an Angry Woman Get Ahead? Status Conferral, Gender, and Expression of Emotion in the Workplace," *Psychological Science* 19, no. 3 (2008): 268–275.

50. Victoria L. Brescoll, "Who Takes the Floor and Why: Gender, Power, and Volubility in Organizations," *Administrative Science Quarterly* 56, no. 4 (2011): 622–641.

51. David G. Smith, Judith E. Rosenstein, Margaret C. Nikolov, and Darby A. Chaney, "The Power of Language: Gender, Status, and Agency in Performance Evaluations," *Sex Roles* 80 (2019): 159–171.

52. Anne Morriss and Frances X. Frei, *Unleashed: The Unapologetic Leader's Guide to Empowering Everyone around You* (Boston: Harvard Business Review Press, 2020).

53. Martha Foschi, "Double Standards in the Evaluation of Men and Women," *Social Psychology Quarterly* 59, no. 3 (1996): 237–254.

54. Monica Biernat, M. J. Tocci, and Joan C. Williams, "The Language of Performance Evaluations: Gender-Based Shifts in Content and Consistency of Judgment," *Social Psychological and Personality Science* 3, no. 2 (2012): 186–192.

55. Paola Cecchi-Dimeglio, "How Gender Bias Corrupts Performance Reviews, and What to Do about It," *Harvard Business Review*, April 12, 2017, from https://hbr.org/2017/04/how-gender -bias-corrupts-performance-reviews-and-what-to-do-about-it.

56. Herman Aguinis, Young Hun Ji, and Harry Joo, "Gender Productivity Gap among Star Performers in STEM and Other Scientific Fields," *Journal of Applied Psychology* 102, no. 12 (2018): 1283–1306.

57. M. Ena Inesi and Daniel M. Cable, "When Accomplishments Come Back to Haunt You: The Negative Effect of Competence Signals on Women's Performance Evaluations," *Personnel Psychology* 68, no. 3 (2015): 615–657.

58. Janice Fanning Madden, "Performance-Support Bias and the Gender Pay Gap among Stockbrokers," *Gender & Society* 26, no. 3 (2012): 488–518.

59. John T. Jost et al., "The Existence of Implicit Bias Is beyond Reasonable Doubt: A Refutation of Ideological and Methodological Objections and Executive Summary of Ten Studies That No Manager Should Ignore," *Research in Organizational Behavior* 29 (2009): 39–69; Mahzarin Banaji and Anthony Greenwald, "Implicit Gender Stereotyping in Judgments of Fame," *Journal of Personality and Social Psychology* 68, no. 2 (2009): 181–198.

60. Michelle M. Duguid and Melissa C. Thomas-Hunt, "Condoning Stereotyping? How Awareness of Stereotyping Prevalence Impacts Expression of Stereotypes," *Journal of Applied Psychology* 100, no. 2 (2015): 343–359.

61. Aguinis, Ji, and Joo, "Gender Productivity Gap among Star Performers in STEM and Other Scientific Fields."

62. Cecchi-Dimeglio, "How Gender Bias Corrupts Performance Reviews"; Shelley J. Correll and Caroline Simard, "Research: Vague Feedback Is Holding Women Back," *Harvard Business Review*, April 29, 2016, https://hbr.org/2016/04/research-vague-feedback-is-holding -women-back.

63. Lily Jampol and Vivian Zayas, "Gendered White Lies: Women Are Given Inflated Performance Feedback Compared with Men," *Personality and Social Psychology Bulletin*, doi:10.1177/0146167220916622.

64. Shelley J. Correll, "SWS 2016 Feminist Lecture: Reducing Gender Biases in Modern Workplaces; A Small Wins Approach to Organizational Change," *Gender & Society* 31, no. 6 (2017): 725–750.

65. Emilio J. Castilla, "Gender, Race, and Meritocracy in Organizational Careers," *American Journal of Sociology* 113, no. 6 (2008): 1479–1526.

66. Karen Lyness and Madeline Heilman, "When Fit Is Fundamental: Performance Evaluations and Promotions of Upper-Level Female and Male Managers, *Journal of Applied Psychology* 91, no. 4 (2006): 777–785.

67. Alexia Fernández Campbell, "They Did Everything Right—and Still Hit the Glass Ceiling. Now, These Women Are Suing America's Top Companies for Equal Pay," Vox, December 29, 2019, https://www.vox.com/the-highlight/2019/12/3/20948425/equal-pay-lawsuits-pay-gap-glass -ceiling; Michael Sainato, "Walmart Facing Gender Discrimination Lawsuits from Female Employees," *The Guardian*, February 18, 2019, https://www.theguardian.com/us-news/2019/feb /18/walmart-gender-discrimination-supreme-court; Anastasia Tsioulcas, "Top Flutist Settles Gender Pay-Gap Suit with Boston Symphony Orchestra," National Public Radio, February 21, 2019, https://www.npr.org/2019/02/21/696574690/top-flutist-settles-gender-pay-gap-suit-with -boston-symphony-orchestra.

68. Samantha Schmidt, "'Victory for Equal Pay': Judge Rules Trump Administration Must Require Companies to Report Pay by Gender, Race," *Washington Post*, March 5, 2019, https:// www.washingtonpost.com/dc-md-va/2019/03/05/victory-equal-pay-judge-rules-trump -administration-must-require-companies-report-pay-by-gender-race/?utm_term=.7e18bb0dd295.

69. Lisa Nagele-Piazza, "EEOC Reduces Employee Pay Data Requirements," Society for Human Resource Management, September 11, 2019, https://www.shrm.org/ResourcesAndTools

/legal-and-compliance/employment-law/Pages/Employers-Should-Review-EEO-1-Guidance
-Before-Pay-Data-Reporting-Deadline.aspx.

70. "Senate Bill 973 (Jackson), California Women's Law Center, 2020, https://www.cwlc.org
/2020/03/senate-bill-973-jackson/.

71. Rebecca Greenfield, "Citigroup Reveals Female Employees Earn 29% Less Than Men Do,"
Fortune, January 16, 2019, https://www.bloomberg.com/news/articles/2019-01-16/citigroup
-reveals-its-female-employees-earn-29-less-than-men-do.

72. Hannah Riley Bowles, Linda Babcock, and Kathleen L. McGinn, "Constraints and
Triggers: Situational Mechanics of Gender in Negotiation," *Journal of Personality and Social
Psychology* 89, no. 6 (2005): 951–965.

73. Andreas Leibbrandt and John A. List, "Do Women Avoid Salary Negotiations? Evidence
from a Large-Scale Natural Field Experiment," *Management Science* 61, no. 9 (2015): 2016–2024.

74. Nina Rousille, *The Central Role of the Ask Gap in Gender Pay Inequality,* University of
California, 2020, https://ninaroussille.github.io/files/Roussille_askgap.pdf.

75. Boris Groysberg, Paul Healy, and Eric Lin, "Determinants of Gender Differences in
Change in Pay among Job-Switching Executives," *Industrial & Labor Relations Review,*
doi:10.1177/0019793920930712.

76. Cecilia Kang, "Google Data-Mines Its Approach to Promoting Women," *Washington Post,*
April 2, 2014, https://www.washingtonpost.com/news/the-switch/wp/2014/04/02/google-data
-mines-its-women-problem/.

77. Cristian L. Dezső, David Gaddis Ross, and Jose Uribe, "Is There an Implicit Quota on
Women in Top Management? A Large Sample Statistical Analysis," *Strategic Management Journal*
37, no. 1 (2015): 98–115.

78. Michelle K. Ryan, Alexander Haslam, Thekla Morgenroth, Floor Rink, Jank Stoker, and
Kim Peters, "Getting on Top of the Glass Cliff: Reviewing a Decade of Evidence, Explanations,
and Impact," *Leadership Quarterly* 27, no. 3 (2016): 446–455.

79. Kathleen L. McGinn, Deborah M. Kolb, and Cailin B. Hammer. "Cathy Benko: WINning
at Deloitte," Harvard Business School Case 907-026, September 2006, https://www.hbs.edu
/faculty/Pages/item.aspx?num=33577.

80. Trond Petersen, Ishak Saporta, and Marc-David L. Seidel, "Offering a Job: Meritocracy and
Social Networks," *American Journal of Sociology* 106, no. 3 (2000): 763–816.

81. Jane Giacobbe Miller and Kenneth G. Wheeler, "Unraveling the Mysteries of Gender
Differences in Intentions to Leave the Organization," *Journal of Organizational Behavior* 12, no. 5
(1992): 465–478.

82. Rita Mano-Negrin, "Gender-Related Opportunities and Turnover: The Case of Medical
Sector Employees," *Gender, Work & Organization* 10, no. 3 (2003): 342–360.

83. Kathleen L. McGinn and Katherine L. Milkman, "Looking Up and Looking Out: Career
Mobility Effects of Demographic Similarity among Professionals," *Organization Science* 24, no. 4
(2013): 1041–1060.

84. Frank Dobbin and Alexandra Kalev, "Training Programs and Reporting Systems Won't
End Sexual Harassment. Promoting More Women Will," *Harvard Business Review,* November 15,
2017, https://hbr.org/2017/11/training-programs-and-reporting-systems-wont-end-sexual
-harassment-promoting-more-women-will.

85. Marianne Cooper, "The 3 Things That Make Organizations More Prone to Sexual
Harassment," *The Atlantic,* November 27, 2017, https://www.theatlantic.com/business/archive
/2017/11/organizations-sexual-harassment/546707/.

86. Robin J. Ely, Pamela Stone, and Colleen Ammerman, "Rethink What You 'Know' about
High-Achieving Women," *Harvard Business Review,* December 2014, 101.

87. Correll, Benard, and Paik, "Getting a Job."

88. Pamela Stone, *Opting Out? Why Women Really Quit Careers and Head Home* (Berkeley:
University of California Press, 2007).

89. Sara A. Rogier and Margaret Y. Padgett, "The Impact of Utilizing a Flexible Work
Schedule on the Perceived Career Advancement Potential of Women," *Human Resource Development Quarterly* 15, no. 1 (2004): 89–106.

90. Leslie A. Perlow and Erin L. Kelly, "Toward a Model of Work Redesign for Better Work and Better Life," *Work and Occupations* 41, no. 1 (2014): 111–134.

91. Boris Groysberg and Sarah L. Abbott, "Canada Mortgage and Housing Corporation: 'One CMHC' and Version 3.0," Harvard Business School Case 9-419-068, May 2019, https://www.hbs .edu/faculty/Pages/item.aspx?num=56155.

92. Nick Bastone, "Salesforce's Chief People Office Explains How and Why the Company Has Spent $8.7 Million to Close Its Gender Pay Gap," *Business Insider*, December 15, 2018, https://www .businessinsider.com/cindy-robbins-salesforce-equal-pay-2018-11.

93. Tina Lee and Julie Sweet, *Advancing Women as Leaders in the Private Sector*, Canada–United States Council for Advancement of Women Entrepreneurs & Business Leaders, 2018, https:// advancingwomeninbusiness.com/wp-content/uploads/2018/10/Advancing-women-as-leaders-in -the-private-sector_report.pdf.

94. Melonie Parker, "How Retention Helps Make Google More Representative," Google Blog, February 28, 2019, https://blog.google/perspectives/melonie-parker/how-retention-helps-make -google-more-representative/.

95. Rebecca Glasman, Tina Shah Paikeday, Harsonal Sachar, Alix Stuart, and Cissy Young, *A Leader's Guide: Finding and Keeping Your Next Chief Diversity Officer*, Russell Reynolds, 2019, https://www.russellreynolds.com/en/Insights/thought-leadership/Documents/Chief%20 Diversity%20Officer_1218_FINAL.pdf.

96. Rosabeth Moss Kanter, "The Interplay of Structure and Behavior: How System Dynamics Can Explain or Change Outcomes by Gender or Social Category" (presentation at Gender & Work: Challenging Conventional Wisdom, Harvard Business School, Boston, February 28 and March 1, 2013).

97. *Dandan Pan, Carrie Haluza, Carolina Dealy, Laura Paquin, Wei Shi, Blanche Matulich and Connie Jacobson on Behalf of Themselves and All Others Similarly Situated v. Qualcomm Incorporated & Qualcomm Technologies, Inc.*, No. 3:16-cv-01885-JLS-DHB (United States District Court Southern District of California 2016).

98. "Equal Pay Act Charges (Charges Filed with EEOC) (Includes Concurrent Charges with Title VII, ADEA, ADA, and GINA) FY 1997–FY 2019," Equal Employment Opportunity Commission, 2018, https://www.eeoc.gov/eeoc/statistics/enforcement/epa.cfm.

99. *Dandan Pan et al. v. Qualcomm Incorporated & Qualcomm Technologies, Inc.*

100. "Sanford Heisler and Tech Giant Qualcomm Agree to $19.5 Million Gender Discrimination Settlement." Sanford Heisler Sharp, July 26, 2016, https://sanfordheisler.com/press-release /qualcomm-gender-discrimination-settlement/.

101. *Dandan Pan et al. v. Qualcomm Incorporated & Qualcomm Technologies, Inc.*

102. Sara Randazzo, "Qualcomm to Pay $19.5 Million to Settle Claims of Bias against Women," *Wall Street Journal*, July 26, 2016, https://www.wsj.com/articles/qualcomm-to-pay-19-5 -million-to-settle-claims-of-bias-against-women-1469571756; Qualcomm, *2019 Corporate Responsibility Report*, https://www.qualcomm.com/documents/2019-qualcomm-corporate -responsibility-report.

Chapter Six

1. Boris Groysberg and Katherine Connolly, "JPMorgan Chase: Tapping an Overlooked Talent Pool," Harvard Business School Case 415-066, May 2015 (revised May 2018), https://www .hbs.edu/faculty/pages/item.aspx?num=48876.

2. Frank Dobbin and Alexandra Kalev, "Why Diversity Programs Fail," *Harvard Business Review*, July–August 2016, 52–60.

3. Klea Faniko, Naomi Ellemers, Belle Derks, and Fabio Lorenzi-Cioldi, "Nothing Changes, Really: Why Women Who Break through the Glass Ceiling End Up Reinforcing It," *Personality and Social Psychology Bulletin* 43, no. 5 (2017): 638–651; Belle Derks, Naomi Ellemers, Colette van Laar, and Kim de Groot, "Do Sexist Organizational Cultures Create the Queen Bee?," *British Journal of Social Psychology* 50, no. 3 (2011): 519–535; Robin J. Ely, "The Effects of Organizational Demographics and Social Identity on Relationships among Professional Women," *Administrative*

Science Quarterly 39, no. 2 (1994): 203–238; Rosabeth Moss Kanter, *Men and Women of the Corporation* (New York: Basic Books, 1977).

4. Rachel Thomas, Marianne Cooper, Ellen Konar, et al., *Women in the Workplace 2019*, https://wiw-report.s3.amazonaws.com/Women_in_the_Workplace_2019.pdf.

5. Terry Stone, Becky Miller, Elizabeth Southerlan, and Alex Raun, *Women in Healthcare Leadership 2019*, Oliver Wyman, 2019, https://www.oliverwyman.com/content/dam/oliver -wyman/v2/publications/2019/January/WiHC/WiHCL-Report-Final.pdf.

6. John T. Josta, Laurie A. Rudmanb, Irene V. Blair, et al. "The Existence of Implicit Bias Is beyond Reasonable Doubt: A Refutation of Ideological and Methodological Objections and Executive Summary of Ten Studies That No Manager Should Ignore," *Research in Organizational Behavior* 29 (2009): 39–69.

7. Michelle M. Duguid and Melissa C. Thomas-Hunt, "Condoning Stereotyping? How Awareness of Stereotyping Prevalence Impacts Expression of Stereotypes," *Journal of Applied Psychology* 100, no. 2 (March 2015): 343–359.8

8. Stefanie K. Johnson and Jessica F. Kirk, "Dual-Anonymization Yields Promising Results for Reducing Gender Bias: A Naturalistic Field Experiment of Applications for Hubble Space Telescope Time," *Publications of the Astronomical Society of the Pacific* 132, no. 1009 (2020): 034503.

9. Jeff Green, "Managers Pick Mini-Me Proteges of Same Race, Gender," Bloomberg, January 8, 2019, https://www.bloomberg.com/news/articles/2019-01-08/managers-pick-mini-me -proteges-of-same-gender-race-in-new-study.

10. Catherine H. Tinsley and Robin J. Ely, "What Most People Get Wrong about Men and Women: Research Shows the Sexes Aren't So Different," *Harvard Business Review*, May–June 2018, 114–120.

11. Ibid.

12. Thomas et al., *Women in the Workplace 2019*.

13. Zoë B. Cullen and Ricardo Perez-Truglia, *The Old Boys' Club: Schmoozing and the Gender Gap*, Working Paper No. w26530, National Bureau of Economic Research, September 2020, https://www.nber.org/papers/w26530.

14. Ashish Nanda, Boris Groysberg, and Lauren Prusiner, "Lehman Brothers (B): Exit Jack Rivkin," Harvard Business School Case, 906-035, January 2006 (revised January 2007), https:// www.hbs.edu/faculty/Pages/item.aspx?num=32960.

15. Robin J. Ely, Debra Meyerson, and Martin N. Davidson, "Rethinking Political Correct-ness," *Harvard Business Review*, September 2006, 78–87.

16. John F. Dovidio, Erin L. Thomas, Corinne A. Moss-Racusin, Victoria L. Brescoll, Mark J. Graham, and Jo Handelsman, "Included but Invisible? The Benefits and Costs of Inclusion," paper presented at Gender & Work: Challenging Conventional Wisdom, Harvard Business School, 2013.

17. Audrey Gelman, "'Where I Got It Wrong': The Wing's Audrey Gelman Confronts the Realities of Rapid Growth," *Fast Company*, February 26, 2020, fastcompany.com website: https:// www.fastcompany.com/90466019/where-i-got-it-wrong-the-wings-audrey-gelman-confronts-the -realities-of-rapid-growth.

18. Anna T. Mayo, Anita Williams Woolley, and Rosalind M. Chow, "Unpacking Participation and Influence: Diversity's Countervailing Effects on Expertise Use in Groups," *Academy of Management Discoveries* 6, no. 2 (2020): 300–319.

19. Thomas et al., *Women in the Workplace 2019*.

20. David A. Garvin, Alison Berkley Wagonfeld, and Liz Kind, "Google's Project Oxygen: Do Managers Matter?," Harvard Business School, Case 313-110, April 2013 (revised October 2013), https://www.hbs.edu/faculty/Pages/item.aspx?num=44657.

21. Melissa Harrell and Lauren Barbato, "Great Managers Still Matter: The Evolution of Google's Project Oxygen," re: Work, February 27, 2018, https://rework.withgoogle.com/blog/the -evolution-of-project-oxygen/.

22. This profile draws on the following Harvard Business School cases: Ashish Nanda, Boris Groysberg, and Lauren Prusiner, "Lehman Brothers (A): Rise of the Equity Research Department," Harvard Business School Case 906-034, January 2006 (revised June 2008), https://www.hbs.edu /faculty/pages/item.aspx?num=32959; Nanda, Groysberg, and Prusiner, "Lehman Brothers (B)";

Ashish Nanda and Boris Groysberg, "Lehman Brothers (C): Decline of the Equity Research Department," Harvard Business School Case 902-003, July 2001 (revised January 2007), https://www.hbs.edu/faculty/Pages/item.aspx?num=28331; Boris Groysberg and Laura Morgan Roberts, "Leading the Josie Esquivel Franchise (A)," Harvard Business School Case 404-054, November 2003 (revised October 2005), https://www.hbs.edu/faculty/Pages/item.aspx?num=30567.

23. Boris Groysberg, *Chasing Stars: The Myth of Talent and the Portability of Performance* (Princeton, NJ: Princeton University Press, 2010); Boris Groysberg and Linda-Eling Lee, "Star Power: Colleague Quality and Turnover," *Industrial and Corporate Change* 19, no. 3 (2010): 741–765.

24. Nanda, Groysberg, and Prusiner, "Lehman Brothers (A)."

25. Groysberg and Morgan Roberts, "Leading the Josie Esquivel Franchise (A)."

26. Nanda, Groysberg, and Prusiner, "Lehman Brothers (A)."

27. Groysberg and Morgan Roberts, "Leading the Josie Esquivel Franchise (A)."

28. Nanda, Groysberg, and Prusiner, "Lehman Brothers (A)."

29. Groysberg, *Chasing Stars.*

30. Groysberg and Morgan Roberts, "Leading the Josie Esquivel Franchise (A)."

31. Groysberg, *Chasing Stars.*

32. Nanda, Groysberg, and Prusiner, "Lehman Brothers (B)."

33. Nanda and Groysberg, "Lehman Brothers (C)."

34. Ibid.

Conclusion

1. "Domestic Box Office for 1980," Box Office Mojo, n.d., https://www.boxofficemojo.com/year/1980/.

2. Kim Borjorquez, "Put People of Color on California Boards or Pay $100K, Proposed Law Says," *Sacramento Bee*, July 23, 2020, https://www.sacbee.com/news/politics-government/capitol-alert/article244255597.html; Heidrick & Struggles, "Board Monitor US 2020," September 9, 2020, https://www.heidrick.com/Knowledge-Center/Publication/Board_Monitor_US_2020; Sir John Parker and the Parker Review Committee, *Ethnic Diversity Enriching Business Leadership: An Update Report from the Parker Review*, February 5, 2020, https://assets.ey.com/content/dam/ey-sites/ey-com/en_uk/news/2020/02/ey-parker-review-2020-report-final.pdf.

3. Eshe Nelson, "In Britain, an Idea to Reduce Racial Inequality Gains Momentum," *New York Times*, August 26, 2020, https://www.nytimes.com/2020/08/26/business/britain-pay-gaps-racial-inequality.html.

4. Kristen Bellstrom and Emma Hinchcliffe, "Black Women Are Bearing the Economic Brunt of the Pandemic," *Fortune*, June 3, 2020, https://fortune.com/2020/06/03/black-women-coronavirus-economy/; Michelle Miller and Vidya Singh, "Gender Pay Gap May Not Close 'for More Than 100 Years' for Black and Latina Women, and Pandemic Could Make It Worse," CBS News, August 8, 2020, https://www.cbsnews.com/news/gender-pay-gap-covid-pandemic-black-latina-women/.

5. Matthew S. Schwartz, "Trump Tells Agencies to End Trainings on "White Privilege" and "Critical Race Theory," National Public Radio, September 5, 2020, https://www.npr.org/2020/09/05/910053496/trump-tells-agencies-to-end-trainings-on-white-privilege-and-critical-race-theor.

6. Abby Ohlheiser, "How James Damore Went from Google Employee to Right-Wing Internet Hero," *Washington Post*, August 12, 2017, https://www.washingtonpost.com/news/the-intersect/wp/2017/08/12/how-james-damore-went-from-google-employee-to-right-wing-internet-hero/.

7. Titan Alon, Matthias Doepke, Jane Olmstead-Rumsey, and Michèle Tertilt, "The Impact of COVID-19 on Gender Equality," Northwestern University, March 2020, http://faculty.wcas.northwestern.edu/~mdo738/research/COVID19_Gender_March_2020.pdf; Jessica Bennett, "'I Feel Like I Have Five Jobs': Moms Navigate the Pandemic," *New York Times*, March 20, 2020, https://www.nytimes.com/2020/03/20/parenting/childcare-coronavirus-moms.html; Caitlyn Collins, Liana Christin Landivar, Leah Ruppanner, and William J. Scarborough, "COVID-19 and the Gender Gap in Work Hours," *Gender, Work & Organization*, 2020: 1–12, doi:10.1111/

gwao.12506; Lucia Graves, "Women's Domestic Burden Just Got Heavier with the Coronavirus," *The Guardian*, March 16, 2020, https://www.theguardian.com/us-news/2020/mar/16/womens -coronavirus-domestic-burden; Liz Hamel, Lunna Lopes, Cailey Muñana, Jennifer Kates, Josh Michaud, and Mollyann Brodie, "KFF Coronavirus Poll: March 2020," Kaiser Family Foundation, March 17, 2020, https://www.kff.org/global-health-policy/poll-finding/kff-coronavirus-poll -march-2020/; Scott Keeter, "People Financially Affected by COVID-19 Outbreak Are Experiencing More Psychological Distress Than Others," Pew Research Center, March 30, 2020, https://www .pewresearch.org/fact-tank/2020/03/30/people-financially-affected-by-covid-19-outbreak-are -experiencing-more-psychological-distress-than-others/; Itika Sharma Punit, "Social Distancing from House Helps Is Exposing the Indian Family's Unspoken Sexism," Quartz India, March 26, 2020, https://qz.com/india/1823823/with-coronavirus-lockdown-working-indian-women-face -family-sexism/; Laura M. Giurge, Ayse Yemiscigil, Joseph Sherlock, and Ashley V. Whillans, "Uncovering Inequalities in Time-Use and Well-Being during COVID-19: A Multi-Country Investigation," Harvard Business School Working Paper No. 21-037, September 2020, https:// www.hbs.edu/faculty/Pages/item.aspx?num=58886.

8. "Coronavirus Lockdown: Sierra Leone 'Role Model' Minister Carries Baby and Holds Zoom Meeting," BBC News, April 30, 2020, https://www.bbc.com/news/world-africa-52487213.

9. Jordan Siegel, Lynn Pyun, and B. Y. Cheon, "Multinational Firms, Labor Market Discrimination, and the Capture of Outsider's Advantage by Exploiting the Social Divide," *Administrative Science Quarterly* 64, no. 2 (2019): 370–397.

10. Michelle K. Ryan and S. Alexander Haslam, "The Glass Cliff: Exploring the Dynamics Surrounding the Appointment of Women to Precarious Leadership Positions," *Academy of Management Review* 32, no. 2 (2007): 549–572; Michelle K. Ryan and S. Alexander Haslam, "The Glass Cliff: Evidence that Women Are Over-represented in Precarious Leadership Positions," *British Journal of Management* 16, no. 2 (2005): 81–90.

11. Boris Groysberg, "How Star Women Build Portable Skills," *Harvard Business Review*, February 2008, 74–81.

12. Laura Morgan Roberts, Anthony J. Mayo, Robin J. Ely, and David A. Thomas, "Beating the Odds," *Harvard Business Review*, April 2018, 126–131.

13. Rachel Thomas, Marianne Cooper, Ellen Konar, et al., *Women in the Workplace 2019*, https://wiw-report.s3.amazonaws.com/Women_in_the_Workplace_2019.pdf.

14. Robin J. Ely, "The Effects of Organizational Demographics and Social Identity on Relationships among Professional Women," *Administrative Science Quarterly* 39, no. 2 (June 1994): 203–238.

15. Colleen Walsh, "Hard-Earned Gains for Women at Harvard," *Harvard Gazette*, April 26, 2012, https://news.harvard.edu/gazette/story/2012/04/hard-earned-gains-for-women-at-harvard/.

16. Eileen Shanahan, "AT&T to Grant 15,000 Back Pay in Job Inequities," *New York Times*, January 19, 1973, https://www.nytimes.com/1973/01/19/archives/att-to-grant-15000-back-pay -in-job-ineouities-women-and-minority.html.

Epilogue

1. This chapter draws upon the following Harvard Business School teaching materials: Boris Groysberg, Kerry Herman, and Annelena Lobb, "Women MBAs at Harvard Business School: 1962–2012," Harvard Business School Case 413-013, February 2013 (revised May 2014), https:// www.hbs.edu/faculty/Pages/item.aspx?num=44334; Boris Groysberg, Kerry Herman, Matthew Preble, "Women MBAs in the Workplace," Harvard Business School Industry and Background Note 413-089, February 2013 (revised May 2014).

2. "Black Faculty Members at Harvard Business School, 1954–Present," Harvard Business School, 2018, https://www.library.hbs.edu/hc/AASU/thought-leadership/hbs-faculty-members/.

3. Letty Cottin Pogrebin, *How to Make It in a Man's World* (Garden City, NY: Doubleday, 1970).

4. John A. Byrne, "HBS Dean Makes an Unusual Public Apology," Poets and Quants, January 28, 2014, https://poetsandquants.com/2014/01/28/hbs-dean-makes-an-unusual-public -apology/.

5. "MBA Class of 2020 Baker Scholars," Harvard Business School, Commencement 2020, https://www.hbs.edu/commencement/awards/Pages/baker-scholars.aspx, accessed November 30, 2020.

6. Denise Lu, Jon Huang, Ashwin Seshagiri, Haeyoun Park, and Troy Griggs, "Faces of Power: 80% Are White, Even as U.S. Becomes More Diverse," *New York Times*, September 9, 2020, https://www.nytimes.com/interactive/2020/09/09/us/powerful-people-race-us.html?.

7. "Building the Foundation: Business Education for Women at Harvard University: 1937–1970," Baker Library Special Collections, Harvard Business School, 2013, https://www.library.hbs.edu/hc/wbe/index.html.

8. Philip Galanes, "Ruth Bader Ginsburg and Gloria Steinem on the Unending Fight for Women's Rights," *New York Times*, November 14, 2015, https://www.nytimes.com/2015/11/15/fashion/ruth-bader-ginsburg-and-gloria-steinem-on-the-unending-fight-for-womens-rights.html.

9. Catherine Cerach, "The History of Women at Harvard Business School." *WSA Newsletter*, Summer 1989.

10. Ellen Marram, "Female B-Schoolers Get Screw-tinized, *The Harbus*, September 12, 1969.

11. Groysberg, Herman, and Lobb, "Women MBAs at Harvard Business School: 1962–2012."

12. Anthony J. Mayo and Laura Morgan Roberts, "Spheres of Influence: A Portrait of Black MBA Program Alumni," Paper presented at the Conference on African American Business Leadership, Harvard Business School, 2018.

13. Groysberg, Herman, and Lobb, "Women MBAs at Harvard Business School: 1962–2012."

14. Ilene Lang, "Women at HBS: A Woman's View," *The Harbus*, February 10, 1972.

15. "Harvard Business Women Organize New Association," *The Harbus*, April 1, 1971.

16. "Harvard Business Women," *The Harbus*, April 1, 1971.

17. Judith. Gehrke, "Women in Management: Some Gains Being Made," *The Harbus*, May 11, 1972.

18. Karen Passage, "Discrimination Guidelines Presented," *The Harbus*, January 20, 1972.

19. "Women's Student Association," *WSA Newsletter*, October 11, 1975.

20. Women's Student Association, "WSA Case Editing Committee Report," December 1980.

21. *Barbara Jackson v. Harvard University and John McArthur*, No. Civil Action No. 84-4101-WD (US District Court for the District of Massachusetts 1989).

22. Nancy Chandler, "President's Summary 1981–1982," *WSA Newsletter*, April 1982.

23. Women's Student Association, "Help Needed for New Admit Brochures," *WSA Newsletter*, January 1981; Women's Student Association, "Phone-a-thon for 1989–1990 Women Admits," *WSA Newsletter*, March 13, 1989.

24. Karen Cmar, "WSA Targets Participation," *The Harbus*, May 20, 1985.

25. Robert J. Dolan, "Heading down the Stretch," e-mail message to students, March 24, 1997; Steven C. Wheelwright and Janice McCormick, letter to students. May 6, 1997.

26. Peter Howley and Andrew Farquharson, "Harassment Case Explodes One Year Later," *The Harbus*, April 13, 1998; Wheelwright and McCormick, letter to students.

27. Faculty and Staff Standards Committee to HBS Community, memorandum, April 9, 1998; Steven Wheelwright, "Community Standards Case Update," e-mail message to students, November 26, 1997.

28. Groysberg, Herman, and Lobb, "Women MBAs at Harvard Business School: 1962–2012."

29. Julia Brau, Paayal Desai, Alex Germain, and Akmaral Omarova, "Gender Discrepancies in Academic Performance," *The Harbus*, May 2010; Ruhana Hafiz, "WSA Academic Initiative Survey," *The Harbus*, December 7, 2009, https://harbus.org/2009/wsa-academic-initiative-survey-4737/.

30. "As Academic Gender Gap Declines, There Is Still Work to Be Done," *The Harbus*, April 25, 2011, http://www.harbus.org/2011/gender-gap/.

31. Monisha Kapila, "Three Ways Harvard Business School Can Change the World for Women," Quartz, April 6, 2013, https://qz.com/71684/three-ways-harvard-business-school-can-change-the-world-for-women/.

32. Katherine Baldiga Coffman, "Evidence on Self-Stereotyping and the Contribution of Ideas," *Quarterly Journal of Economics* 129, no. 4 (2014): 1625–1660.

33. Jodi Kantor, "Harvard Business School Case Study: Gender Equity," *New York Times*, September 7, 2013; Anne Morriss and Frances X. Frei, *Unleashed: The Unapologetic Leader's Guide to Empowering Everyone around You* (Boston: Harvard Business Review Press, 2020).

34. Poorvi Vijay and Anoothi, "Record-Breaking Women Class Presidents: Is the World Ready for This Change," *The Harbus*, December 5, 2019, https://harbus.org/2019/record-breaking -women-class-presidents-is-the-world-ready-for-this-change/.

35. "MBA Profile and RC Case Protagonists," Harvard Business School, 2020, https://www .hbs.edu/racialequity/data/Pages/mba.aspx.

36. Ioana M. Latu, Marianne Schmid Mast, Joris Lammers, and Dario Bombari, "Successful Female Leaders Empower Women's Behavior in Leadership Tasks," *Journal of Experimental Social Psychology* 49, no. 3 (2013): 444–448; Penelope Lockwood, "Someone Like Me Can Be Successful: Do College Students Need Same-Gender Role Models?," *Psychology of Women Quarterly* 30, no. 1 (2006): 36–46.

37. Lesley Symons, "Only 11% of Top Business School Case Studies Have a Female Protagonist," *Harvard Business Review*, March 9, 2016, https://hbr.org/2016/03/only-11-of-top-business -school-case-studies-have-a-female-protagonist.

38. Colleen Sharen and Rosemary McGowan, "Invisible or Clichéd: How Are Women Represented in Business Cases?," *Journal of Management Education* 43, no. 2 (2019): 129–173.

39. Association to Advance Collegiate Schools of Business, *Business School Data Guide 2018*, 2018; Shelby Colby and Paula Burggeman, *What Women Want: A Blueprint for Change in Business Education*, Graduate Management Admission Council, 2017, https://www.gmac.com/-/media /files/gmac/research/research-report-series/2017-gmac-white-paper_what-women-want-web.pdf.

40. Ilana Kowarski, "U.S. News Data: A Portrait of the Typical MBA Student," U.S. News, March 14, 2017, https://www.usnews.com/education/best-graduate-schools/top-business -schools/articles/2017-03-14/us-news-data-a-portrait-of-the-typical-mba-student; Elizabeth Olson, "Women Make Up Majority of U.S. Law Students for First Time," *New York Times*, December 16, 2016.

41. Robin J. Ely, Pamela Stone, Laurie Shannon, and Colleen Ammerman, *Life & Leadership after HBS*, Harvard Business School, 2015, https://www.hbs.edu/gender/faculty-research/life -and-leadership-after-hbs/Pages/default.aspx.

42. Mayo and Roberts, "Spheres of Influence."

43. Nancy M. Carter and Christine Silva, *Pipeline's Broken Promise*, Catalyst, 2010, http://www .catalyst.org/system/files/Pipeline's_Broken_Promise_Final_021710.pdf.

44. Marianne Bertrand, Claudia Goldin, and Lawrence F. Katz, "Dynamics of the Gender Gap for Young Professionals in the Financial and Corporate Sectors," *American Economic Journal: Applied Economics* 2, no. 3 (2010): 228–255.

45. Andrew Garthwaite, "Masters in Management Data Highlights Gender Pay Gap," *Financial Times*, October 20, 2019, https://www.ft.com/content/794ee6a8-ea4b-11e9-85f4 -d00e5018f061.

46. Mayo and Roberts, "Spheres of Influence."

47. "Community Conversation on Race: June 11, 2020," Harvard Business School, 2020, https://www.hbs.edu/news/articles/Pages/community-conversation-on-race-june-2020.aspx.

48. "The First Tenured Women Professors at Harvard University," https://hwpi.harvard .edu/files/faculty-diversity/files/timeline-final_32.pdf.

49. Regina Herzlinger and Joel Klein, "The IRS Can Save American Health Care," *Wall Street Journal*, July 1, 2018, https://www.wsj.com/articles/the-irs-can-save-american-health-care -1530477705; "Health Reimbursement Arrangements and Other Account-Based Group Health Plans," *Federal Register* 84, no. 119 (June 20, 2019), https://www.federalregister.gov/documents /2019/06/20/2019-12571/health-reimbursement-arrangements-and-other-account-based-group -health-plans; Alexander Acosta, Steven Mnuchin and Alex Azar, "New Health Options for Small-Business Employees," *Wall Street Journal*, October 22, 2018, https://www.wsj.com/articles /new-health-options-for-small-business-employees-1540249941.

INDEX

Note: The letter *t* following a page number denotes a table and the letter *f* following a page number denotes a figure.

Abe, Shinzo, 116
ABI/ProQuest database, articles on workplace inequality, 13
academia, 142
advancement barriers. *See* gender barriers to advancement, in early and midcareer
advertising bias, backlash against, 114
agency, sense of, 14
Amazon, Rooney Rule, 77–78
anger, expressions of, 146
Anyoku, Chichi, 247–248
Applegate, Lynda, 233
apprenticeship model, 18
"Are Women Executives People?" (*HBR*), 96–97
AT&T, class-action gender discrimination lawsuit against, 215–216
Atkins, Ros, 119–127
attrition indexes, 160
Australia
    advocates for targets for women board members in, 75
    board gender diversity in, 68
    study on gender equality, 111–112

baby boomers, with plans for career interruption for parenting, 21
BBC, Atkins's 50:50 Project, 119–127
Benko, Cathy, 156
Best Buy, Results Only Work Environment (ROWE) program, 158–159

bias
    first-generation forms of, 131
    against men taking parental leave, 100–101
    mental minimization of, 51–52
    by men with nonworking wives, 23
    in performance evaluations, 110, 145–149
    review of résumés and, 90, 138
    second-generation forms of, 130–131, 170
    training on how to overcome, 148, 181
    unconscious type, 148, 161, 180–181, 237, 241
    See also discrimination
BiasWatchNeuro.com, 97
Biden, Joseph, 97
Bishop, Julie, 43–44
BlackRock, 77
Black women
    attrition rates, 160
    as board members, 67
    disparities in HBS alumni study, 247
    as *Fortune* 500 CEOs, 40
    inclusive cultures and, 189–191
    navigation through barriers, 52–53
    need for improved male sponsorship of, 144
    on promotion decisions, 195
    scrutiny and burden of proof on, 47–48
    study on resilience, 211
    white mentors of, 141
blind screening, in hiring, 90, 138, 182
boards of directors. *See* corporate boards, women on
Boston College, Center for Work and Family, on co-parenting, 114

Boston Symphony Orchestra, 150
Brandt, Beverly, 229
Brougher, Françoise, 44
Buffett, Warren, 69, 70
*Building on a Culture of Belonging: 2020 PwC
        Diversity & Inclusion Transparency Report*
        (PwC), 40
Burnham, Elizabeth Abbott, 227
Burns, Ursula, 40
Bush, George H. W., 36–37

California
    Fair Employment and Housing
        Department, 169
    law on board composition, 75, 76, 78, 207
    proposed law on company reports on
        gender inequality factors, 150–151
    Public Employees' Retirement System, 77
Campbell, Phyllis, 73
Campbell Soup, 98–99
Canada, board diversity at Desjardins Group, 72
Canada Mortgage and Housing Corporation,
        Results Only Work Environment
        (ROWE) program, 159
Canada–United States Council for Advance-
        ment of Women Entrepreneurs &
        Business Leaders, survey on talent
        management, 130
caregiving. *See* work-life balance
Caremark, 88
Carli, Linda, 17
Case Centre, 241
Catalyst, 215, 218–220
    Men Advocating for Real Change program,
        105
Center for Talent Innovation, report on
        professional development, 182
Chamberlain Group, 109
Change.org petition, 114
chief diversity officers (CDOs), 160
Chirac, Bernadette, 72
Citigroup, gender pay differentials, 151
CNN, parental leave lawsuit against, 101
coauthored papers, credit for, 136
collaborative work approaches, 141, 146
college degrees, awarded to women, 2
Collins, Francis, 97–98, 132–133
commitment myth, 184–185
compensation
    gender pay gap, 2, 113–114, 150, 247
    negotiations for, 151–152
    promotions and, 152–153, 161–162
    racial/ethnic minority pay gaps, 150

retention and, 156, 160
    severance pay, 48, 95
competence vs. likability, 50–51, 145–146
Conant, Doug, 98–99, 107, 108
coronavirus pandemic
    impact on careers of mothers, 22
    impact on women and families, 209
    impact on women of color, 208
corporate boards, women on, 5–6
    drawbacks of homogeneity, 224–225
    governance gap and, 66–69
    government/regulatory/social pressures,
        74–78
    marginalization of, 72–74
    percentage as board chairs, 72
    percentages of, 65–66, 67
    power of corporate sisterhood, 78–84
    scenarios of, 61–62
    twokenism, 68, 73
    window dressing vs. culture renovation,
        69–74
crony capitalism, 69–70
cross-training programs, 141

daddy bonus, 26
daughter effect, 107–108
Daum, Alexandra, 244, 245
Davies Review, 75
Dawes, Karen, 233
Dayton-Hudson Corporation (Target), 87
Deloitte
    survey on male parental leave, 102
    Women's Initiative, 156
Desjardins Group, 72
Digital Equipment Corporation, 218
discrimination
    AT&T, class-action gender discrimination
        lawsuit, 215–216
    in hiring processes, 135–139
    Qualcomm, discrimination lawsuit and
        settlement, 169–172
    in staffing decisions, 112–113
    See also bias; Black women; Equal
        Employment Opportunity Commission
        (EEOC); racial/ethnic minorities;
        women of color
Dot Foods, 108–109, 131–132
dual-career families, 21–22, 114–117
Duchossois, Craig, 109

Eagly, Alice, 17
Eisenman, Elaine, 81

Ely, Robin J., 185–186
Emory, Kyle, 105–106, 107, 245–246
emotions, 47–48
England, requirement for company reports on
        gender pay differentials, 150
Equal Employment Opportunity Commission
        (EEOC)
    data collection suspended by Trump
        administration, 150
    discrimination complaints, 169, 215–216
Equal Pay Act, 169
Esquivel, Josie, 200–201, 203, 204
European Union, proposal to mandate quota
        for women board members, 75
Eveillard, Betty, 228, 229

fair play, sense of, 106–107
Federation of Women Shareholders, 73
feedback, 186
"Female B-Schoolers Get Screw-tinized" (The
        Harbus), 224
female CEOs
    proportions of, 1–2, 17
    as role models, 54
    women of color as Fortune 500 CEOs, 40
    See also corporate boards, women on;
        women in leadership; specific individuals
Ferraro, Geraldine, 97
50:50 Project (BBC), 119–127
Financial Times, on gender pay gap, 247
first-generation bias, 131
flexibility stigma, 23–26, 48, 114–115, 157–158
Fore, Henrietta Holsman, 69
Fornelli, Cindy, 68
Forté Foundation, 27
Fortune 500 companies
    former CEOs as board members, 78–79
    number of gender-balanced corporate
        boards, 66
    percentage of racial/ethnic minority board
        members, 66
    percentage of women board members,
        65–66, 76, 78
    percentage of women executives, 40
Fraenkel, Fred, 202–203, 204
France, requirement for company reports on
        gender pay differentials, 150
Franklin, Barbara Hackman, 11, 33–38,
        224–225
Frei, Frances, 147
FTSE 100 companies
    percentage of racial/ethnic minority board
        members, 66

percentage of women board members, 75
UK company boards with voluntary
        targets, 75
FTSE 250 companies, board diversity policies
        of, 76–77

Gallup poll, on perception of gender parity, 102
Gelman, Audrey, 192–193
gender barriers to advancement, in early and
        midcareer, 4–5
    gender dynamics in business school, 26–29
    double bind, 29–31
    lowered horizons, 16–20
    organizational barriers, 20–26
    scenarios of, 16, 17–18, 20–21, 23–24, 27
gender gap, in perceptions on gender equality,
        102
General Motors, 66
Generation Xers, with plans for career
        interruption for parenting, 21
George, Bill, 68, 91
Ginsburg, Ruth Bader, 223
glass ceiling, 43–44, 154
glass cliff, 154–155, 211
glass-shattering organizations, 6, 166–167
    attraction of candidates, 130, 132–135
    compensation and promotion, 150–155
    cyclical reviews of systems, 159–162
    hiring practices, 135–139
    integration of new employees, 139–142
    management process, 166–167t
    performance evaluations, 145–149
    professional development, 142–145
    Qualcomm profile, 169–172
    retention of top talent, 130, 156–159
    summary conclusion, 205–213
    surveys of women executives, 163, 164t, 165,
        166
Global Educators Network for Health
        Innovation Education, 225–226
Goldman Sachs, 77, 138
golf, 140, 187
Gompers, Paul, 108
good woman vs. good leader, 29–31
Google, 150, 153
government mandates, on board composition,
        74–75
Graham, Ginger, 230–231
Grant, Adam, 106
Greyser, Stephen, 97
Grogan, Nicole, 111
groupthink, 69, 71
Grupo Globo, 57–61

"Guidelines for Avoiding Discrimination against Women in Written Materials" (WSA), 230

Hacke, Robin, 234
Hagan, Tara, 244–245
Hajim, Ed, 35
Hall, Tony, 125
Hammond, Mary Ellen, 237
Hampton-Alexander, 67–68
Harbus, The
    articles on gender equity, 228, 237
    "Female B-Schoolers Get Screw-tinized," 224
    survey on gender inequality, 103–104
Harris, Kamala, 97
Harvard Business Review
    "Are Women Executives People?," 96–97
    on men's expectations for work and family, 100
Harvard Business School (HBS), 2–3
    admission of women students, 223–27, 229, 236, 246
    African American Student Union, 223, 232
    alumni study, 15–16, 19–20, 21–22, 103, 104, 113, 246–247
    Baker Scholars, 222, 226
    as case study in organizational change, 221–249
    Committee to Increase the Number of Women at HBS, 232
    Community Values, 235–236
    complaints about sexual harassment, 234–235
    courses covering board gender diversity, 66
    early treatment of students of color, 221, 223, 224, 226, 227
    Franklin's comments on, 38
    Gender & Work Research Symposium, 162
    gender discrimination lawsuit against, 231
    gender parity gains during 2010s, 238–244
    How Star Women Succeed course, 240, 242–243
    Innovating in Health Care MBA course, 255
    majority male faculty in, 28, 221, 227, 229, 252–253
    survey of women executives, 163, 164t, 165, 166, 175–178, 176f, 183, 187
    underrepresentation of women in cases for discussion, 230–231, 233, 240–243
    Women on Boards program, 79–80, 240
    Women Students' Welcome events, 233–234

See also Harbus, The; Women's Student Association (WSA); *specific alumni*
Harvard College
    as male only school, 215
    HeForShe campaign (UN), 105
Herzlinger, Regina E., 231, 251–256
higher education, gender dynamics in, 27–29
hiring practices
    blind screening, 90, 138, 182
    diversity in interview panels, 135–137
    drawbacks of unstructured interviews, 137
    gender-based language in job descriptions, 133–134, 135
    interview formats and rubrics, 137–138
    tips for managers, 138–139
hoarding of power, 176
homophily, 132
homophobia, 231
Hooper, Michele, 79, 85–92, 207
Humanyze, 115–116

IBM, study on gender parity, 102
Illinois, law on board composition, 76
implicit bias. *See* unconscious bias
inclusive cultures, 187–191
inclusive management. *See* managerial roles, attributes of inclusive
international assignments, 19
interpersonal exclusion, 187–191
interview panels, diversity in, 137
investment banking industry, barriers to integration of women, 139
investment firms, diversity disclosure requirements, 77
Ivey, 241

Jaber, Fatima Al, 79
Japan, womenomics initiative, 116
job descriptions, gender-biased, 133–134, 135
Johnson, Brad, 106
Jones Day, parental leave lawsuit against, 101, 114
JPMorgan Chase
    career reentry program, 173–174
    gender inequality in, 129
    parental leave lawsuit against, 100

Kanter, Rosabeth Moss, 69–70, 162
Keating, Susan, 83–84
Klein, Joel, 225
KPMG, 82
Kullman, Ellen, 27

Lambert, Lillian Lincoln, 223–224
Lang, Ilene H., 215–220, 227–228
Larson, Henrietta, 227
Latinx
    attrition rates, 160
    Illinois law on board composition inclusion
        of, 76
leadership archetypes and masculinity, 42–45,
    50, 146
leadership roles. *See* corporate boards, women
    on; women in leadership
Lean In Together program, 105
Leffler, Libby, 239
Lerner, Teena, 199–200, 202
Leroux, Monique, 72
Levy, Leslie, 228
Light, Jay, 225
likability. *See* competence vs. likability
Lotus, 217–218
LVMH, 72

male advocacy in gender equality, 6
    daughter effect and, 107–108
    examples of, 96–98
    masculine norms and parental leave,
        98–102
    men as change agents, 108–113
    programs for, 105–107
    redefining the goal, 113–117
    shifts in psychological standing and, 101–104
    in WCD's efforts, 83–84
managerial roles, attributes of inclusive, 7,
    173–179
    championing values of diversity, equity,
        and inclusion, 194–197
    development of objective lens, 179–182
    foster inclusive culture, 187–191
    HBS survey of women executives, 175–178,
        176f, 183, 187
    leveraging diverse perspectives, 191–194
    percentage of inclusive managers, 176f
    provision of equitable developmental
        opportunities and feedback, 182–187
Manbassadors program (WSA), 105–106,
    244–246
Marc, LaToya, 239
Marcoux, Isabelle, 73–74
masculine norm, 42–45, 50, 55, 99–102, 146
MBA (master of business administration),
    27–28
McArthur, John, 230–231
McGinn, Kathleen, 237
Men Advocating for Real Change program, 105

Men and Women of the Corporation (Kanter), 162
men of color. *See* racial/ethnic minorities
mentorship
    apprenticeship model vs., 18
    cross-race relationships, 141
    examples of, 54–55, 86–87, 99, 109, 185, 219
    by inclusive managers, 182–183
    lack of access to, 144
    post #MeToo movement, 110
#MeToo movement
    backlash to, 110–111
    corporate responses to, 95–98
    impacts of, 179, 207
    systemic nature of gender inequity, 245
    as viewed through zero-sum lens, 103
    WCD's response to, 83
Mexico, study on gender equality, 112
Microsoft, 150
millennials
    on consequences of using work-life balance
        programs, 23
    on diminished expectations for attaining
        senior leadership positions, 17
    masculine norm and, 100
    on men as change agents, 113
    with plans for career interruption for
        parenting, 21–22
Mondale, Walter, 97
Morrison, Denise, 99
Morriss, Anne, 147
motherhood penalty, 25–26, 136, 157–158, 170
MSCI ACWI Index, 65

Nasdaq stock exchange, 77
National Association of Corporate Directors
    (NACD), 88, 91
National Institutes of Health (NIH), 97,
    132–133
negotiation skills, 151–152, 185
network disruption, 68–69, 132–133
Nike, 150
9 to 5 (film), 205, 212
Niv, Yael, 97–98
Nixon, Pat, 36
Nixon, Richard, 36
Nohria, Nitin, 222, 236, 237, 238
no-jerk policy, 201
Nooyi, Indra, 27, 40
Norway, law on board composition, 67, 75

Obama, Barack, 101
Ocejo, Santiago, 112–113, 245

office housework, 143
Ohanian, Alexis, 115, 117
online job postings, 133–134, 152
outlier effect. *See* women in leadership
overwork, culture of, 20–21, 116, 170

parental leave, 98–102, 114–116
parenthood. *See* work-life balance
Parton, Dolly, 205–206
pay gaps, requirements to disclose, 207, 208.
    See also compensation
pedestal effect, 106
pension funds, 77
people management. *See* glass-shattering
    organizations; managerial roles,
    attributes of inclusive
perception management, 45–46
performance evaluations
    bias in, 110, 145–149
    checklist systems, 149
    promotions and, 150
    ratings based on stereotypes, 15
    self-assessments by women, 148
personal brands, 46
Pessoa, Ana Paula, 50, 57–63
Pew Research Center
    poll on perception of gender parity, 102
    study on gender equality (2020), 103
Piltch, Matt, 104, 105, 245–246
pink ghettos, 143
police chiefs, hiring of, 136
Porgrebin, Letty Cottin, 221–222
Posner, Susan, 228–229
PricewaterhouseCooper (PwC), report on
    culture of belonging, 40
professional development, 142–145, 182–187
professional service firms
    percentage of women leaders in, 31, 40
    performance evaluations, 148–149
profiles
    Atkins, Ros, 119–127
    Franklin, Barbara Hackman, 11, 33–38,
        224–225
    Herzlinger, Regina E., 231, 251–256
    Hooper, Michele, 79, 85–92, 207
    Lang, Ilene H., 215–220, 227–228
    Pessoa, Ana Paula, 57–63
    Qualcomm, 169–172
    Rivkin, Jack, 189, 199–204, 210
promotions
    compensation and, 152–153, 161–162
    gender inequality in, 17, 42, 136
    inclusive managers and, 179–180, 183–184

retention and, 156
    self-nomination for, 152–153
Promundo, study on gender equality (2019),
    111
psychological standing, men's sense of,
    101–104

Qualcomm, discrimination lawsuit and
    settlement against, 169–172
queen bee behaviors, 176–177

racial/ethnic minorities
    attrition rates, 160
    among board chairs, 72
    on corporate boards, 66–67, 71–72, 76
    pay gaps, 150
    subject to glass cliff effect, 154–155
    See also Black women; women of color
Radcliffe College, 215, 223, 224
Rawlinson, David, 117
Rawlinson, Nadia, 117
resilience-building environments. *See* women
    in leadership
Results Only Work Environment (ROWE)
    program, 158–159
retention of top talent, 156–159
risk-aversion, 185
Rivkin, Jack, 189, 199–204, 210
role models, 16–17, 53–55
Rubin, Julia Sass, 232

S&P 500 companies
    percentage of chief diversity officers with
        access to employee demographic data, 160
    percentage of women board members, 68
    percentage of women executives, 40
S&P 1500 companies
    shareholder proposals on board
        composition, 77
    study on implicit ceilings for women, 154
Salesforce, annual compensation audits, 160
Sandberg, Sheryl, 27, 105
Sanders, Judy, 200
Santoni, Erica, 246
Schwartz, Carol, 232
Schwartz, Felice, 218–219
second-generation bias, 130–131, 170
Securities and Exchange Commission (SEC),
    requirement for companies to explain
    diversity considerations in board
    appointees, 76, 77

self-assessments, by women, 148
self-confidence, 53
self-directed teams, 141, 146
severance pay, 48, 95
sexual misconduct, 95, 157, 190, 234–235. *See also* #MeToo movement
shareholders, on board composition, 77, 90–91
Shearson, departmental innovations, 199–204
Siebert, Muriel, 230
Singer Company, 34
Slaughter, Anne-Marie, 20, 113, 114
Smith, David, 106
social interactions, 140
Society for Human Resource Management, on parental leave, 100
Society of Women Engineers, formation of Men's Auxiliary, 97
Sohovich, JoAnna Garcia, 109
Soss, Wilma, 73
SoulCycle, parental leave lawsuit against, 101
South Korea
  parental leave policies, 115
  study on women managers, 210–211
Spain, law on board composition, 75
State Street Global Advisors, 77
Stautberg, Susan, 80–84
Steel, Joan, 82
Steinem, Gloria, 230
stereotypes of women's innate capabilities, 46–47. *See also* good woman vs. good leader
Stiegel, Herta von, 74
Stone, Pamela, 23–24
stretch assignments, 15, 24, 142–143, 182–183
surveys
  on board gender diversity, 66–67
  of millennial women (2015), 12, 17
  on talent management, 130
  of unmarried, childless men/women (2015), 12–13
  Women in the Workplace survey (McKinsey and Lean In), 17, 179
  on work-life balance, 20
  See also Harvard Business School (HBS)
Symbolics, 217
systemic approaches. *See* glass-shattering organizations

talent management. *See* glass-shattering organizations
task segregation, 143
Tattersall, Marnie, 228, 229, 230

technology firms, performance evaluations, 148–149
30% Club, 75, 79
Time's Up, 212
Tinsley, Catherine H., 185–186
Tracy, John, 108–109, 131–132
Trewstar, 220
Trillium Asset Management, 77
Trotter, Donne, 101–102
Trump, Donald, 150
2020 Women on Boards, 79–80
twokenism, 68, 73

Uber, job ad study, 134
unconscious bias, 148, 161, 180–181, 237, 241
underrepresentation. *See* corporate boards, women on; women in leadership
Unfinished Business: Men Women Work Family (Slaughter), 113
United Kingdom
  requirement to disclose gender pay gaps, 207, 208
  voluntary quota targets for women board members, 75
United Nations HeForShe campaign, 105
University of Chicago, study of MBAs (1990–2006), 247
University of Pennsylvania, Small Communities Talent Search program, 85–86
US Federal Reserve, hiring practices, 138
US Naval Academy, study on bias in performance evaluations, 146
US Transportation Department, parental leave lawsuit against, 101

Valantine, Hannah, 133

Walmart, 150
Washington State, law on board composition, 75, 76, 207
Weiner, Edie, 80–81
Wellcome Trust, 98
"Why Women Still Can't Have It All" (Slaughter), 20
Wing, The, 192–193
Winston, Mary, 40
Winter, Alison, 81
Wolfer, Alexis, 246
Wolfish, David, 245
Women Corporate Directors (WCD), 80–84

women in leadership, 5
  development of resilience, 48–53
  late-career barriers, 44–48
  the outlier effect, 41–44
  resilience-building environments, 53–56
  study on decline of, 212
Women in the Workplace survey (McKinsey and Lean In), 17, 179
Women of Campbell events, 99
women of color
  as board members, 66, 76, 207–208
  challenges for executives, 41–42
  disadvantaged by less managerial support/guidance, 186
  as *Fortune* 500 CEOs, 40
  need for improved integration of, 140, 141
  need for improved male sponsorship of, 144
  percentage as board chairs, 89
  scrutiny and burden of proof on, 47–48
  study on decline in leadership pipelines, 212
  study on resilience in managers, 211
  subject to glass cliff effect, 154–155
  See also Black women
Women's Student Association (WSA)
  address to hostile environment, 234–236
  Admitted Student Days, 232
  Career Day, 230
  Case Editing Committee, 230–231
  "Guidelines for Avoiding Discrimination against Women in Written Materials" (WSA), 230

Harvard Business Women club as forerunner to, 228
  impacts of, 228–232, 248–249
  Manbassadors program, 105–106, 244–246
  recruitment of Black applicants, 232
  recruitment of female applicants, 229, 232
  study on honor recipients, 236–237, 238
  survey on dissatisfaction with case discussions, 233
  Women in Management Day, 229–230
  See also Harvard Business School (HBS)
Women's Venture Capital Fund, 220
work-life balance
  as barrier to advancement narrative, 19–23
  egalitarian partnerships, 254
  flexibility stigma and, 23–26
  housework and caregiving, 21, 100–102, 113–116
  motherhood penalty, 25–26, 136, 157–158, 170
  as social problem, 12
  varying age group perspectives on, 21–22
workplace masculinity contest, 146
work redesign, 158–159
World Economic Forum, on women in senior positions, 17

zero-sum thinking, 103, 176

ACKNOWLEDGMENTS

Like any intellectual work, this book is the product of many minds. We are deeply indebted to the people who have contributed their stories, their ideas, and their time to this project and whose encouragement and counsel lifted our spirits along the way. Any new knowledge contained in the preceding pages has been created not by us alone but in and through the collective insights of the scholars, practitioners, and advocates who have generously spent time with us and with this project.

The two of us met nearly a decade ago when we joined a small work group spearheading W50, Harvard Business School's (HBS) commemoration of the fiftieth anniversary of women's admission to the MBA program. We began researching the history of women's experiences as students and faculty, discovering how far the school had come in fostering gender equality on campus but also finding that women had long been trying to dismantle obstacles that remain to this day. What we learned is reflected in the epilogue, which traces HBS's journey and attempts to shed light on the milestones we have not yet reached. That W50 year fostered new conversations about the state of the school and galvanized renewed attempts to make progress. In the years since, we have been honored to help institutionalize some of these programs, including the annual Gender & Work Research Symposium and ongoing efforts to ensure that our curricula reflect gender, race, and other kinds of diversity in leadership. With our colleague Robin Ely we helped launch the Gender Initiative in 2015, which serves as a hub for the school's work on multiple forms of inequality in the workplace.

Working together on the W50 commemoration turned out to be just the start of a partnership between the two of us. We have continued writing and pursuing new research ideas together, many of which became part of this book. The growing list of articles and cases we had written or planned to write about gender inequality was in part the impetus for this book. So too was our sense that the pattern we had observed in researching women at HBS mirrored that of society more broadly: When it comes to gender at work so much has changed, yet parity remains elusive. It seemed to us the right time to explore why that pattern persists and provide clear guidance about how to change it.

We believe that much is known about how to effect that change, and we are deeply indebted to the scholars whose work we have endeavored to explicate and synthesize in this volume. By seeking to understand the contexts in and mechanisms through which inequality persists, they have provided essential clues about how we can mitigate or even eradicate it. One reason we wrote this book was to make the insights and implications of their research more accessible and actionable for people who want to make change in their companies and beyond. We are confident in this book's descriptions and prescriptions because we are confident in the rigor and robustness of the scholarship from which it draws. At various points we also reference our own prior work. While we are collaborators on some of these projects, others are sole-authored or undertaken with other colleagues. For simplicity's sake we refer to any such prior study as "our research," but a look at the sources cited in the notes will clarify authorship for any interested readers.

We owe special thanks to the people who read portions and versions of this manuscript with care and provided important critiques, including Robin Abrahams, David Alworth, Christina Bermingham, Siri Chilazi, Allison Elias, Robin Ely, Gretchen Gavett, Pamela

Joyner, Deborah Kolb, Reynold Levy, Tony Mayo, Laura Moon, Jennifer Nash, Nitin Nohria, In Paik, Laura Morgan Roberts, Kim Scott, and Matt Segneri as well as three anonymous reviewers. Their reactions put pressure on our thinking in the most productive ways. In addition, the feedback of Amy Bernstein and Sarah Cliffe at *Harvard Business Review* helped to develop many of the ideas in this volume. Our first editor at Harvard Business Review Press, Tim Sullivan, believed in this project and helped us think about what kind of book it could and should be. Melinda Merino, in whose capable editorial hands we have spent most of this journey, cheered us on and also asked hard questions that shaped and reshaped the book into the best version of itself.

Many other kinds of support made this book possible. We would not have been able to undertake, much less sustain, the years of work the book necessitated without the backing of leaders at the school who believed in its value and the time our colleagues spent in conversation with us. Countless formal and informal discussions influenced our thinking and created space for the book to evolve. In particular, our immediate colleagues in the HBS Initiatives department and the Organizational Behavior Unit were invaluable thought partners. In addition, the research we conducted specifically for this book was a team effort. Numerous collaborators helped conduct interviews, run statistical analyses, and interpret archival materials, while yet others made sure that logistics ran smoothly and seamlessly. We would especially like to thank Sarah Abbott, Ethiopiah Al-Mahdi, Xiang Ao, Shelby Austin-Manning, Kate Connolly Baden, Deborah Bell, Jean Cunningham, Vicki Good, Elizabeth Johnson, Jan Hammond, Kalpana Jain, Juemin Luo, Erica Mirabitur, Dory Nemitz, Jan Rivkin, Laurie Shannon, and Debora Spar. We also received assistance from the Case Research & Writing Group and Baker Library, and HBS's Division of Research and Faculty Development provided funding.

Moreover, we have built on the work of many organizations long committed to advancing women in business, and several have been valuable sources of advice and insight. Chief among these groups are

Catalyst, the Committee of 200, the Forté Foundation, Lean In, the Stanford VMware Women's Leadership Lab, Women Corporate Directors, and the Women and Public Policy Program at Harvard Kennedy School. We would also like to thank Linda Rabbitt, through whose generosity the HBS Executive Education program Women on Boards was launched and who continues to champion our work and the goal of advancing women in leadership.

Most of all, we wish to thank the people we interviewed and surveyed for this book, who number well into the hundreds. While we cannot name them all (and some wish to remain anonymous), we are immeasurably grateful to them. They include Harvard College and HBS graduates, participants in HBS's Executive Education programs, and women and men working at organizations of all sizes around the world. A number of our subjects helped us find other people to interview; we owe a special note of thanks to Susan Stautberg for introducing us to several key people who enriched this book. We are especially grateful to the profile subjects who spent several hours speaking with us about their career journeys and their efforts to advance gender equity: Ros Atkins, Barbara Hackman Franklin, Regina Herzlinger, Michele Hooper, Ilene Lang, and Ana Paula Pessoa. (Jack Rivkin passed away in 2016; his profile is based on earlier interviews and public sources.) Our interviewees' experiences and observations are at the heart of this book. Their stories remind us that inequality is not abstract. It limits, frustrates, and diminishes real people, robbing them and the world of their full potential. Yet we complete this book with a sense of hope and possibility precisely because we have had the privilege of hearing from so many who are doing their best to advance equality—women and men at all career stages, from all over the world, in just about every industry imaginable. We are honored and humbled to share what we have learned from them with the readers of this book.

Finally, we close with acknowledgments to our loved ones.

First, from Colleen: I am deeply grateful to my friends and family, whose interest and delight in hearing about this project never flagged even when my own enthusiasm did. They celebrated every milestone and offered encouragement at every roadblock. In particular I thank my parents, whose excitement about the publication of this book exceeds my own. Most of all I am indebted to my mother, Patricia Carroll Swalley, who has nurtured my own ambition, intellect, and independence since the day I was born. She gave me a voice, and everything I do is an effort to honor her belief in its power.

Second, from Boris: Family is always important to me, but with this project it was even more important. I especially want to thank my parents, who have always taught me about the deep importance of equality and inclusiveness. They are the people who helped me appreciate diverse points of view, and in my mind they are the most inclusive people I've ever met. I also want to thank my sister and my wife, who were the first ones to help me appreciate the challenges women face in the workplace. They have helped to shape my view on this subject more than anyone else. I always wanted to be like my sister, and there is no question in my mind that I married up.

One of the reasons I wrote this book is for my kids, my daughters and my sons. They are my deepest passion and purpose. When I look at them every morning, how different they are and how talented they are in their own ways, I am motivated more than anything else to research, write, and work with organizations in the journey of becoming more inclusive.

ABOUT THE AUTHORS

COLLEEN AMMERMAN is director of the Harvard Business School Gender Initiative, which catalyzes and translates cutting-edge research to transform practice; enable leaders to drive change; and eradicate gender, race, and other forms of inequality in business and society. Ammerman oversees the initiative's portfolio of activities, including events, programming for practitioners, and research dissemination. She has authored various articles and teaching materials on gender and work and is a researcher with *Life and Leadership after HBS*, a longitudinal study of the post-MBA paths of Harvard Business School alumni, examining how race, gender, and other factors shape their lives and career experiences.

BORIS GROYSBERG is the Richard P. Chapman Professor of Business Administration at Harvard Business School and a faculty affiliate at the Harvard Business School Gender Initiative. He has won numerous awards for his research, which focuses on the challenge of managing human capital in small and large organizations across the world. Groysberg is the author of the award-winning book *Chasing Stars: The Myth of Talent and the Portability of Performance* and the coauthor (with Michael Slind) of *Talk, Inc.: How Trusted Leaders Use Conversation to Power Their Organizations*. A frequent contributor to *Harvard Business Review*, he has written many articles, notes, and case studies on how firms hire, develop, retain, engage, communicate, and leverage diverse talent to create inclusive cultures. Professor Groysberg was inducted as a fellow into the National Academy of Human Resources in 2016. Before joining Harvard Business School, he worked at IBM.